MediaSpeak

By the same author:

The Joy of Words
InWords and OutWords
Music through the Looking Glass
Keep taking the Tabloids
A Small Book of Grave Humour
Dead Funny
Lern Yerself Scouse (Ed.)
Scally Scouse (Ed.)

Typeset on an Apple Macintosh II with Microsoft Word 3.00 /4.00 and Aldus Pagemaker
by the author, who therefore takes full responsibility for *all* errors.
Acknowledgments to Sharon Quayle and Ian Jones of the AppleCentre Liverpool.

Changing Sounds and Trends in English Speech

MediaSpeak

**Basically, yer-know-I-mean,
a book in terms of
spoken English-if-you -like:
radio, television, eck-settera**

With a Free Supplement on MediaWrite

Fritz Spiegl

FRAM, Dus. Moc.

Elm Tree Books · London

ELM TREE BOOKS

Published by the Penguin Group
27 Wrights Lane, London W8 5TZ, England

Viking Penguin Inc, 40 West 23rd Street, New York, New York 10010, U.S.A.
Penguin Books Australia Ltd, Ringwood, Victoria, Australia
Penguin Books Canada Ltd, 2801 John Street, Markham, Ontario, Canada L3R
1B4

Penguin Books Ltd, Registered Offices: Harmondsworth, Middlesex, England

First published in Great Britain 1989 by
Elm Tree Books

British Library Cataloguing in Publication Data
CIP data for this book is (!) available from the British Library

ISBN 0-241-12704-1

This book is dedicated to wife,
petite blonde vivacious artist, stunning Ingrid Spiegl (39)
with all my love
(see *ATTRIBUTIVE QUEUE*, *AGEISM*, STUNNING)

INTRODUCTION

Here are two books for the price of one: *MediaSpeak* and *MediaWrite* - both titles satirical of the current typographical fad of running words together and sticking a capital letter in the middle. To get your second book free, all you have to do is turn the volume upside-down and start again. The contents occasionally overlap, but you may find cross-references drawing attention to this. Some of the entries presented me with a quandary. Should I, for the sake of the kind of completeness even a light-hearted reference-book must strive for, include subjects I had already touched upon in my previous books, *The Joy of Words* and *In-Words and Out-Words*? I decided to compromise by putting in, on the whole, only those about which I felt I had something new to say. That applies to both sections. Some of the more obvious idiocies of newspaper English have appeared in my *Keep taking the Tabloids* (Pan Books, 1983, now out of print); and that title, too, was ironic, but in those days I did not know that irony is the last thing readers and writers of our smudgier prints understand.

As the air-waves become ever more crowded (or "de-regulated") we are constantly reminded that quality comes in inverse proportion to quantity: where broadcasting is concerned more always means worse. It happened first with the advent of "independent" (meaning *commercial* and therefore totally *dependent*) television, and again with local radio, both BBC and commercial (not to mention "community") stations: devoted to pop, pap and prattle, with little or no programmes to feed the mind, few offer information or give a public service, as Radio Four and its predecessors have been doing since the 1920s and Radio Three for nearly two generations. And now that the skies are opening to rain down from satellites the sort of rubbish people are said to demand, things can only get worse. All non-BBC channels are trying to capture the mass market, all shout for a pitch in the market place, and all under-estimate public taste.

In this book I ignore (for once) junk music and concentrate on speech. For whereas newspapers are written in an unchanging, stilted English, the spoken language as heard on radio and television is constantly changing before our very ears. Such is the power of the spoken-word media that as soon as someone hits on a cliché, vogue-word or catch-phrase, we all seem to to fall upon them and worry them to death, as a dog would a bone. The same goes for new fads in pronunciation. The great but gradual vowel shift which English underwent during the middle ages is as nothing compared to the loosening and flattening of the vowels in the 1980s, as well as the modifications of consonants. And the changes happen so fast that one is made aware of them as dramatically as plant-growth can be observed when cinema film is speeded up. The BBC takes much trouble in training its microphone staff (TV presenters are selected according to other criteria too contentious to be treated here...). But distinction must be made between announcers, who are carefully chosen and schooled in all aspects of speech (including phonetics) and are an example to us all (see *RP*); and many other broadcasters on both radio and television: reporters, correspondents, freelance presenters (not to mention local-radio reporters who are often gifted all-rounders but vocally untrained because straight out of school, or worse, the local newspaper office). The BBC is often obliged to engage staff broadcasters who are woefully under-educated. Much is expected of applicants, but the attributes so hopefully listed in job advertisements are becoming rarer year by year. Of the many graduate (i.e. post-university) aspirants to news-trainee positions some 98 per cent usually fail. Some of those who *are* successful and go on to become reporters on this or that specialist subject, or are sent to important centres like Moscow, Berlin or Paris, sometimes bring to mind the American tourist's reaction on seeing the statue of Winged Victory in the Louvre: "GEE if that's *victory* I'd like to see the one that *lost*!" (And many foreign postings seem to go to those with little aptitude for foreign languages.) No-one seems any longer to train reporters to read their scripts as if they understood the meaning of the words (words which they themselves wrote down!) Intonation is flat, monotonous and unvarying, and the least important words, especially those at the end of phrase, get the strongest stress (indeed their use of last-word stress is one of the most puzzling manifestations of current radio and TV speech!) With woeful ignorance of elementary poetry, internal word-stress differences, too, (e.g. *con*trast/con*trast*) are disregarded. Phrases are cut into short, bite-sized lengths: breath is taken not where the sense but their lung-capacity demands. The result is an inane, chanting singsong that spells death to meaning, for each phrase "sings" exactly like the previous one, landing on the identical note. Young women reporters with light, "jolly-hockey-sticks" voices seem to be specially prone to this: you can hear them everywhere - on TV, Radio Four, and especially on local radio - reporting from Westminster, on consumer and travel programmes, etc. Some of these fads are described under their own headings, e.g. *LAST-WORD STRESS* and *REPORTERS' SINGSONG*.

In these speakers (and only these, for there are many *excellent* ones) the lack of education shows in the way they both write and present news and current-affairs items. That a reporter or correspondent has not been to Balliol or Caius College or is not a member of the Atheneum club should not be held against him, but as a news-gatherer he should have kept his ears open and known that they are not pronounced "Bally-all" ,"Kay-us" and "Ath*een*-yum". And many betray their inadequate education in their *pronunciation*: not by their accent but because they had clearly never encountered certain words before, e.g. "Altdorfer's painting, the Adoration of the *Maggie*"; or "the Pope has *beautified* a Roman Catholic priest"; or (a sports reporter) "He must have discovered the secret of *euthanasia* - he seems to go on and on for ever". The man who says "the ship was *tethered* a mile from the shore" and (in the same report) that it had "heaved to" could not have read any of C.S. Forrester's maritime adventure stories. One does not expect masterminds, but some of the simpler questions from that programme MIGHT well be used in their initial training so as to sort out the worst ignoramuses (in this book internal cross-references to both halves are in SMALL CAPS).

No Radio Four news reporter should be allowed to get away with "He had sawed through the bars of his cell"; or "The pilot ejaculated over the North Sea"(WHAT - at 30,000 feet?); or "There was not hardly any smoke"; or (nervous of the common LAY/LIE confusion)"police lay siege to the bank"; or (a sports reporter): "His medals should be stricken from the record-books". An MP's broadcast statement "The Chancellor has woven a tangled web" was summarised moments later by the FRONT MAN as "He said the Chancellor had weaved a tangled web". One must, of course, make allowances. When the reporter under fire in a Nicaraguan trouble-spot said, "The President held up an empty baby's bottle" one would hardly expect his London editor to ask him to re-record that part of his despatch. But - "Mrs Thatcher had a meeting with Mr Haughey described as Frank" could and should have been corrected - if only to "Charles". So should "Their reactions have been *one* of anger" and "The situation can be summed up in *one* word - *absolute chaos!*" (see *PLURAL CONFUSIONS*). A broadcaster, whether local reporter, news-reader or Radio Three presenter, who says "seck-a-tree", "fillum", "arthuritis", "febb-you-airy" or "lawranorder" has no more right to his job than a violinist who is unable to cross his strings or play a simple scale with accuracy.

Perhaps where the training of reporters and correspondents is concerned the BBC clings to its old, Reithian courtesy. For a gentleman may draw attention to a colleague's undone flies but must never, but never, comment on careless errors in grammar or pronunciation, let alone point out a more junior colleague's solecisms. Also, to judge by the aural evidence of reporters who keep making the same mistakes over and over again, one must assume, too, that many producers no longer *produce* in the sense theatre or music producers do. Actors and musicians expect to receive "notes" after a performance, and do not generally repeat their errors. If they do they expect to find themselves replaced. I hope I have not been too hard on the foibles of weather forecasters (see *WEATHERBABBLE*) but as they are now part of "showbiz" they will understand that they may be loved or hated like any other comedian or entertainer; and many would make *excellent* comedians.

ACKNOWLEDGEMENTS

I am grateful to many colleagues, professional users of words, for help and advice, with special thanks to Harriet Cass of Radio 4 and Peter Barker of Radio 3, whose faultless diction and delivery, and pleasant, friendly voices are known and admired nationwide. In between announcing and reading the news they read my typescript, made many suggestions and comments, and in several instances saved me from a RED FACE (as has my Editor at Elm Tree Books, Caroline Taggart). The same applies to Piers Burton-Page, formerly a BBC producer and announcer, now Radio 3 Presentation Editor; and to his colleagues at Radio 4, Helen Wilson and Peter Donaldson. If readers need to imagine what *kind* of sounds I had in mind when referring to "the best kind of English" (see *RP*) they need only to recall those speakers: fortunately "BBC English" is still a model to the nation and the English-speaking world (again, see *RP*) ; and especially to those Britons who (like me) had to *learn* English instead of merely "picking it up". With Jim Black, too (formerly Presentation Editor of Radio 4, i.e. in charge of announcers), I have over the years discussed such things endlessly; and countless "Did you hear that?" notes passed between us all. Broadcasters and producers (or ex-producers) and others who work or worked for the BBC, like Barrie Hall, Cathy Wearing, Gillian Hush, Mark Rowlinson, Paul Hindmarsh, Andrew Lyle and Graham Melville-Mason, have also made useful suggestions; as did many listeners, like Mrs Dorothy Stanton, Professor Peter Fellgett FRS, David Stuckey and Philip Towell. Where I was unable to find verses to illustrate word-stressing Wendy Cope helped me by composing some - and a few I invented myself. It is now customary for people who are heard and seen on radio or television, especially TV *PERSONALITIES*, to have books "researched" (meaning *written*) for them, to which they add little except their name. This is not such a book. Apart from the acknowledgements mentioned above I stand or fall by my own research, including the illustrations. Thanks to the computer revolution I was even able to produce both the typesetting and page layout, with the help of the Apple Macintosh and a laser printer. This also means that all "keyboarding" errors, too, are necessarily mine. As an 18th-century author put it more elegantly (the extract discovered and kindly sent to me by Mrs Lisa Cox):

THe faults efcaped in the printing, wee had not fuch meanes to prevent, as we defired, nor could we conveniently collect them, by reafon of our haft, or hazard, and other interruptions : wee therefore leave them to be amended, cenfured, and winked at, according to the Readers courtefie or difcretion.

A

A for *ARTICLES, STRESSED* English has many delightful variations of pronunciation, both social and regional. There is no "right" or "wrong" way (although this never stops people complaining when others do not conform to their own ideas). But over many centuries there have developed certain traditions dictated by euphony and rhythm which have become part of *RP* because great poets and authors have enshrined them in their writings and celebrated actors spoken them. According to these traditions there are two ways of pronouncing the definite article. The elongated *the* ("thee") when preceding a word beginning with a vowel: "thee" apple, "thee" importance, "thee" only, "thee" unvarying, "thee" excellent; and the almost voiceless *the* ("thuh") before words starting with a consonant: "thuh" man, "thuh" woman "thuh" child, "thuh" good, "thuh" bad. So when Wordsworth wrote "The child is father of the man" he would not have expected to hear it spoken *"Thee* child is father of *thee* man" because it ruins the rhythm of his verse. Yet that is how many people now over-emphasise "thee" definite article. Can you imagine Gray's *Elegy written in a Country Churchyard* spoken as follows?

> *Thee* curfew tolls *thee* knell of parting day,
> *Thee* lowing herd wind slowly o'er *thee* lea,
> *Thee* ploughman homeward plods his weary way
> And leaves *thee* world to darkness and to me.

Only when one hesitates or pauses while selecting the next word does one naturally elongate the *the*: "Thee [...pause...] child is father to thee [...pause...] man". However, politicians and media persons habitually elongate as a form of emphasis, not only "thuh" into "thee" but change the indefinite article *a* "uh" into an elongated *a* rhyming with "hay". Even the most eloquent speakers give the impression that they are re-punctuating their sentences. The great parliamentarian Michael Foot would say things like "Is thee. Prime Minster aware that thee. Most urgent priority in thee. Defence of thee. Realm is ay. Close observance of ay. Strategy for..." - thus turning flow and rhythm into an almost asthmatic wheeze, but at the same time sounding both compelling and breathlessly urgent.

A for ARTICLES, MISSING The space-saving newspaper habit of omitting definite/indefinite articles (to produce an "attributive queue") copied on radio and TV. Any small savings in time are outweighed by a loss in sense and meaning. Instead of saying "John Williams, a producer of oven-ready chickens..."; or "Mrs Gordon, the specialist in reconditioned pianos..."; speakers save a comma or two and tell us in one breath, "Oven ready chicken producer John Williams yesterday..."; or "Reconditioned piano specialist Mrs Gordon..." It looks silly enough in print, but when *spoken* sounds not only absurd, angular and ugly, but also reveals that the writer/speaker has no feeling for the rhythm of words. Possessive pronouns, too, are omitted: "...this was confirmed by sister Beryl, who said brother Darren told how father Arthur always cleaned the gun..." - making them sound like nuns, monks or priests - Sister Beryl, Brother Darren and Father Arthur. The dropping of articles, definite and indefinite, has even spread even to Radio Three presentation. Although officially discouraged, scripts by some (younger?) producers may require announcers to say things like: "Today's recital is given by soprano Emma Crosby with harpsichordist Johann Goldberg, theorbo-lutenist Robert South and contrabass-piano-accordionist Ulf Halvorsen". (NO THIS IS NOT an exaggeration!) It makes "Harpsichordist" and "Theorbo-lutenist" sound as if they were grandiose titles, like "General Secretary Gorbachev". Not even journalists themselves (see *MediaWrite*) use such unnatural constructions when they *talk to each other* so why address intelligent listeners in the language of tabloid newspapers?

A for *ARTICLES, REDUNDANT* At the other extreme is the needless *duplication* of articles, definite and indefinite (or even mixed): "*A* half *a* million pounds..." or "During *the* next half *an* hour" or "*A* good, brisk, half-*an*-hour walk..." or implied: "It's available from *all a* hundred branches". There is also the redundant article combined with a redundant preposition: "*A* half *a* mile *off of* the Isle of Wight".

'ABBZZOULVE' "A subsequent inquest abbzzoulved the police..." (Radio 4 *News*) combines the *BUZZINGS* with the new modified *o* sound: from solve as in *holler* to an *o* as in *whole*.

ABSENT/ABSENT "He *ab*sented himself from his unit..." said a radio reporter who had read English at university (though perhaps not enough of it). Verb/noun stress differences printed in this book, have been tested where possible with poetry, because metre usually confirms established stressing. But changes are constantly taking place which will no doubt come to be accepted, whether Shakespeareans like it or not.

> From you I have been *ab*sent in the spring,
> When proud-pied April, dress't in all his trim,
> Hath put a spirit of youth in every thing.
> Shakespeare: *Sonnet 98.*

> If thou didst ever hold me in thy heart
> Ab*sent* thee from felicity awhile...
> Shakespeare: *Hamlet*.

ABSOLUTELY DISGUSTED See WHY (OH WHY) OH WHY?

*AB*STRACT/AB*STRACT*

> Who is the *ab*stract of all faults
> Shakespeare: *Antony and Cleopatra*.

> When, looking ab*stract*ed,
> You push those spectacles back into place,
> I am strongly attracted
> To the idea of a passionate embrace.
> Wendy Cope: *The Life of the Mind*.

'ACK-SHLEE' Speech-opener or meaningless filler, like IN (POINT OF) FACT. Both are being ousted by BASICALLY, although the time-honoured "well" shows no sign of decline. The factual "actually", indicating that something is actual or factual, or is a slight revision of what one has just said, is under threat from the fashionable HAVING SAID THAT. See also COR! and LICH-LEE.

ACOUSTIC See STATISTIC.

ACRONYMS Making words from initials has become a sport, and politicians, scientists, sociologists, charitable workers and pressure-groupers (especially they) vie with each other to make silly new words. The word *acronym* is Greek-based but a modern formation, first recorded in 1943: for an outline of its often sinister history please see my previous book, *The Joy of Words* (Elm Tree Books). When newspapers use acronyms they print an explanation of the initials in parentheses so that the reader can check back when it appears subsequently. The radio listener is unable to do this. If he tunes in after an acronym has been mentioned and explained - once - he may be perplexed by apparent gibberish. For example, a presenter of a medical programme about anorexia said,"They have devised a test they call the Eating Attitude Test, or EAT, which will..." etc. And thereafter (in a programme about eating!) he kept using the verb "eat" in what appeared to be a totally nonsensical way, as a noun. In other programmes "age" and "sad" were bandied about with barely an explanation that they meant "Action Group for the Elderly" (AGE) and "Seasonal Affective Disorders" (SAD), respectively. Broadcasters assume that 1) listeners know what they themselves know (in which case why are they giving the talk?); 2) that they never switch on late; 3) that the telephone or doorbell never makes them miss a single word. Some modish abbreviations are not acronyms but words chosen because they are somehow connected with the aims or activities of an organisation, like "Provide" or "Conduct"; or "Relate" (as we must now call the Marriage Guidance Council!). Like acronyms, these phoney nouns are used as if they had been in the dictionaries for centuries; and of course make nonsense to most listeners.

ACTUALITY Extraneous noises in radio programmes or programme items to add atmosphere, drama or realism. They take, broadly, two forms: continuous background with which speech has to compete, or (more often) a few seconds of opening introductory noise, perhaps only vaguely related to the subject and faded out as soon as the speaker embarks on his story. From that moment it is never heard, or referred to, again. Thus an item about the summit of Everest is sure to start with a fragment of howling wind - possibly from the Sound Effects Catalogue (No. EC18Af, one of 50-odd kinds of wind available). A few seconds later the gale mysteriously abates and the speaker continues unhindered. News from the picket-line is always precded by a burst of angry chanting or baying. Dispatches from wars and revolutions start with a stutter or two of machine-gun fire or a couple of explosions (No. EC 146A b02 in the Sound Effects Catalogue?), then faded, leaving the correspondent alone with his tape-recorder. World War II home front atmosphere is evoked by a brief up-and-down wail of an air-raid siren, mixed with the throb of enemy bombers overhead. A few seconds of morse-code dots and dashes (plus concertinas, the long-established "French Atmosphere" noise) effortlessly transport us to the French resistance. World War I atmosphere? Half a dozen bars of "It's a long Way to Tipperary" (with the tramp-tramp-tramping of army boots) set the scene. Nostalgic plays about childhood are introduced by a playground singing-game, rendered as tunelessly as only today's cloth-eared young can "sing" (indeed, children singing out of tune are always good value). Whenever a soldier, sailor or airman is buried we are sure to hear part of the Last Post. Train journeys begin and end with the obligatory choo-choo of appropriate vintage (enthusiasts will spot the slightest anachronism) and programmes about prisons begin and/or end with the inevitable clang of a cell door. If a telephone-call is made, e.g. in an investigative piece, we get *brr-brr, brr-brr*, twice. Always twice, though telephone bells are changing fast. For the seaside the old *DESERT ISLAND DISCS* seagull or one of her sisters is wheeled out (See NO THIS IS NOT...). The ludicrous thing about stock radio clichés in news or features is that they are introduced in such a way that the listener is led to believe the first sounds he will hear are those of the presenter whose name has just been announced. Instead of which we get that old seagull, a horse's neighing, a cockerel's crowing or a chuntering ape. The listener wonders - is the presenter an animal impressionist or a lunatic? So when the melancholy Last Post is sounded again, and it is preceded by the words, "This report from Christopher Smooth" - we hear what we think is Mr Smooth himself blowing a burst on the bugle, then wiping his lips and embarking on his description of the scene. Actuality has been cheapened by the advent of simple, self-adjusting, hand-held cassette tape-recorders which any reporter can point in the direction of a sound. The result is mixed with his speech later, in the studio, and that is why the effect sounds artificial and contrived. See also *LIBRARY FILM*.

'ADDAWL' See NODDADAWL.

AFFIRMATIVE The American *yes*. See also INDEED and DEFINITELY.

'AHBEE' As used for *MENUS*. "In today's *You and Yours* ahbee talking about..." Its declension is youbee, heebee, sheebee, weebee, theybee (some of which see separately). Also WHOBEE, as in "Jonathan Smith whobee back next week..." and DURBEE, an essential element in *WEATHERBABBLE*. On commercial radio and TV - "WEEBEE back after the BREAK".

'AH-BEE-TREE' *SYNCOPATION* of arbitrary.

AITCHES See *HAITCHES*.

'ALCOHOLE' See *GENTEEL O MODIFICATION*.

'ALLIANCE/ALLOWANCE' *(THE) NAY LONGER RIND O* makes the two sound almost the same.

ALSO Like ONLY, a word often mis-stressed: "Max Belgrave, who *also* presented the programme..." has a different meaning from "Max Belgrave, who also *presented* the programme..."

ANCHORMAN The chairman of a magazine or discussion programme, a PRESENTER who links the contents or contributions and ensures that everyone gets his say: now a little dated. It is one of 151 "sexist" words banned by Radio New Zealand in 1988 by order of its Director General Beverley Wakem, who also banished gamesmanship, heroine, maiden voyage, father-land, mother nature and even mothering (the latter doubtless replaced by PARENTING). Yet the words "Director" and "General", two eminently male-associated titles, appear not to be on Ms Wakem's hit-list.

AND - VARIETIES OF The *OED* gives more than 46 inches to this little word, listing its connective and additive meanings, etc. But it fails to define the radio and TV "and", unless you reinterpret its definition,*"And*, introductory, continuing the narration, from a previous sentence, expressed or under-stood..." For in broadcasting this may be not just a previous sentence but a previous programme. PRESENTERS walk into a cold studio and start their recording with a cheery, breezy "*And* hello THERE..." There is also the Radio Exclamatory "A-a-a-a-nd...!" barked in schools programmes in the way a drill sergeant - and the German *Achtung!* - give warning that a command is to follow: "A-a-a-a-nd... stop!" But the most nonsensical *and* is that which has no function at all, merely a punctuation-mark in news reports: "Tennis-*and* Britain's seeds are all out of the tournament..." or "The weather-*and* it will be mostly dry".

AND FROM ... TO ... See *LINKS*.

AND NOW IF YOU'LL EXCUSE ME Drama cliché, used chiefly in radio plays as a scene-changing device. Usually followed by "I've got work to do", which makes it all the more contrived: people in real life would find some polite excuse.

AND WITH THAT ... Investigative reporters' cliché: "And with that he banged the door in my face."

AND I QUOTE ... This parenthetic interjection is unnecessary if the speaker can change inflexion and *PACE* to indicate a quotation. On TV "and I quote" may be replaced by the now fashionable, quaint "I quote" gesture: both hands raised aloft, first and second fingers sticking up like rabbit's ears and brought down once or twice to meet the thumb. See also WAIT FOR IT! and *PUNCTUATION-BY-INTONATION*.

AND THERE WE (MUST) LEAVE IT News and current affairs PRE-SENTERS' often peremptory way of telling guests that their discussion or argument must come to an end.

*A*NNEXE/ANN*EX* The first is the noun (an added building) and stressed on the first syllable; the second the act of annexation, firmly stressed on the second. But many announcers and newsreaders say both in the same way: "The Russians *an*nexed Afghanistan".

A NONSENSE People used to declare that some idea, argument or view was "nonsense", and often did so with vehemence. But German-American has given the word a nonsensical indefinite article; also "a coffee" (though not "a tea").

'ANOREXIC' Should surely be anorectic - and the same applies to dyslectic, but the persistent misusers always win. Let us be thankful they did not also force us into "epilepsic", "dyspepsic", "sythesic" and "pathesic"?

APPLICABLE/APPLICABLE The former is preferred by RP-speakers, though for no good reason.

ARE YOU SITTING COMFORTABLY? Cliché catch-phrase from the lamented *Listen with Mother* radio programme. The follow-up is, "Then I'll begin".

ARISTOCRAT Has the stress on the *first* syllable; aris*toc*racy on the third; and aristo*crat*ic on the forth. Anyone who puts it anywhere else, especially the second syllable, is either American or not an aristocrat.

'ARTHURITIS' See *INTRUSIONS AND SUPERFLUITIES.*

'ARTIC' Also "antartic": one of the omitted-consonant group of words, like "lenth", "strenth", "fith", "elettric", etc.

'ASHFELT' Almost universal, time-honoured mispronunciation of "asphalt", especially among those who work with the material, so it is probably traditional. ("Ashfelt" is often covered with "bitch-you-men".)

'AZSHOO' Increasingly common way of saying "as you", sounding like the French word *ajout*. Try saying "as you" separately and you need to move the position of the tongue on your palate, whereas with "*ajout*" you hardly need to move it at all. This is how the language shifts, and how pronunciations like "station" (originally "stass-y-on" - with two tongue-movements) came about.

AS IT WERE See IF-YOU-LIKE.

(THE) AS ... OPENER See *CAUSE-AND-EFFECT OPENERS.*

'ASSESSORIES' In fashion-experts' talk, what complete a woman's wardrobe, e.g. hat, handbag, shoes, a poodle, etc. Perhaps we owe it to the Access Card that we still distinguish between "access" and "assess". See also SUSSINCT.

ATE The standard *RP* English pronunciation is "et", an ancient form probably going back to Germanic *essen*. Scottish and rural English speakers prefer the "purer" pronunciation "eight", and look askance at Englishmen who say they "et" their meal. However, a magn*ate* is not the same as a magn*et*, and the separate pronunciations may be worth preserving. See also EXPA-TRIATE.

-ATION See *INFLUX OF -ATIONS*.

AT THE END OF THE DAY As a Radio 4 educationist said: "At the end of the day school dinners are not likely to be very popular with pupils..." (especially when they've already gone home and had their tea...) This is a common but meaningless prelude to a statement which is unlikely to be a profound one - a mere filler, like the ubiquitous BASICALLY. Also "In the final analysis", "When all is said and done", etc.

AT THIS (VERY)(PRESENT) MOMENT IN TIME American translation of German longwindedness (*Zu diesem Zeitpunkt*). It has been satirised, ridiculed and lampooned but refuses to LAY down and die. Now chiefly heard from trades unionists, captains of industry, soldiers, sports reporters and sundry PUNDITS wheeled out to face microphone and camera. They will do anything to avoid the little word "now". See PERIOD OF TIME. CURRENTLY has also had a good run, and PRESENTLY continues to confuse.

(TO) AUTHOR Recent verb-from-noun formation, like PARENTING, which saves a little time but generates much irritation, at any rate until we all get used to it.

(AND) A VERY SPECIAL HELLO! By all means let us be friendly to each other but no listener or viewer is taken in by a pretence that he is the *only* one the presenter cares about (any more than a newspaper reader falls for an "exclusive" offer): satirised by Sir Robin Day, ONE-TIME presenter of *The World at One*, who used to end the programme with the words, "And a *very* good afternoon - especially to YOU!" See also THANK YOU.

'AVERZSHON' See *SOFTENED SH*.

AXE A tedious and over-used *MediaWrite* cliché which *sounds* even more foolish when spoken, e.g. "The Prime Minister will probably axe two of her senior ministers".

B

(THE) BACKCHAT EFECT Has been fashionable for some years: listener/viewer participation, e.g. when letters from listeners/viewers are read aloud but broken up into short phrases and interspersed with, and interrupted

by, smart, arch or even sharp remarks from the *PRESENTER*. It was used for some years on *Feedback* (Radio 4) and is still the mannered way of *Points of View* on BBC TV. Many good ideas become boring when over-used.

BALANCED ON A KNIFE EDGE Five words better expressed by one: "uncertain". Also WALKING A TIGHTROPE.

BALLS IN COURTS Meaninglessly overused sports cliché, as in "The ball is very firmly in the opposition's court". Ballgames, recently imported from USA, are, well, "a different kind of ballgame altogether".

BALLS(-UP) See *RUDE WORDS*.

BASICALLY The most common opener, especially when replying to questions, and now a full-blown plague. It comes in many ways, from the cockney "by-sickly" to the Welsh "bäsically" (sung with a different note for each of its four syllables!), the flat, bleated Geordie "bäääsically", and any number of foreign accents. It is often followed, somewhere in the middle of a statement, by the interjection IF-YOU-LIKE; and at the end (especially from footballers, managers, boxers, snooker-players, etc.) by -LIKE, YER KNOW, or "yerknowlike".

(THE) BBC COFFEE JOKE All disc jockeys and most serious broadcasters with an opportunity for voicing impromptu asides are sure to mention the "awful BBC coffee". It is in fact very good - "real" (not instant): probably the best and certainly the cheapest institutional coffee in the country.

(THE) BBC'S PHILHARMONIC ORCHESTRA See YOB'S *POSSESSIVE*.

BELIEVE YOU ME USA (from German, *Glauben sie mir*) alternative to "no kidding". In the middle of a sensible discussion, perhaps between politicians or B'SN'SSM'N, it sounds like a lapse into pidgin.

BEST-SELLING AUTHOR As in "WEEBEE talking to best-selling authors Jeffrey Archer, Monica Dickens and Barbara Cartland..." They can't all be *best*-selling. Barbara Cartland, for one, sells "better" than the other two. The best-selling author must be God who AUTHORED ("holy-ghosted"?) the Bible. See also AWARD-WINNING in *MediaWrite*.

BID Headline word meaning "attempt" or "try". Like other newspaper abbreviations it does not sound good in spoken English. But many, like PLEA, PROBE and VOW, have crept into radio and TV news. I wish they would creep out again. Good broadcasters can do without newspaper puns, juvenile joke-riddles and time-saving clichés.

'BISHARLES' England, Scotland, Wales and AH-LAND, in WEATHERBABBLE.

'BITSA' RAIN *WEATHERBABBLE.* When rain comes in "bits" it is called hail.

BLACK-EDGED VOICE A kind of INTONATION reserved for bad news, chiefly death announcements. The voice starts on a slightly higher note than usual for the deceased's forename and drops an octave for his surname: "Doug [octave-drop] Smith, the well-known racehorse trainer, has died at the age of 99"; whereas "Doug [no drop - voice remains level] Smith, the well-known racehorse trainer, has CLOCKED UP another Derby winner". Unfortunately few announcers now use this effect and it must itself be pronounced dead. See also NEWS INVERSIONS.

BLAH BLAH BLAH The threefold blah is a variant of ECK-SETTERA, especially when the speaker reports verbatim.

BLAST Newspapers use this for "explosion" because it is shorter. But a blast is the movement of air that *follows* the explosion. In spoken English such small inaccuracies are more readily noticed than in print.

'BRAHM' Mythical German composer sometimes featured on Radio 3, as in "Brahm's Fourth Symphony". The script may say *Brahms'* but the genteelly-soundless apostrophe destroys the distinction. Surely "Brahmses"?

'BRAZZIA' See *BUZZING S.*

BREAK As in "SEE YOU after the break!" dissembling euphemism meaning advertisements on commercial stations. See also AHBEE and WEEBEE.

(VERY) BRIEFLY Interviewer's warning to the person he is interviewing that the interview is approaching its conclusion and he had better be brief, e.g. my all-time favourite: " Very briefly, Reverend, JUST what *are* the implications of two thousand years of Christianity?" See also the section about interviews in my previous book, *The Joy of Words* (Elm Tree Books).
BROADCASTER See PERSONALITY.

'B'SN'SSM'N' Common *SYNCOPATION* of "businessman". When the speaker uses the *BUZZING S* it becomes *b'zzn'zzm'n* - see below for further examples of buzzing bees.

(THE) BULK OF Best avoided in certain applications, like "The bulk of women taking the slimming course reported little or no success..." Try "most of".

(THE) BUZZING S Consonant modification adopted by many communicators and possibly related to the *SOFT-BOILED X*. The Buzzing *S* makes chrysalis into *chryzzalis*, brassière into *brazzia*, bassoon into *buzzoon*, desolate into *dezz' late*, dose into *doze*, forensic into *frenzic*, virtuosity into *virtuozzity*, gristle into *grizzle*, parsley into *pahzzlee* (this one pioneered by a well-known TV cook), dissertation into *dizzertation*, divisive into *de-veye-zive* (or *d' vizzive*), dissolve into *dizzolve* (or *dizzoulve* - see *GENTEEL O*). I have also noted down *compulzzory, dezzision, perzuazive, permizzible, philozzophy, ele' trizzity, azzma* (asthma!), *unprezzedented* and many more. The personal pronoun "us" was one of the earliest victims of this creeping genteelisation: for many it rhymes not with "bus" but "buzz". *NAMES*, too, are being turned into buzz-words. The Russian composer Mussorgsky has become *M' zzorgsky*, and Heseltine *Hezzle-tine*, which is not how the Right Honourable Michael of that family introduces himself. The BBC always prides itself on pronouncing surnames in the way the families say them but now even some respected broadcasters buzz round such names like swarms of angry bees. See also the *SOFTENED SH*.

BY This book is *by* me, not the excellent printer whose presses produced the copy you are reading. But on music announcements "by" may mean the performer(s), not the composer. So you get announcements like *"Feelin' high on Dope Baby?* by the Rolling Stones" or *"Polovtsian Dances* by the London Philharmonic Orchestra". Even the lamented Roy Plomley used this solecism in his *DESERT ISLAND DISCS*.

C

CACHE Try a *hoard* or a *store* of arms. You will then be talking English - and if you say *cache* like "cash" you are not talking French anyway. See also COUP.

CAMEO ROLES See *SPECIAL APPEARANCE*.

CAN I JUST SAY ONE WORD? As I was compiling this book a politician made that request on *Any Questions?* His wish was granted and he spoke without hesitation or interruption for a good four minutes.

CAN I/LET ME MAKE ONE THING ABSOLUTELY CLEAR? Politicians' meaningless noise: a mere delaying device when replying to an awkward question. On *Today* an interviewer once countered this with a brusque, "No. I'd rather you answered my question".

(THE) CAN'TARDLIES See *REDUNDANCIES AND PLEONASMS*.

'CAPSHOOLS' *YOD DROPPERS* take their medicine in this form. *Medicine Now* (Radio 4) is positively rattling with capshools, dripping with inshlin and raging out-of-control with demensha; while its sister-programme YOU 'N' JAWS is full of CONSHOOMER items. Blame the "Jeshooits". However, I have also heard the American "Caps'l'", which is almost the same sound as the German *Kapsel*.

CAPTIONS See *GRAPHICS, LIBRARY FILM* and *TALKING HEADS*.

CAREER DIPLOMAT Sounds like a tautology - at any rate when applied to British diplomats, who go through a rigorous selection procedure and may rise to dizzy heights only after menial jobs as third secretaries in obscure countries. But there is always the chance that a prime minister may appoint his non-career, non-diplomat, son-in-law to be Ambassador in Washington..

'CAR-*RICK*-A-TYOOR' The *OED* says "the stress was, and is often still, on the *u*, especially in the verb and derivatives, especially *caricaturing*, etc". It says nothing about a stress on the *ic*, which is placed there by communicators who are clearly not AR-*IS*-TOCRATS - or are merely unfamiliar with the word.

CARING A beautiful word irretrievably politicised. The jingling, rhyming reduplication "caring-sharing", once a favourite in the same quarters, has been satirised out of existence.

CAUSE-AND-EFFECT OPENERS Cliché intended to lend continuity and urgency to news stories. The trick is to manufacture sentences that begin with "As...", "With..." or "After..., followed by a long string of words: "As rain disrupts the third test, England are 79 for six..." or "With polling coming to an end in the local elections it is becoming clear that...", etc. This is the way journalists write in newspapers, not how they converse.

(THE) CHAIN LINK EFFECT "An effect which reporters use to add drama to their reports, reports that often come from foreign countries, coun-

tries in turmoil, a turmoil they feel may be conveyed by this kind of bogus continuity, continuity derived from repeating the last element of each phrase, a phrase that amplifies what ..." Reporters can go on like this for ever, and some do.

'CHARD' As in "chard abuse". The process of flattening the *i* sound into *ah* may have been speeded by the curious diction of pop-singers. Their vocal apparatus usually ranges from the inadequate to the nonexistent, and they are therefore unable to produce a singing (*singing?*) tone except with a fully-open *ah* (the easiest vowel to sing on): e.g. "Mah sweet Laahd".

'CHARL' As above, but legal process, as in "The charl has opened of two alleged terrorists..."

CHAT SHOWS Guests are generally showbiz *PERSONALITIES* "opening this week in the West End" (which impresses listeners in the North of Scotland hardly at all) or authors with books "just out". Hosts are likely to be even more famous than guests, and the ultimate accolade is having the show named after him in an awesome, single-word title, e.g. "I saw him on *Wospel*". There is also a small catchment group of regular, proven chat show (also panel games) guests - some of whom also spend their whole lives on TV and radio *GAME SHOWS*). Some programmes, like the Radio 4 *Midweek*, specialise in exposing amiable eccentrics or harmless lunatics intending to do something unusual, eccentric or lunatic, or who are made into a contrived "birthday guest". On chat shows DIDN'T YOU ONCE? is often used, a phrase with which the host reminds a guest of some anecdote rehearsed beforehand, which the host has in his notes but the guest forgets to bring up, e.g. "Didn't you once lend Elizabeth Taylor a pair of knickers?"

CHEERS! See THANK YOU.

'CHEW MALT' As in "There was chew malt in the Commons when Mr Kinnock clashed with Mr Heffer on Chewsday". "The first Chewsday in FEBB-YOU-AIRY" perhaps? See *YOD-DROPPING*.

'CHINEE SHARDS' *YOD-DROPPERS'* Chinese yards. Also *SYNCOPATIONS* like "Chineeshculpture" and "Chineeshipyards" - only a few examples of a common trend in the evolution of informal English, a development which offends some listeners but is happily accepted by many more. However, the effort expended on separating the *s* from the *y* sound is MINIMAL: a simple drawing-back of the tongue by a millimetre or two.

'CHOOPS' As in "Russian choops are moving out of Afghanistan". Scots are proud of the rolled *r* - and so, to a lesser extent, are the Irish. But English and Welsh prefer to skate over the *r* altogether, e.g."jigh" weather. But see *INTRUSIVE R*.

'CHRIS-CHIN' *SYNCOPATION* of the same order as "stay-shun", i.e. so long established that anyone now saying "Chriss-tee-ann" sounds almost mannered. Other examples will be found throughout this book: I include them for the record, not to criticise.

'CLAHDY' Cloudy - see *NAY LONGER RIND O*.

CLOCKING UP (e.g. a century) See *MediaWrite*.

CLOUD CUCKOO LAND Imaginary place where difficult interviewees are thought to live; which is why, when their interviewers have run out of questions, they ask, "But aren't you living in cloud cuckoo land?" See also other favourite questions, e.g. HOW WORRIED ARE YOU? or DOES THAT WORRY YOU? And, of course, the stock question of stock questions, HOW DO YOU FEEL?

COCK A HOOP What mediamen think we feel when pleased: "Neil Kinnock was cock a hoop yesterday as..." Real people in real life seldom if ever feel cock a hoop.

COCK UP See *RUDE WORDS*.

*COM*BAT/COM*BAT*

> The *com*bat deepens. On, ye brave,
> Who rush to glory, or the grave!
> > Thomas Campbell: *Hohenlinden*.

> To com*bat* a poor famish'd man
> > Shakespeare: *Henry VI*.

COM*BINE*/COM*BINE*

> God, the best maker of all marriages,
> Com*bine* your hearts in one.
> > Shakespeare: *King Henry V*.

The accentuation on the second syllable is confirmed by countless poems, farmers stress "*com*bine" (i.e. harvester) on the first; and this has absurdly been taken up by reporters: "Christian militia forces have *com*bined with

Israeli troops" - suggesting that they brought in the harvest together.

COMING ON STREAM From the oil industry but used as a cliché for "starting to work", even when no liquid is involved: "The first cars have been coming on stream".

COMMAS From aural evidence it seems that some radio news scripts use commas and full-stops interchangeably, this is a deplorable practice, it only makes it more difficult for the reader to use proper inflexions and for the listener to understand his meaning, perhaps the idea is to give an impression that news items are presented in the urgent form of a shopping-list, I don't like it, see also RIP AND READ.

COMMENT/COMMENTATOR/COMMENT "In an impromptu *com*ment the *com*mentator com*ment*ed upon the situation..." is what Alvar Lidell would have said. But most speakers now stresses the verb on the first syllable.

COMMUNITY RADIO See *JUNK RADIO*. And for an interpretation of the catch-all sociological word "community" please see *The Joy of Words*.

COMPACT/COMPACT Rousseau's *Social Compact* as well as a lady's powder *com*pact stress the word on the first syllable, but the verb and adverb are stressed on the second. But although the BBC advises Radio 3 speakers to say "Com*pact* Disc" practice is about evenly divided.

> Sweet spring, full of sweet days and roses,
> A box where sweets com*pact*ed lie.
> George Herbert: *Virtue*

COMPOUND/COMPOUND Cattle are kept in *com*pounds, but actions are com*pound*ed.

> Com*pound* for sins they are inclin'd to
> By damning those they have a mind to.
> Samuel Butler: *Hudibras*.

CONCEITS Or better, the conceit of some who make radio and TV programmes. They hold the view that the listener or viewer always switches on at the beginning of the programme and remains captivated until the end, and that his attention never wanders. The telephone never rings in mid-programme, no persons from Porlock arrive unannounced at his front-door . Thus, in a discussion programme the speakers may be identified *once*, at the beginning, verbally by the presenter or chairman on radio, and on TV by means of a briefly superimposed *CAPTION*. After that, a distracted or late switcher-on must guess who is taking part. The folly of this is compounded when those who take part in the programme (probably strangers to each other) decide immediately to be on first-name terms, according to the custom of INSTANT MATEYNESS. So all we know is that John is speaking to Michael, with interjections from Ros, Dave and Jane. See also GOOD TO BE BACK! and TALKING TO.

CONCERT PIANIST Equestrians do not speak about HORSE(BACK) RIDING but simply "riding"; similarly musicians add no qualification to "pianist", unless a consciously distinguishing between a "classical" pianist and, say, a pub pianist, jazz pianist or honky-tonk pianist, etc.

*CON*DUCT/CON*DUCT*

> Sir Plume, of amber snuff-box justly vain,
> And the nice *con*duct of a clouded cane.
> Alexander Pope: *The Rape of the Lock*

> Con*duct*or, when you receive a fare,
> Punch in the presence of the passnjare!
> N.G.Osborn: *Isaac H. Bromley*

> Con*duct* yourself with due decorum
> Talking to the Great Panjorum.
> Anon.

CONFERRING TOGETHER A *REDUNDANCY*. "Conferring" on its own means exactly that.

*CON*FLICT/CON*FLICT* The same differences apply as above.

CONSHUMERS See *YOD-DROPPING*.

*CON*SORT/CON*SORT* See above.

*CON*TEST/CON*TEST*

> What dire offence from am'rous causes springs
> What mighty *con*tests rise from trivial things.
> Alexander Pope: *The Rape of the Lock*

> In spite of the codicils granny requested,
> Where there's a will there's a way to con*test* it,
> Anon.

*CON*TRACT/CON*TRACT*

> Come, temperate nymphs, and help to celebrate
> A *con*tract of true love: be not too late.
>> Shakespeare: *The Tempest*

> To whom the Angel with con*tract*ed brow
> Accuse not Nature, she hath done her part;
> Do thou but thine, and be not diffident
> Of wisdom, she deserts thee not if thou
> Dismiss not her.
>> John Milton: *Paradise Lost*

*CON*TRAST/CON*TRAST*

> Let the loud drum in *con*trast beat
> While trumpets blare in battle's heat.
>> Anon.

> I know not how long the gay dance might have lasted
> With the semibreve's gravity strangely con*trast*ed.
>> Anon.

CONTROVERSY/CON*TROV*ERSY One of the most heatedly discussed stress differences containing perhaps an element of verbal class-warfare, for *RP*-speakers tend to say *con*troversy, while con*trov*ersy is considered more down-market/journalese. (See also line three of the verse by Matthew Prior printed under the heading DISPUTE). But once you examine analogous words you will find that the controversy controversy is a lot of fuss about nothing. People who hate con*trov*ersy probably say in*trav*enous instead of *intra*venous, and certainly ex*trap*olate. But as people do complain about con*trov*ersy, never about *con*troversrsy, speakers who have no strong feelings either way might consider stressing the *first* syllable and lead a quiet life. Better still, say "argument, debate, disagreement", etc. (See *RE-PHRASING*). And also KILOMETRE and *SPLIT INFINITIVES*.

'CONVERZSHON' See *SOFTENED SH*.

*CON*VERT/CON*VERT*

> Charming women can true *con*verts make,
> We love the precepts for the teacher's sake.
>> George Farquhar: *The Constant Couple*

> And be you blithe and bonny
> Con*vert*ing all your sounds of woe
> Into Hey nonny, nonny.
>> Shakespeare: *Much Ado about Nothing*

CONVICT/CONVICT

> Banished he was for ever more
> To the distant *con*vict shore.
> Anon.

> Lose no time to contradict her
> Nor endeavour to con*vict* her
> Jonathan Swift: *Daphne*

COR! With or without the optional "Blimey", a favourite introductory noise of one or two disc-jockeys, where others might prefer the ubiquitous BASICALLY or the almost obsolete ACK-SHLEE.

COUP Like CACHE, an unnecessary foreign word. *Revolt, uprising...?*

COURTESY TITLES See *TITLES*.

CRUNCH (SITUATION) A monstrosity at last on the wane, to be satirised into oblivion, and not before time.

'CUVVENTRY' Common among older *RP* speakers for Coventry; also "Cuvvent" Garden and "cunvents". But most of those who live in Coventry, Covent Garden or convents seem to disagree. Perhaps there is some ancient reason for the eccentricity: after all, witches speak about their "cuvven" and we bake our buns in the "uvven".

CURRENTLY One of several ways of avoiding the short word "now". See PRESENTLY and AT THIS (VERY)(PRESENT) MOMENT IN TIME.

D

'DAY-EE-TEE' Now almost standard for "deity", though older listeners insist on "dee-ee-tee" (and "spontan-ee-eeity"). But as Latin *deus* is pronounced "day-us", not "dee-us" I suspect that "dee-i-tee" springs from the idiosyncratic Latin pronunciation taught in the big old public schools, like "weeny, weedy, weakie"; "Tee Deeum and Joo-bilah-tay" are widely accepted.

DE- See *ELONGATED PREFIXES*.

DEAD MEN "The dead man was seen driving away from the town at about noon". Clever of him, but was the TV reporter quite *sure* the man was *dead*?

And "The widow watched helplessly as they coldbloodedly shot her husband..." gets its chronology in a twist. One does not wish to quibble about tragic events but when the unfortunate woman watched she was not yet a widow.

DEFINITELY Dated and downmarket form of an emphatic "yes". It came into fashion during the early days of TV interviews, spread by a foolish *GAME-SHOW* in which contestants "lost" if they said "yes" or "no". Other "yes" clichés include INDEED and POSITIVELY; and Americans like to bark AFFIRMATIVE (after the German "*Jawohl!*"?) See also OF COURSE.

'DER-EYE-ZORY' New, genteel, *BUZZING S* sound that makes *s* into *z* , like "chryzzalis", "explozive", etc. Wages offers are sometimes called "de-rizz-ory", by analogy with DIVIZZIVE.

DESERT/DESERT

> What ailed us, O gods, to de*sert* you
> For creeds that refuse and restrain?
> Come down and redeem us from virtue,
> Our Lady of Pain.
>   Charles Algernon Swinburne: *Dolores*

> Fret not to roam the *desert* now,
> with all thy winged speed:
> I may not mount on thee again -
> thou'rt sold, my Arab steed!
>   Caroline Norton: *The Arab's Farewell to his Steed*

DESERT ISLAND DISCS One of the longest-running radio programmes, a national institution and favourite subject for cartoonists, parodies and spin-off programmes ("Desert Island Discards", "Desert Island Risks", "Desert Island Duds", etc). D.I.D. was devised by Roy Plomley and postulates the banishment of some well-known *PERSONALITY* to an imaginary remote island, with nothing but a gramophone, eight records, a book (other than the big dictionaries), the Bible, Shakespeare, and one luxury. This, the rules state, must not have a roof in case the castaway makes it serve as a house, or be converted into one. So upright pianos are allowed, grands prohibited, as the castaway might sleep under it. ("Are you good with your hands - could you build a shelter?"). The programme goes back to the early days of radio when gramophones and records were less widely available, and tape-recorders unheard of. Earlier castaways therefore genuinely welcomed the rare opportunity of hearing their favourite records from the unrivalled BBC Gramophone Library. Plomley always took much trouble to find out what he could about his guest, gave him lunch at his club and enjoyed talking to people who shared his love of classical music. When pop-entertainer guests were unavoidable he tolerated them and their choice with courtesy. After his death *Desert Island Discs* moved in various directions and, some said, began to lose its way. His successors relied more on the work of RE-SEARCHERS, making nonsense of the original idea of a conversation between friends. The fame of the presenters often over-awed their subjects; whereas Plomley laid no claim to any fame except as presenter of *Desert Island Discs*. He devoted all his time to it, seldom broadcasting on other programmes; and not only made his name with the programme, but made it totally his own. Thus, however good his successors, he is irreplaceable.

'DETERIATION' Common *SYNCOPATION* occasionally so mis-spelt.

'DEZZOLATE' See *BUZZING S*.

DIALECT Is not the same as "accent". See *RP*.

'DICK ENGINE' "Conditions are positively dick engine". *LAZY TONGUE* pronunciation of Dickensian. See also GILBERSHUN and SHOOBERSHON; and DEMENSHA.

DIDN'T YOU ONCE...? Said by *CHAT SHOW* hosts nudging guests to tell a story previously rehearsed, e.g. "Didn't you once stroke Hitler's cat?"

'DIE-LAY-TORY' Common alternative pronunciation of "dilatory", normally either "dill-a-tory" or the three-syllable "dill-a-tree". A confusion with "dilation" and between two Latin-based words: *dilatorius*, a loiterer and *dilatus*, wide apart.

'DIE-SECT' There is no argument about this, a creeping *mis*pronunciation of dissect, spoken even by some medics. *Dis + sect* is from Latin for "cutting up". "Die-sect" would have only one *s* and be "cutting across". The culprit is the false analogy with *bi*sect = cut in two.

'DIFFERENT THAN/TO' Americans like it, but English purists say only "from" will do. But this doesn't always work satisfactorily, especially when in longer sentences the differing things or ideas are so far apart that "from" sounds awkward. "Homer is different than a pigeon" and "Homer differs to a pigeon" both sound wrong; but, "The word Homer means something different for a student of philosophy than it does for a fancier of racing-pigeons" is acceptable. The alternative would have to be the clumsy "...means something different from what it does..." See 'IN THE SAME WAY THAT'.

DIRECT/DIRECTLY The first means "by the straightest route", the second, "soon". The false "directly" is analogous to the absurd (and absurdly common) IMPORTANTLY. But "The concert comes to you direct from the Royal Albert Hall" is BBC jargon meaning "live" transmission. Pop musicians oxymoronically speak of a "live recording", though one knows what they mean.

DISCOURSE/DISCOURSE

> Not by your individual whiskers
> But by your dialect and *dis*course.
> Samuel Butler: *Hudibras*

> Bid me dis*course*, I will enchant thine ear,
> Or like a fairy trip upon the green,
> Or, like a nymph with long dishevell'd hair,
> Dance on the sands, and yet no footing seen...
> Shakespeare: *Venus and Adonis.*

DISCOUNT/DISCOUNT

> Walter works in the *dis*count trade -
> A surefire thing and he's got it made.
> Lichtenstein: *The Discount Trade*

> Dis*count* the rumours, whisper it not
> Some like it tepid, some like it hot.
> Arden: *Penny*

DISGUSTED, TUNBRIDGE WELLS See WHY (OH WHY) OH WHY?

'DISHEER' This year: an example of *YOD-DROPPING*, like 'larsheer', 'necksheer' and 'ee-cheer' - not to mention the apparently ailing 'sick shears'. No longer confined to vulgar yobs' speech: many young professionals and old politicians affect them, too.

DISINVITATION An invitation withdrawn. Why not say so, since the time saved is both MARGINAL and MINIMAL?

DISPUTE/DISPUTE In the "best" speech, or *RP,* there is no stress difference between noun and verb, both having the stress on the second syllable:

> Waste not your Hour, nor in vain pursuit
> Of this and That endeavour and dis*pute*...
> Edward FitzGerald: *Omar Khayyám*

He his fabric of the Heavens
Hath left to their dis*putes*, perhaps to move
His laughter at their quaint opinions wide...
John Milton: *Paradise Lost*

He religion so well with her learning did suit
That in practice sincere, and in controverse mute,
She shewed she knew better to live than dis*pute*.
Matthew Prior: *The Lady who offers her
Looking-Glass to Venus*

But the trend is now towards *dis*pute, suggesting a kind of negation of "pute" (which in archaic English is a strumpet or whore!) See also RE-.

'DISS' As in "Diss gummunt": Common opening words of frustrated politicians. If you listen carefully to vehement or angry words you will find that the *th* usually comes out as *d*.

'DIZZIDENTS' Dissidents, according to the *BUZZING S* fashion.

DJ BABBLE Disc jockeys and other presenters of live, unscripted programmes are required to have what Bishop Henson described as "The fatal facility for continuous utterance"; and when that facility is under strain they fill gaps with meaningless interjections like "It's all go!" or "That's the way it is", or "KEEP THOSE LETTERS COMING IN", etc. When even the clichés fail they can always SPIN another disc, or slot in a cassette to pound out the station jingle. BBC Radio 2, incidentally, does not admit to having disc-jockeys. They are called "presenters"; and a few do "present" and are very good at their job. The rest - babble. See also *WEATHERBABBLE*.

DOES THAT WORRY YOU? Stock question (of the HOW DO YOU FEEL? and CLOUD CUCKOO LAND group) asked of interviewees who clearly *are* worried. Also "*JUST* HOW worried *are* you?", as if worry could be precisely quantified.

DOING WELL/DOING GOOD There is a difference between the two, except among *SPORTS COMMENTATORS*: "Didn't the lad do good?" does not refer to his charitable works.

DOWNING As in "After the downing of an Iranian airliner ..." (Radio 4 *News*). Ale is colloquially downed, workers may down tools in hope of having their wages upped. But in serious news bulletins "shooting down" is surely to be preferred, especially on the BBC.

'DOZE' *BUZZING S* pronunciation of dose.

DRAMATIC Newsmen like to elevate every event into a DRAMA (or a SAGA if ONGOING). But over-used words lose their force. A "dramatic improvement" is no improvement on a "big improvement" - or perhaps a sudden one. See also STAGGERING.

DRAMATIC PRESENT (PRESCIENT FUTURE) TENSE Stilted, foolish fad favoured by news-editors who formerly worked for newspapers: "Also within the next half-an-hour, a man is gunned down on the streets of Paris..." or "Tonight, Britain is swept by storms and torrential rains..." "Daphne du Maurier dies in Cornwall, that's in a couple of minutes" (ITV *News at Ten*). Do they talk to their wives and families in headlines? No: they say, as we all would, "This morning baby filled his pottie and in the afternoon the cat ate the budgie", not "This morning, the baby fills his pottie and in the afternoon the cat eats the budgie"; nor "Guess what. That novelist, what's-her-name, dies in Cornwall!" So why do they talk to *us*, the listeners, in this ridiculous way?

DRINK THIS - IT'LL DO YOU GOOD The recovery cliché in radio and TV plays, following shock, an accident or fainting-fit, illness, etc.

'DRORING' See *INTRUSIVE R*, but this is one of the commonest, even among educated speakers, and deserves an entry to itself. Even art experts lecturing on TV have been known to speak of "William Blake's delicate drorings..." See also JAWRING.

DUE TO/OWING TO "The landing had been delayed due to a technical fault..." Some say this is pompous and stilted journalese. Why not the simpler "because of" and give them less to complain about?

'DURBEE' See AHBEE.

DYSLEXIC See ANOREXIC.

E

'ECK-SETTERA' Who started it, this fashion for pronouncing *et cetera*, (Latin for "and the rest") as though it had a *ck* or an *x* in it? No wonder people are clamouring to have elementary Latin restored to schools.

'EDWAAHDIAN' Some older speakers prefer this apparently authentic Edwardian pronunciation. Even if people did talk like that in 1905, most *RP*-speakers today say "Ed-*waugh*-dee-an". Imagine your neighbour calling to his child, "Ed*waahd*! Cum 'ere at wunce!"

'EFTA' A curious class (or "cless") compromise. A speaker who wants to sound neither "posh" by elongating his *a* ("ahf-ter", or "claah-ss") nor too working-class by flattening it ("ufta", "cluss") chooses something in between, making it "efta" and "cless". It is now very commonly heard, especially from politicians who wish to sound more "working-cless" than they really are. They hear "chents" at football matches, take their partner for a "dents, and their holidays in "Frents". See also *RP*.

'EGG-SIZE' As in "egg-size officers". See *SOFT-BOILED EGGS.*

'EGG-ZOOMED' *YOD-DROPPER'S* exhumed.

'EGG-ZOOBERANCE' More *SOFT-BOILED EGGS,* combined with *YOD-DROPPING.*

EH See ER.

EJECT/EJACULATE Two words with the same Latin origin ("to throw out") but with two different meanings. The reporter on a commercial local-radio station who claimed "The pilot ejaculated over the North Sea" clearly did not know which was which.

ELECTED AS/APPOINTED AS "She was elected as an MP in 1985" and in "He was elected as Lord Mayor..." are nonsense. She was elected *as* a private citizen, he *as* a councillor or alderman. Only *after* their election did they become MP and mayor, respectively. See *REDUNDANCIES.*

ELEGANT VARIATION Old-fashioned term for using a synonym to avoid using the same word twice in close proximity. "The minister is likely to take issue on that issue" (BBC reporter) would have sounded more euphonious rephrased. But better to repeat the same word than use another one which *sounds* as if it meant the same. It seldom does. See EJECT/

EJACULATE, and other confusibles.

(THE) ELIDED S As in "crewship" for "cruise ship": difficult to avoid without one's sounding like an over-pedantic elocutionist. But as with so many problems of English pronunciation, compromises are readily to hand.

ELONGATED PREFIXES Pronunciation may be a matter of taste, age, class, region or opinion, and no-one can say that one way is right and another wrong: think of example "eye-ther/ee-ther" and "nye-ther/neether" which co-exist happily. But some pronunciations militate not against taste or class but sense and meaning, especially of words beginning with a prefix: *de-*, *re-* and *dis-*, etc. To say "dee-nigh-grate" for "denigrate" is *wrong* because it turns the meaning upside down. Denigrate means "to blacken", from Latin *niger* - the de- prefix being the French intensification *de*, whereas the English de- (pronounced "*dee*") is the cancelling, undoing prefix (as in "deefuse" and "dee-contaminate"). Thus "*dee*-nigh-grating" would be an *un*blackening process: to "*dee*-nigrate" a black man is to *whiten* him. The same goes for deprivation: "*dee*-prye-vation" would be a cancellation of privation, so "*depp*-ree-vation" is surely to be preferred. The same goes for "*dee*-lectation", which would be a *loss* of taste, not the enjoyment of it. Other elongated prefixes can confuse meaning: a body is recovered, but an eiderdown "*ree*-covered"; drunkards are reformed but battle lines "*ree*-formed"; you may resign your job - but then change your mind and "*ree*-sign" your contract: in the first instance you would have been replaced, in the second, "ree-placed" - in another position. An offer may be refused, but an electrical appliance "*ree*- fused". The Americans, with their informal, devil-may-care approach to English, like to lengthen prefixes, often implying them where none is meant, e.g. "*cree*-mation". They also gave us the nonsensical "*ree*—search", which all but the most meticulous English-speakers seem to have adopted. Also "*ee*-lec-TOral" and "ee-lectricty": faulty "ee-ducation", perhaps? See also EXPATRIATE, and INFLAMMABLE.

'ENCOURGE' Rhyming with "purge": an affectation of the American-English pronunciation of "encourage" and a frequent British-English two-syllable *SYNCOPATION* of a three-syllable word.

'ENTERPRIZONES' Some say this is an example of a creeping laziness, a laid-back form of pronunciation, a reluctance of the tongue to stop and start again between the "enterprise" and "zones". But in reality it is one of the more natural elisions, difficult to avoid (see above) without a self-conscious effort.

EQUALLY AS... *REDUNDANCY* used perhaps in the belief that an extra word may add emphasis, as in "The Irish Prime Minister was equally as quick to condemn the outrage..." - and that was in a scripted, *recorded* radio report which could have been edited if the news editor had spotted it, or been offended by it. But most such solecisms now go unnoticed by editors, and therefore uncorrected, to be repeated *ad nauseam*.

'EQUAYZHUN' An equation is a mathematical/algebraic formula some (at least those who learnt "old" mathematics) remember with dread. Today's equation is nothing but a trendy way of saying "situation", "position", "problem", "comparison", etc., especially in interviews. And as if to emphasise the misuse it is also fashionably mispronounced to rhyme with "persuasion". Before long, maybe, we shall be catching a train at a "stayzhun". The softened *sh* is spreading fast, e.g. the "Perzhing Missile", named after the World War II US General Pershing, a hard man who would have hated to be turned into a whooshing softie.

ER In impromptu speech it is human to "er" (also to "um" and to "e-e-e-h") when seeking a word that momentarily eludes one. Some speakers unknowingly make a habit of it - and are astonished when they hear themselves recorded. And if that doesn't help, an edited tape from which everything is removed *except* the er's, um's and e-e-e-h's, works wonders! Scottish and foreign English-speakers seem to prefer "e-e-eh" for filling-in thought gaps - a cross between the German ä-ä-ä-ä-h and a sheep in distress.

EVACUATE This is a transitive verb. You evacuate someone or something, including the bowels. For these, plain "evacuate", on its own, has become the accepted euphemism, so it is misleading to say, in a news-bulletin, "Because of danger of gas Red Adair and his men were obliged to evacuate".

EXACTLY Interviewese. As in "*Exactly* what happened when you woke up next morning?" - and as often as it is asked, replies begin with (WELL) BASICALLY. See also JUST HOW...?

'EXCREESHA' I suspect that those who pronounce excreta like this think it is spelt "excretia". The word rymes with Rita, not Lucretia.

EXPATRIATE Commonly mispronounced *ex-patriot* - which is a *former patriot* who no longer loves his fatherland and (it is tacitly suggested) may even harm it. An *ex-patriate* merely no longer lives there, though his love for it may be undiminished. A carefully enunciated "ex-pay-tree-eight" might save the speaker a lot of money. Better to shorten the word to "ex-pat" than be sued! Saying *magnet* for magnate can also confuse.

EXPORT/EXPORT "After the last war the slogan was '*EXPORT* OR DIE!', said an economist on the radio. It wasn't. The catchphrase was '*EXPORT* OR DIE!' Public speakers, politicians and journalists observed the old-established stress difference between ex*port* (verb) and *export* (noun) well into the 1960s and 70s, except perhaps when emphasising the difference between the two, e.g. "In his speech the Prime Minister referred not only to ex*port*ing but also to *im*porting consumer goods".

EXPLOSIONS These always "rock" the neighbourhood, just as shots "ring out".

EXPOSÉ One of many foreign-word traps for the unwary. When the French use the noun *exposé* they are more likely to refer to an analysis, statement or exposition. But why use a French word (needing an acute accent) when there is a plain English word "exposure"? Also *extraordinaire* for "extraordinary" - see *MediaWrite*.

'EYELAND' *WEATHERBABBLE* for Ireland, a *SYNCOPATION*.

'EYE-TINNERY' *SYNCOPATION* of "itinerary". Whenever a word contains more than one *r*, at least one usually falls by the way, e.g. FEBB-YOU-AIRY, SECK-A-CHEE, etc. and the process appears to be natural.

'EYE-THER/EE-THER' Both pronunciations cheerfully co-exist, an example of British freedom and tolerance. Most dictionaries, however, tend to give the first as preferrable, on grounds of Old and Middle English spellings, and because David Garrick used it. The *OED* says "eye-ther" is "somewhat more prevalent in educated speech".

F

FEATURE/FUTURE With some speakers the two sound almost the same: a combination of the *NAY LONGER RIND O* and *YOD-DROPPING*.

'FEBB-YOU-AIRY' A much complained-about mispronunciation, formerly heard mostly from babies unable to say their *r*. See SECK-A-CHEE. **FFHHH** See PFHHH.

FIGHTER The "neutral" word devised by the evenhanded BBC to get round the FREEDOM-FIGHTER/TERRORIST problem.

FIGHTING FOR (HIS) LIFE See the *MEDIAWRITE* section for the alleged fighting spirit of a person who may be unconscious and on a life-support machine. As a reporter once said: "A MAJOR battle is now underway in hospital to save the lives of the survivors".

'FITH' The omission of the second *f* in fifth annoys some listeners (as do "lenth", "strenth", and "Wilsha" for Wiltshire); but then some object to the *presence* of the *t* in "Hertfordshire", traditionally called "Hah-f'd-sha", although the *BBC Pronouncing Dictionary of British Names* also give "Hart-f'd-sha". When a local pronunciation is in doubt the BBC telephones the local vicar or postmistress.

FLAMMABLE See INFLAMMABLE.

FLYING INTO (LONDON) Perhaps best reserved for the short take-off and landing aircraft which *are* able to fly *into* the docklands of London; or helicopters (or the disaster one hopes will never happen). Passengers spending hours in motor-cars on jammed roads leading from outlying international airports see the irony of having flown "into" a city.

FOLLOWING SUIT "Shell are [!] increasing the price of petrol and other companies are likely to follow *suit*". Following suit is a card-playing term now almost automatic in news scripts, maybe because a twin-term lends extra emphasis. "Other companies are likely to follow" seems perfectly adequate.

FOREIGN WORDS The BBC is more careful about pronouncing foreign words (and especially names) than foreigners are about English ones. An advisory Pronunciation Unit staffed by linguists is available to producers at the touch of a telephone key-pad. They can instantly tell broadcasters the most acceptable pronunciation of regional Finnish or Hungarian words, or the appropriate Chinese inflexion for Deng Xiaou Peng. Behind it lies more than the BBC tradition of accuracy and reliability Lord Reith strove for. The British have always treated foreigners with courtesy. When they speak to them they raise their voice to make quite sure they are understood; and are tolerant of that great basic disability, the foreigners' disadvantage of not having been born British. But things are changing. "Franglais" *oo* versions of the French *u* (which *should* be something like the German *ü*) are becoming more the rule than the exception, e.g. Auguste (as in Rodin) usually comes out as "Oh goosed" and Albert Camus seldom gets beyond "*Al* Bear *Cam*oo". Legitimate anglicising, eg. Nessles for Nestlés, and Soo-shard for Suchard (not "suck hard"!) is surely to be encouraged: no-one suggests we prononunce Waterloo (i.e. the London railway station) in the Belgian manner, like their Waterloo, the scene of the battle just South of Brussels (or Bruxelles) to rhyme with "batter low". To most Englishmen Emile Zola's famous article in defence of Dreyfus was headed "Jack Hughes" (not to mention the philosopher "Mark Hughes"). German fares a little better, though important *internal* word-stressings are often wilfully changed (e.g. *Klavierübung*, or *Klavierübung*). But the philosopher Immanuel Kant must always be "Immanuel *Can't*": and here it is not that they can't pronounce it properly - they daren't (just as *SPORTS REPORTERS* never mispronounce "Grand Prix"). We can find consolation, however, in the knowledge that foreign radio stations mangle English words and names a lot more comprehensively than we do theirs. But the gender of foreign words cannot be unisexed: Radio Three presenters have been heard to describe Sir George Thalben-Ball as "the *doyenne* of English organists".

FORMER/ONE-TIME "Her former lover" is not the same as "Her onetime lover" - unless her former lover really managed it only once.

FORWARD PLANNING Planning by definition means to contrive, project or arrange something beforehand. You would hardly indulge in backward planning? Surely therefore a *REDUNDANCY*.

FREEDOM-FIGHTERS See TERRORISTS.

FREQUENT/FREQUENT

> The auld wife sat at her ivied door,
> (Butter and eggs and a pound of cheese)
> A thing she had frequently done before
> And her spectacles lay on her apron'd knees.
> C.S. Calverley: *Ballad*.

> Myself when young did eagerly frequent
> Doctor and saint, and heard great argument
> About it and about: but evermore
> Came out by the same door as in I went.
> Edward Fitzgerald: *Rubayat*

FRESH Try new, renewed, further, increased, more, etc. for a change - and avoid idiocies like "Three weeks after the earthquake fresh bodies have been discovered in the wreckage".

FRONT (MAN) "Fronting" a programme means introducing it, that is, reading and saying the words that roll up the autocue: often little more than that. Behind every front man there is a backing-group carrying out painstaking research and writing his script. Front men thus acquire a reputation for expertise in many subjects. One was even offered an honorary degree by a university - in a subject he never studied nor claimed expertise in.

FUNDAMENTAL RIGHT Another twin term, like FULL ENQUIRY, GRUELLING TRIP etc. Politicians feel that "right" on its own is too short a word to make much impact. Most rights are, alas, anything but fundamental.

FURORE The English pronounce this semi-foreign word in three syllables, whereas the Americans prefer "few-roar". There is good old English word, "furor", and plenty of synonyms, like "uproar".

G

GAME SHOWS Pretentious term for panel games or quiz shows. Like TALK SHOWS and old films they form the staple diet of junk TV, and increasingly also radio, although a little more intelligence is expected of listeners than of viewers.

'GATES' The animals which, according to the *NAY-LONGER RIND O*, the Bible separates from the sheep.

GAY Once again I deplore the loss of a lovely English word, especially when there are so many AIDS-afflicted *sad* men. But at the end of the 19th century "gay" did briefly enjoy connotations of illicit, though heterosexual, pleasure.

GEE Contrary to common belief, not all Americans preface all their statements with this abbreviation for "God", and not many KRAUTS these days say SIEG HEIL! or Spaniards OLE! - see *MediaWrite*.

(THE) GENTEEL O MODIFICATION This turns the *o*-before-*l* sound as in "moll" into that of "hole" or "soul". Involve thus turns into "involve", solve into "soulve", revolve into "revoulve", alcohol into "alco-hole" and aerosol into "aero-sole" and "Interpole" for Interpol. There was a celebrated COCK UP at the end of a televised *Eurovision Song Contest* brought about by the director's pronouncing revolve "revoulve" - which an assistant misheard on his earphones for "roll" and started to "roll the credits", much

too soon. The director's ill-tempered ranting in the control-box is preserved on tape.

GETTING OFF THE GROUND Becoming operational: "The new Margam colliery has yet to get off the ground" (Mr Arthur Scargill, on BBC TV). See also ON STREAM.

GINORMOUS See GUESSTIMATE and SHAMBOLIC. Also LIKE SO and LOOK SEE.

(THAT'S A) GOOD QUESTION Not a compliment to the interviewer but the interviewee's admission that he has no answer. Experienced politicians do not waste time on the *quality* of a question. They ignore it and score some other - irrelevant - point; or answer a question the interviewer did not ask.

GOOD TO BE BACK! Said by presenters on their return to a programme after returning from holiday, sickness, etc. But are they *sure* everybody noticed their absence? And see CONCEITS.

'GRADGLY' *SYNCOPATION* heard in *WEATHERBABBLE* and elsewhere: "A front of TICKLY high pressure is gradgly moving in from the south..."

GRAPHICS/CAPTIONS Specially-prepared illustrative TV pictures and drawings. Until recently these were comparatively primitive: painted or drawn illustrations with stick-on or rub-down lettering, the whole thing mounted on (usually black) cardboard and placed on something like a music-stand in front of a camera. If anything moved it was pushed about by an un-seen operator. Computer graphics have changed all that. Many previously unattainable effects suddenly became not only possible but instant clichés. Nothing on the screen stands still: imitation pages or postcards turn of their own accord, twist and tumble; sheets of "paper" fly through space, zoom into view before disappearing again into the distance. Presenters themselves may suddenly shrink into two-dimensional postcard pictures that revolve, turn and somersault towards (or away from) the viewer in a seasick-making flurry of unnatural activity. Much the same devices are used for programme captions, especially for news and current-affairs programmes. The whole restless melange is often accompanied by noisy junk-music. No wonder viewers are deserting TV in droves to seek the calm of information radio, like BBC Radio 4, or "real" music on Radio 3.

GREAT No longer denotes merely size or abstract greatness (i.e. a great ship, or a great composer) but alleged excellence("We're having a great time!") or is merely an exclamation of approval ("Great!").

(THE) GREAT UNWASHED W.M. Thackeray invented that calumny on the working man, in *Pendennis*: "Gentlemen, there can be but little doubt that your ancestors were the great unwashed". He was probably alluding to Shakespeare's line in *King John*, about "another lean unwash'd artificer", which William Cowper later appropriated and modified.

GREMLINS As in "Sorry about the gremlins THERE" when something goes wrong, perhaps a tape or record played at the wrong speed. Gremlins were invented by the RAF in the last war - mischievous sprites who got the blame for unforeseen (minor) mishaps.

GRIMACE/GRIMACE A new trend (perhaps USA from the German *Grimasse?*) places the stress on the first syllable ("*grim*ass"), but although it is gaining ground in media speech it is unsupported by any poetry I could find: "In their high, musty place/Grim gargoyles gri*mace*".

GROUND RULES The first word is surely no more than a meaningless makeweight, an aid to rhythm. See *REDUNDANCIES*.

GRUELLING TRIP Any uncomfortable journey described by a reporter.

GUESSTIMATE See SHAMBOLIC.

'GUMMAN' *SYNCOPATION* of "gunman".

'GUM'T' When Handel in his *Messiah* sang "And the government shall be upon his shoulder" he spread the three-syllable word "government" over three notes. By conversational *SYNCOPATION* it has been reduced to two: "gov'n-ment"; but more recently it has suffered a further cut, usually from politicans, to one syllable, as above.

H

HAD As an aid to the grammatical expression of tenses this little word is fast disappearing, and its use all but forgotten: "he did it" where "he had done it" would be appropriate. As the schoolboy said, "I had 'had' where I should have had 'had had', though 'had had' had had the teacher's approval."

HADNAVES and **OFFOFS** As in "If Tony and I hadnave stood for election" and, from another well-known politician, shadow foreign-secretary and journalist, who said on TV after an adverse by-election result: "If he hadnave thought he'd win..." Also (a BBC reporter): "He took the mace off of the table as a form of protest". Older grammarians railed against "Who has *got* my inkstand?" and "conversing *together*" - both considered *REDUN-DANCIES* but now accepted.

HAITCHES AND AITCHES Voice and comprehension tests for aspiring news-reporters might include a check on the aspirants' aspirates. Not only do many aitch-droppers slip through the net but some are "haitch"-adders, which is worse - a sign of nervous pseudo-gentility: "Gee Haitch Q" is common (though not on Radio Three). But usage changes here, too. A language text-book of 1909 lists Heir, Honesty, Honour and Hour as having a silent *h*, but then adds Humour and says it must be pronounced "Yumour". One frequent and highly articulate broadcaster on Radio Four and TV always selfconsciously says "An 'otel" and "The 'otelier".

HALF (ONE) As in "AHBEE back with you at half one to play you some more of the latest ALBUMS". That is how the young (and some not-so-young) now say "half past one". There is no law against it, although the more fastidious don't like it. If it is American it must be confusing for their German-speakers (see OUT THE DOOR and WRITE US) for in German *halb-eins* is not "half *past* one" but "half *before* one", i.e. "half past twelve". This practice has made many an international assignation go awry by an hour. The American "a quarter of one" confusingly means "a quarter to one".

HAVING SAID THAT Heralds a slight revision of a statement or opinion just expressed, and also (usually) a dangling participle: "Having said that the mice are probably on their way out". Clever little mice! See also IF-YOU-LIKE and YERKNOW.

HEADMASTER/HEADMISTRESS Now outmoded (perhaps outlawed) terms. The equality industry and some education authorities sternly insist we say "head teacher" or "head"; and of course the chairman has become a "chair".

HEAVY BREATHERS See *PFHHH*

'HEEBEE' *MENU* ingredient, as in "On *Newsround* today heebee talking to teenagers whobee..." See also its declensions, AHBEE, YOUBEE, SHEEBEE, WEEBEE, WHOBEE and THEYBEE.

'HERE'N'DARE' "DURBEE bitsa rain here'n'dare": *WEATHERBABBLE*.

HE WOULD, WOULDN'T HE Often coupled with "As Mandy Rice-Davies said", to dismiss an excuse or explanation as obvious. The remark was by no means original when Miss Davies uttered it (in a much publicised case) but now appears in dictionaries of quotations as if it had been a profound statement. See also TO COIN A PHRASE.

HHH See PFHHH.

HIM/HIS One does not have to be a poet, or aware of such old-fashioned technical terms as "possessive gerunds", to sense that the lines

> The manner of his leaving of the room
> Was a matter of his going to his doom.

would sound absurd as "The manner of *him* leaving" and "a matter of *him* going". But such niceties are seldom observed: a sign not so much of increasing informality but of decreasing literacy. See also WAS/WERE.

HOPEFULLY American mistranslation of the German *hoffentlich*," in-the-hope-that", but confused with *hoffnungsvoll*, "full-of-hope". One travels hopefully, i.e. in the hope of arriving; listeners hopefully complain about the misuse of "hopefully", but SADLY (see *MediaWrite*) in vain.

HORSE(BACK) RIDING This separates the horsemen from the rest. The former assume we know that it's not a bicycle, tram or bus they ride, and simply speak about *riding*. See CONCERT PIANIST.

HOW...? See JUST HOW...?

HOW DO YOU FEEL? This universal, inevitable, relentlessly meaningless and totally unanswerable question has been ridiculed since the mid-1970s but sooner or later every news interviewer seems to ask it - no matter whether the interviewee has just been bereaved, injured, escaped injury, divorced, rescued, awarded a prize, or been acquitted of some offence: a microphone is sure to be stuck in his face and out comes the idiocy: "How do you feel?" It was asked of an airline pilot who had just landed *Concorde* with part of its tail missing, and of the Liverpool football manager immediately after he had witnessed 95 of his supporters killed. A more recent variation is "What was going through your mind when...?" Newspaper reporters, too, ask people how they feel but at least we do not hear them doing so - we only read the "replies" they manufacture (see FALSE VERBATIM in *MEDIAWRITE*). See also JUST HOW..? and HOW WORRIED ARE YOU?

HOW MANY "We have a report on how many people are starving in Ethiopia". Will it quantify how *many* are starving or tell us *how* they are suffering their misfortune?

HOW WORRIED ARE YOU? Stock interviewers' question. Also DOES THAT WORRY YOU? and above.

I

IF-YOU-LIKE This interjection now garnishes almost every impromptu statement, interview, discussion and often even the briefest comment. (Most answers to questions seem to begin with BASICALLY). "If-you-like" is the upmarket, educated-if-you-like, equivalent of the older, downmarket YER KNOW, and of the -LIKE suffix of the uneducated. Though it is just as unattractive-like, it appears to have supplanted the older SORT-OF. Variations such as "if-you-will" (favoured by Americans) and "if-you-wish" are also gaining ground-if-you-like, though AS-IT-WERE has almost had its day. Another hesitatory interjection, especially when time or money are under discussion, is WHAT, as in "We're talking IN TERMS OF, what, a thousand pounds", or "This job is going to take at least, what, A HALF AN HOUR". I am not criticising, merely observing-if-you-like: we all have our foibles and habits. But the minister who said "And in this field-if-you-like I'd like to make some changes..." had clearly become so anaesthetized to it that he no longer knew he was saying it. Like it or not, if-you-like is here to stay - until superseded by a different craze-if-you-like.

I HEAR WHAT YOU SAY Five words that are sweeping the world of communicators, politicians, BISN'SSM'N and other articulates who give interviews and engage in public discussion. Phrases like IN TERMS OF and IF-YOU-LIKE have had a similar meteoric rise (as the "shot in the arm" did before it died of an overdose). The implication is "I hear what you say, am sympathetic to your views and I respect your opinion - but I'm not letting on whether I agree with you".

I'LL **GET IT** Kneejerk response by one character or another whenever the telephone rings in a radio or TV play.

I'LL SEE *MYSELF* **OUT** Said in every radio or TV play when a character leaves. This cliché is used so as not to waste time, e.g. by having the microphone or camera follow a character down the hall and out of the front-door, with the often lengthy goodbyes encountered in real life. But YOU BETTER COME IN is just a senseless formula.

I/ME/HE/HIM "And it's goodbye from Brian and I" or "This is a matter between you and he" are common grammatical gaffes - gaffes because they believe that "me" is vulgar and therefore wrong. The only remedy is a crash-course in elementary grammar (if possible with a little Latin) or to listen to/ read good speakers/writers. Or to ask oneself - would anyone say "from I" or "between he?" The same goes for the more common (therefore colloquially more acceptable) "She is older than him". Think of "She is older than he (is)". See also THEM/THEY.

IMPLEMENT/IMPLEMENT Marcellus in Shakespeare's *Hamlet* speaks of the contemporary international arms trade as the "foreign mart for *im*plements of war"; but any measures to counter it would be imple*ment*ed - a difference now almost universally ignored. Everything is *im*plemented, and more's the pity.

IMPORT/IMPORT The same remarks apply as to "implement", above, and indeed to EXPORT.

IMPRINT/IMPRINT The details which appear at the beginning of this book are the *im*print. They are im*print*ed on page iv.

I MUST SAY... A speech-opener, as meaningless as ACTUALLY, BASICALLY, IN FACT, WELL, etc. and almost as meaningless as the I-want-to-say-something *PFHHH*.

INCREASE/INCREASE

> God made the woman for the man
> And for the good and *in*crease of the world.
> Alfred, Lord Tennyson: *Edwin Morris.*

> A thing of beauty is a joy for ever:
> Its loveliness in*creases*; it will never
> Pass into nothingness; but still will keep.
> John Keats: *Endymion.*

INDEED[1] In some circles a modish indication of agreement or affirmation, i.e. "yes". Americans love the one-word AFFIRMATIVE, probably introduced by their armed forces because in the noise of battle a curt "yes" might be missed. But even civilians, in the quiet of an office, say, "The answer is in the affirmative, sir". See DEFINITELY.

INDEED[2] Meaningless and insincere makeweight gush, as in "Thankyou-verymuchindeedHarriet" in *WEATHERBABBLE*.

INDEED[3] A substitute for IN FACT, as in "Indeed he lived to tell the tale..."

INFLAMMABLE The only word *officially* banned from the English language (at any rate for semantic reasons, not to "protect" minority groups). Consumer bodies were worried about possible danger if "in-flammable" were thought to be the same as "non-flammable". Clothing, furniture, etc., must therefore be labelled "flammable".

(THE) INFLUX OF -ATIONS I blame German-Americans, who never use a short word when a long one is available. American authorities reject plain transport, transplant and import for "transportation", "transplantation" and "importation"; and are constantly making up new *-ations* from nouns, like "hospitalisation" and "burglarisation" (whether there is a *z* before *-ation* or an *s* is another matter). "Admitted to hospital" is admittedly a little longer, but "burglary" seems adequate. Most English doctors have accepted "medication" for medicine, and motorists are thought to be more impressed by the "instrumentation" on their cars than mere instruments.

INJURED/WOUNDED Civilians are injured, soldiers wounded, but the second is gaining ground in references to civilian shootings. Both are *hurt*, so a compromise is available.

IN (POINT OF) FACT Like INDEED[3] this is usually - though not always - a meaningless filler whose purpose is to create speech balance.

'INSHLAR' Modish form of "insular", like "inshlin", "peninshla(r)" and other sound-related words.

INSTANT EXPERTS Whatever makes news - an industrial disaster, a new invention, discovery, dispute, war, etc., an Instant Expert is ready to be to be wheeled on, by radio as well as TV, to give an instant expert opinion. He may come from an obscure university faculty (" We asked Dr Mohamed Strabismus, Lecturer in Terrorist Food Preferences at the University of Salford...") or, more likely, from an "Institute". Now, there are many long-established and learned institutes where all manner of disciplines are studied and analysed for the good of mankind (and that - I feel certain - goes for the Lifestyle Enhancement Research Unit of the Polytechnic of the South Bank, from whose director I have a letter before me). But, since Britain is a free country, anyone can set himself up as a consultant, get some headed writing-paper printed and establish an "institute" in his spare bedroom ("...so we asked John Smith, Director of the Institute of Toad Migration..."). When awarded *YOBS' TITLES* Instant Experts can take on a surreal quality. Real example heard on Radio Four: "I spoke to International Disaster Expert Richard Harris..." (name disguised to avoid giving offence).

*IN*SULT/IN*SULT* Another noun/verb stress difference.

> Yet ev'n these bones from *in*sult to protect
> Some frail memorial still erected nigh
> With uncouth rhymes and shapeless sculpture deck'd
> Implores the passing tribute of a sigh.
> Thomas Gray: *Elegy* .
>
> A potent quack, long versed in human ills,
> Who first in*sults* the victim whom he kills....
> George Crabbe: *His Mother's Wedding Ring*

IN TERMS OF See TALKING IN TERMS OF...

INTERRELATED Things (or people) that are related are, by definition, related to each other. So why the Americans' needless *inter-*? We don't talk of "having sexual interrelations" - yet! See *REDUNDANCIES*.

INTO Often used in place of *of* as in "We have an investigation into child abuse in Cleveland..." Also "a survey into..." and even "a report into..."

INTONATION The rise and fall in the pitch of the voice, and in effect a kind of singing (the Germans call it *Sprechgesang*) which, like singing, can become monotonous if repeated without variation or sufficient regard to the meaning of the words spoken. Different speakers have their own characteristics and intonation habits that make them instantly recognisable - and by some instantly liked or disliked (though tastes fortunately vary). Intonation probably cannot be taught, only learnt by imitation: certain groups, like reporters, disc-jockeys and commercial-radio newsmen, have developed their own, characteristic REPORTERS' SING-SONG which they do indeed copy from each other. See BLACK-EDGED VOICE.

(THE) INTRUSIVE R AND OTHER REDUNDANCIES It seems to be a natural thing to slip an *r* between certain vowel sounds, more than mere vocal slovenliness. Every choral society at rehearsal sings *"Hosanna-r-in excelsis"* until told otherwise. Our unlovely old friend "Laura Norder" is joined by the novelist "Ednaro Brien", "Annarof the Five Towns", the "Shower of Iran" and "The Jackdoor of Rheims", and (!) "the areararound the Armeniarearthquake..." - which is really quite difficult to say, but they said it, like "This marks the end of an erarin the history of the cinemarin Italy"). Even a distinguished expert on art speaks of "Picasso's drorings" while *You and Yours* warns that our freezer might be "thawring". A lifelong devotee of (and broadcaster about) G. B. Shaw not only calls him "Shoar" (two syllables!) but manages to give the dramatist's name two syllables. On

Radio 3 a scripted talk informed us that "Dr Howells invited me into his joring-room", and "Aldous Huxley foresore a time..." A story on Radio 4 about a character called Lucia had "...after Luciar arrived"; and there are the "Philadelphiarorchestra" and the "Philharmoniarorchestra". In the financial news "Burmaroil" is going strong ("no stigmarattached") and on ITN the news-reader said, "As far as Syriarisconcerned..." In the end, when a Radio 3 presenter spoke of "a soaring tune on the violins" I began to wonder whether he was praising the composer's melodic gifts or suggesting that the violinists were trying to saw their fiddles in half. Conversely, "The prisoner was seen soaring through the bars" suggested *Superman*, not a convict. A news reporter almost created poetry when he said "As far as lorries are concerned the lawris unclear". "Contractual" is so often said "contractural" that one now often sees it printed that way, for mispronunciations turn into misspellings. The intrusive *r* is undoubtedly a fault, a deficiency in the speaking of formal English. The very fact that intrusives annoy many listeners should make professional communicators try to avoid them, if only as a matter of pride in their craft. After all, what would a musical audience think of a player unable to slur from a D to an E without accidentally touching the D sharp in between? Not much, I suggest; yet the French have adopted this way of "filling in" gaps between vowels in their language and made it "official". And in rural as well as regional dialects/accents, too, a filling-in seems to come naturally: a scouse-speaker asking "Is that Anne?" says "Is tharranne?" (or even "Izzarranne?") Curiously enough the word "February", which does have an *r* in the middle, has been causing people to add an intrusive *y* instead - FEB-YOU-AIRY - almost as common as ECK-SETTERA. Some speakers are unable to cope with adjacent consonants and feel more comfortable if they put a connecting vowel between them, e.g. "Da-vorak" for "Dvorak". Irish (and other rustics) perfer "fil-lum" to "film"; some Scots "perils" to "pearls" (see *RP*) and "perishin" to "Persian". One said, "Oil wells round our coast will make us into another perishin' gulf." The BBC occasionally reminds broadcasters about intrusives, and everyone who mentions the Radio 4 programme *Law in Action* seems to use a nervously staccato: "Law - in - Action". Another curiosity is the gratuitous *r* (both written and spoken) in the noun peninsula, making it "peninsular", like the adjective.

'INVOULVE' Like SOULVE and REVOULVE, an example of the *GENTEEL O MODIFICATION*.

I PUT IT TO HIM Interviewers' jargon meaning "I asked him".

'ISSHOOS' The news world is full of issues, and when two or more *YODDROPPERS* discuss them they make ugly, whooshing sounds as if overtaken by communal sneezing-fits - and perhaps in need of "tisshoos"? I have even heard an attempt, by a non-BBC speaker on *Today,* to turn "eschew" (%es-chew") into "eshoo".

'ISTANGLIA' In *WEATHERBABBLE* East Anglia has all but lost its first element and gets most of the stress on the second.

IT'S ALL GO Meaningless, time-filling interjection in *DJ BABBLE.*

J

'JAMA' See PUR-CHEE.

'JEWEL' As in "jewel carriageway" - see *YOD-DROPPING.*

JUST HOW...? Questions that in ordinary life begin with "how" are in radio and TV interviews intensified with the addition of a "just". *"Just* HOW DO YOU FEEL?" Only once have I heard an interviewee, in pain after being injured and nearly killed in an accident, snarl back, "Just how the hell do you *think* I feel?" Other silly questions include *"(Just)* how important (or serious) *is* this?", "Just how sorry *are* you...?", *"(Just)* how confident *are* you?", and *(Just)* how pleased/angry/disappointed *were* you?" - as if these sentiments could somehow be accurately quantified. Such questions are not meant to make the interviewee quantify the *degree* of seriousness, importance, his anxiety or regret, but to explain *why* he thinks these things are so. When Mrs Norman Tebbit, wheelchair-bound and paralysed in the IRA bombing of the Grand Hotel, Brighton, returned to the place four years later, an ITV reporter cheerfully asked her, "Has this place any bad memories for you?" She sweetly and patiently replied, "What do *you* think?" See also WHERE DO WE GO FROM HERE?

K

KAFKAESQUE Whenever I am tempted to use this word (and it is not very often) I say "nightmarish" instead, remembering that I have read very little of the work of Franz Kafka (1883-1924) and the vast majority of listeners perhaps even less.

(AND) KEEP THOSE LETTERS COMING IN Farewell injunction to listeners at the end of certain current-affairs, news and consumer programmes. It may mean "We're a bit short of material".

(THE) KIDS (OUT THERE) The alleged listeners to Radio 1 and other pop music stations, especially commercial radio.

KI-*LOM*-ETRE When decimalisation came to the UK those unfamiliar with the word put a thumping stress on the middle syllable. The word is a compound of *kilo* and *metre*, hence *kilo*metre: there is no unit called the "lom". We are probably stuck with it now, though if you say *kilo*metre no-one will laugh at you (just as they don't complain about *con*troversy but do about con*tro*versy). I wonder whether the same controversy attended the introduction, in around 1850, of the word "photographer", now stressed with the accent on the *tog*.

'KNOWHARRAMEANLIKE(BRIAN)' Sportsmen's favourite suffix, like -LIKE.

L

LAID/LAY/LIE The distinction between the two forms is perfectly clear to anyone who has read good books and listened to educated speakers (or even learnt a little grammar). He will know that eggs (and, in colloquial American, girls) are *laid*; but having been laid they *lie* - in straw, on a bed, grass, etc. Even an only slightly observant person picks up these "correct" usages, as if by absorption. He will not absorb them by only watching TV or listening to *DJ BABBLE*. Difficulties arise when he has a vague idea that there *is* a difference - as with WHO/WHOM - and in a panic gets it wrong. So he says "The policeman was laying on the ground..." because he feels it sounds more "posh" than "lying"; or "Special Branch men lay siege to the house..." instead of "laid". "Lain", incidentally, has all but disappeared. Some newspaper journalists "correct" it as a suspected misprint. Such confusions may pass several pairs of editorial eyes without being spotted. See also *MediaWrite*.

*LA*MENTABLE/LA*MEN*TABLE An example of class/regional stress distinction. *RP*-speakers go for the first but the second, which follows the stress of the "la*ment*" (never "*la*ment") and seems to me to be *PREFER*-RABLE - and that word suffers from the same social division.

'LARSHEER' Not DISHEER or NECKSHEER. See *YOD-DROPPING*.

(THE) LAST-WORD STRESS In the early days of radio, speakers dared not lower the inflexion of final words of phrases or sentences in a normal, conversational manner for fear of their being lost in the crackle of at-

mospherics. When BBC correspondents later were able to send reports from far-flung places they encountered even worse interference. But in spite of the improvements in transmission, with satellites making the sound as clear as if it came from the studio, the old habits persist, both from abroad and at home. Reporters continue to raise their voice to an unnatural degree, and retain the last-word stress. It is almost their trade-mark, probably to give the impression of urgency and news drama. The worst almost shout their reports, even when speaking to their tape recorders without competing with background noises. This flat intonation has remained almost the norm in *From Our Own Correspondent* and numerous consumer programmes, uninflected except for final words: every last word of every phrase or sentence is given a frenzied emphasis, by lowering the *pitch* of the voice but not the *volume*. Some indeed make a *crescendo* through it and perhaps even elongate it or its final syllable. As a result many reports sound, at best, meaningless, and at worst a monotonous *REPORTERS' SING-SONG*. The reporters give the impression that they find their own words incomprehensible. Some sound as expressionless and flat as 10-year-olds reading aloud their essays in class. English has a natural rise-and-fall, with a preponderance of feminine ending, i.e. *penultimate*-word-stress, but the last-word-stressing reporters' delivery comes over as a kind of aggressive swagger in which the artificial emphasis sounds almost petulant, a sort of verbal foot-stamping. Whether they speak of tragedy or comedy, of good news or bad, the pervading inflexion is flat and unchanging, the pace (which varies when real people in real life talk to each other) monotonously unvaried. The last-word stress habit has been taken up by local-radio reporters, many of them newspapermen, who mistake this delivery for professionalism. And here's a curious phenomenon: on TV the effect is less noticeable. Perhaps the *NODDIES* and other televisual effects distract the viewer's attention.

LEFT DEAD A current fad among news editors. Wherever there is an item about a disaster, a bomb OUTRAGE, etc. the dead are *left*, e.g. "The explosion in Beirut left six people dead..." See also FRESH.

'LENTH(Y)' Length(y). For omissions and alterations of consonants see also ARTIC and ECK-SETTERA, etc.

LESS/FEWER There is a distinction between the two, although so many speakers ignore it that before long another useful language-tool will disappear. "Less" refers to quantity or bulk (" less fruit"), "fewer" to numbers (" fewer apples"). The right way sounds neither pseudo-posh nor stilted (as the correct use of WHOM *does* sometimes) and no-one will give you a funny look if you get it right.

LIBRARY FILM Old film sequences shown to accompany and illustrate news stories for which no pictures are available, because TV hates *TALKING HEADS*. Explanatory *CAPTIONS* saying "Library Film" may be flashed on and off at great speed: look away and you get the false impression that what you see is real news. TV convention also demands that when there is a subsequent reference to some previous news of great moment, an extract from the original TV news is shown, over and over again, *ad nauseam*. And if too horrific to be shown in close-up, an inset still picture of the disaster is shown in a corner of the screen to remind viewers of what most of them know already. Horrors like the football disasters, the Zebrugge ferry sinking, the Piper Alpha oil-rig explosion and the Lockerbie terrorist outrage, are revived at the slightest opportunity, however remotely related - either with reference to the event itself or to some other news item about football violence, fires, explosions, air-crashes, etc. When there is a change in the value of the pound, the frontage of the Bank of England is lovingly shown, in slowly changing focus. If there is news about the Chancellor of the Exchequer, the battered old red despatch-case is brought out; a change in fuel prices, and someone is ludicrously shown filling his tank at a petrol-pump - as if we had to be reminded what *this* looks like. If there is news of a police investigation, the old revolving shop-sign outside New Scotland Yard is sure to be going round and round. If a firm or company is in the news, the camera will start by looking at its name-plate outside the front door, and open out to reveal the whole building. Then it's up the wall, a close-up of a window - and a moment later, the camera is inside. TV people never seem to enter a building by the front door (certainly not up the stairs, which is time-consuming) but scale it on the outside, SAS-like. Most viewers already know what name-plates or business premises look like. They certainly know the faces of political leaders and their premises (especially the White House, the Kremlin, the Palace of Westminster and No. 10 Downing Street), yet up they come - again and again and again, either as a backdrop or sitting in the corner of the screen behind the presenter's left shoulder (why always the left?). In other words, viewers are treated as if they were illiterate, unimaginative idiots, or children unable to understand words without the help of pretty pictures. In this way TV reduces supposedly serious events to the level of strip-cartoon comics. But, as with most radio and TV habits, a precedent can be found in the press. There, no story about any person, however well-known, is complete without yet another appearance of that person's stock photograph. See also *GRAPHICS*.

LICHEN A not unattractive moss-like growth forming on stone and roof surfaces. It used to be pronounced "lye-ken", like the Greek word *leichen* it comes from. But when air pollution made lichen rarer the word was rarely heard, and so people started to call it "litch-en", which is more logical in

English. The *OED* still recommends "lye-ken" but *Chambers's* gives "litchen" as a second form.

'LICH-LEE' Literally. As in "My eyes were lich-lee glued to the set", or "I was lich-lee on cloud nine", or "The *Pride of Kent* is now lich-lee coming through the harbour wall". Whichever way they pronounce it, people nearly always misuse "literally" - unless it is *literally,* ACK-SHLEE and genuinely, happening.

LIEUTENANT According to an old convention the British Army says "leff-tenant" but the Royal Navy insists on "loo-tenant". Naval persons are scornful of the army pronunciation, which pains them almost as much as having Mr Gieves, the old-established naval outfitter, pronounced "Jeeves", like P. G. Wodehouse's manservant. The American armed forces have only one sort of lieutenant, and he is always a "loo-tenant". Broadcasters who follow the navy's convention are often accused by listeners of aping Americans!

LIFE or LIVES? Cats are said to have nine lives, but humans die only once. "Seven people are reported to have lost their lives" always sounds strange to me. Each had only one life to lose.

LIGHTNING STRIKE "Two airport workers were hurt after a lightning strike..." (Radio 4 *News*). Were they struck by lightning or the victims of industrial "action"?

-LIKE The less-educated equivalent of IF-YOU-LIKE. Both suffixes-like are tacked on-like to statements made in interviews-like by sportsmen-if-you-like talking off the cuff-like. Also the fuller form KNOWHARRAMEAN-LIKE. See BASICALLY and SORT OF.

LIKE SO TV PERSONALITIES' baby-talk. Cooks, craftsmen, children's entertainers - all who show viewers how to do something - interject "like so" into their commentaries, especially when fashioning their artefacts. See also LOOK SEE, GINORMOUS, etc.

LIKE TOPSY IT JUST GROWED "JUST HOW did you start your collection of beer-mats?" Answer: "Like Topsy it just growed". Interviewed collectors always seem to invoke Topsy (from *Uncle Tom's Cabin*.)

LINKS A way of getting from one subject to another on radio. TV poses fewer problems because the viewer is simply shown a different picture to indicate a change of subject. The time-honoured radio link goes something like this: "And from wool-gathering in the Pyrenees to the English shire horse..."; or "And from ships to chips - the sort that go into computers that is, not hot fat..."; or "And from football supporters to the kind of support most women of a certain age need up above..." Then there is the "But..." link, too obvious to illustrate, which compares what has gone before to what follows and finds no connection; also the NO-THIS-IS-NOT link, the OH-YES-AND link and the "Guessing-game Link", which is a speciality of *Kaleidoscope* on Radio Four. In this arts programme, which usually contains several unconnected contributions, one item comes to an apparently inconclusive end and is followed by an unannounced, unidentified and, of course, irrelevant piece of music (or other recorded *ACTUALITY*). The listener is momentarily baffled. *Has* the item ended or not? Has someone put on the wrong tape? Only then, perhaps after a couple of minutes of noise, the presenter explains its significance. And it may enable him to get in another cliché, the YES-YOU'VE-GUESSED link. It has become a thoroughly boring cliché. See also AND... and *MENU*.

LIP-LICKING Although a sign of nervousness and stage-fright, even some experienced TV performers persist in it, darting out a tongue in a rapid action that would do credit to an ant-eater.

LIP-READING Many deaf or hard-of-hearing TV viewers rely on firm lip-movements from the *TALKING HEADS* they watch - which makes it all the more surprising that so many of them copy ventriloquists and hardly move their lips. It takes so little effort.

LITTERY Common *SYNCOPATION* of "literary".

LOOK! Radio dramatists' preposterous device for describing what the listener cannot see. Thus, two people might be lying in wait at night - you can tell it is night because the BBC owl has just hooted - when one tells the other, "Look, a light's just gone on at the bedroom window on the first floor. He's undrawn the curtain. He's opening the window. He's got a gun. He's pointing it at the girl. He's gonna shoot. (Sound effect: bang!!!)... Oh my God! She isn't...? You mean...?" and so on. His companion, who is not blind and can perfectly well see for himself what is going on, must respond to this nonsense so that the listener may know what is going on.

LOOKS There are many and various ways of "looking" in radio programmes: "A not-too-serious look..." "A sideways look..." "A quizzical look..." and many more. Looks also occur in MENUS e.g. "We'll be looking at the hepatitis B virus" (and they'll have to look jolly closely!), "Hetty Davis will be looking into the life of Mary Russell Mitford". And, inevitably, on science programmes, "Mike Bonker has been looking into these black holes..."

LOOK-SEE Grown-ups' facetious baby-talk: "Our reporter Karl West went and had a look-see". See also LIKE SO.

LOOT *YOD-DROPPERS'* lute.

(THE) ... MAGAZINE/NEWSPAPER Do we need to be told that it is "the Times newspaper" and "the Guardian newspaper"? BBC news editors also call what used to be their own house-magazine the "Listener magazine" (to distinguish it from one putative listener?) though so far not the "Radio Times magazine". Nor "the New York Times newspaper" or "the Pravda newspaper". (Incidentally - maga*zine* or *mag*azine? *RP*-speakers probably prefer the first, but in Scottish-RP the second seems to be favoured.)

M

MAJOR Vogue adjective denoting size or importance: major earthquakes, major disturbances, major riots, etc., and of course

MAJOR HEADACHES Radio and TV suffer the same news headaches as newspapers (though not HEARTACHES, which are the papers' preserves - see *MediaWrite* section) but they *sound* sillier heard than they look in print. One admires the newsreader who could say (or fail to question beforehand): "If the electricians leave, the TUC has a major headache on its hands".

MAMMOTH Very big indeed, even bigger than MAJOR or the time-honoured news-word "massive". Frequently twinned with "task", when, in non-*RP*, "It's a mammoth tusk..." may give the confusing impression that the speaker is talking about an extinct, hairy elephant.

MANDATORY A class/regional stress difference has established itself: *RP*-speakers say "*man*datory", others, including Northerners, "man*day*tory".

MARGINAL(LY/ISED) "Pertaining to an edge, border, situated at the extreme edge of an area, etc.," says the *OED*. But among *INSTANT EXPERTS*, etc., it means "small" or "unimportant". The introduction of the newer usage is credited by later *OED* editions to the *New Statesman*, though psychologists and sociologists appropriated the word earlier. But language never stands still, and when a cliché can be created it will be. Politicians are now fond of saying that things or people are being "marginalised".

MAY/MIGHT See under this heading in *MediaWrite*. The same remarks apply.

M'BBC RADIO NEWS The prefatory "m" sound is a tiny, barely-noticeable grunt, and helps to start the vocal cords vibrating. Try it when you are sure no-one is listening. Many singers do it, and so do some BBC announcers - perhaps because many of them have trained voices.

ME/I See MYSELF.

'MEATY-LOGICAL' "Meteorological" has seven syllables, which any normal English-speaker with a tongue, a larynx and all the other bits and pieces can negotiate without much trouble, certainly with a little practice. In reality it usually comes out as either "meaty-logical" (or "meaty-rogical"). If, as some say, it is difficulty to pronounce the letter *r* twice in one word, how about "Met Office", a contraction which served us well during World War II? See also FEBB-YOU-AIRY and SECK-A-CHEE.

'M'DEEVAL' Almost standard *SYNCOPATION* into two syllables of the four-syllable "me-di-aeval".

MENU List of contents given at the beginning of a programme (like "headlines" in news bulletins). May include the *WHY OPENER* ("Why tobacconists are fuming at the latest anti-cigarette moves..."); the *HOW OPENER* ("how a publican found himself at the receiving end of a bombshell..."); *WE ASK...* ("We ask where does the Prime Minister stand now?") and the *WE HEAR HOW...* opener ("... and we hear how Mrs Thatcher has reacted to..."). One presenter said on *You and Yours,* without taking breath for any punctuation that may or may not have been in her script: "How doctors are tackling genital warts and we hear why an inventor is trying to tickle your taste buds". See also AHBEE, HEEBEE, SHEEBEE, WEEBEE and THEYBEE.

METAMORPHOSIS/METAMORPHOSIS/METAMORPHOSE Opinion is divided about the stress but Robert Browning made his own view clear in his *Burlesque for Palgrave on the Pronunciation of 'Metamorphosis'*:

>'Twas Goethe told us all by analysis,
>That change in plants we call Metamorphosis.

MILESTONE A mark of progress. As in "Our Motoring Correspondent describes the new model as a milestone".

MINIMAL Small, like MARGINAL.

MISSILE/MISSAL The Americans confuse lethal arms with manuals of the mass; and sad to say, one or two BBC speakers are beginning to ape them.

(THE) MISSING D EFFECT Established in informal regional as well as *RP* speech: goo'show, goo'dog, goo'girl, goo'concert - g'bye", g'night 'n' G'bless...

(THE) MISSING T EFFECT Cockneys like replacing the *t* with a glottal stop, and this ancient dialect effect enables them to say "bottle" without moving the tongue, the second syllable being an ape-like grunt.

MIS-STRESSING One of the besetting sins of modern news-reading and reporting. For no apparent reason the least important words (or the wrong part of a word) are given the strongest stress. This is not a matter of taste or fashion but of meaning. To speak of Mersey*side* or West*minster* is to reveal a misunderstanding of what such place-names denote and how they came into being. And there is a difference between saying, "We have a problem on our *hands*" and "We have a *problem* on our hands". For other complaints see *LAST-WORD STRESS* and *OVERSTRESSED PREPOSITIONS*.

MM The tiny grunt accompanying social kissing on radio and TV as well as in real life. It has a downward inflexion, suggesting effort, not unlike the sound of a person straining at stool. Amorous (i.e.*"*French"[!]) kissing is usually soundless - at any rate to those not directly involved - but on radio, where full-frontal sex is increasing as fast as it is disappearing from TV, soft moaning and heavy breathing are in order.

MMM! Appreciative sound to accompany tasting in food programme items. It is a kind of "do-not-adjust-your-set" message to mean "we're thinking about our verdict". Usually followed by the unattractive noise of talking while chewing.

'MODGIT' Fashionable pronunciation of moderate combining *SYNCOPA-TION* with the almost traditional English reluctance to sound a decent - or even a faked - *r*. Female presenters seem especially fond of it, although the three-syllable "mo-de-rate" sounds neither affected nor elocuted.

'MOLE-CYULAR' (To rhyme with pole-ruler). At least one BBC reporter prefers that pronunciation of molecular. And why not? Most people put the stress on the second syllable, *lec*, but those who say it the other way merely reveal that they do not have much contact with molecular scientists. See also NEW-KEE-LAR.

MONITORING As in "Our Middle East Correspondent has been monitoring the situation from Cyprus". It means the correspondent is, sensibly, a long way from the scene of the action. Much monitoring of trouble-spots also goes on from the well-stocked bars of international hotels.

MY GUEST TODAY... TV is showbusiness and so, to a lesser extent, is radio. There is no guararantee that the words of wisdom that come out of a speaker's mouth were the unaided work of the person who formulates them. Most of the carefully prepared quips with which presenters introduce quiz or discussion programmes are the work of script-writers; and in some programmes (e.g. *Call My Bluff*) the guests as well as the presenter may be supplied not only with questions but also the answers. Interviewers, quizmasters, etc., are always chosen from the ranks of the already famous. They arc thcrcforc too busy for anything so mundanc as writing thcir own scripts, even if perfectly capable of doing so. Once the viewer or listener is aware of this he will marvel at the way in which they introduce their latest fellow-celebrity as "*My* guest today..." He is not *their* guest but the firm's, which also stocks the drinks-cabinet in the hospitality suite. Even the question on the host's clipboard will have been composed by a RESEARCHER.

MYSELF Widely supposed to be a classier alternative to "me" but in fact often betrays misunderstanding of simple grammar or nervousness about being "correct". Thus a well-known politician said to an interviewer after an accident he had witnessed, "Myself and a passer-by ran out into the road to help the motorist..." He obviously wanted to put himself first but felt "I and a passerby..." might sound self-important, and "Me and a passer-by..." would sound - and be - "wrong". But even where "me" is perfectly correct, people like to play safe and say "This is a great day for myself..." or "It was given to my mother and myself..." or "From Brian and myself, goodbye".

N

(THE) NAY LONGER RIND O There is no doubt (date or dight) about ("abate" or "abite") it: the rounded *o* sound is going out (ate or ite) of fashion among the English white-collar, blue-collar, middle and even upper classes: it is no longer rounded but rainded or rinded. Some regional accents have always substituted *ay* for *o*, and "hay nay brain cay" is standard with Ambridge farm-workers in *The Archers*. In the early and middle 1980s this affectation was adopted by many of the newly-prosperous young almost as

a class-badge, just as their elders took to imitating Liverpool Scouse in the 1960s. Thus yuppies and rustics are now united by a common *o*. Even some royals have taken to it; we hear them in our "heppy haimes". There are other variations, e.g. clahdy, claydee or clye-dee for cloudy, as heard in *WEATH-ERBABBLE*. Radio and TV have several otherwise excellent *FRONTMEN* who fail to distinguish between found and find, diary and dowry, alliance and allowance or future and feature. They shop in seepermarkets, hear music by May-tsart and tell us that the cabinet sits in Dining Street.

'NAWSHA' Nausea. See SRI LANKA.

'NECKSHEER' See DISHEER.

NEWS INVERSIONS In the belief that radio listeners have a ten-second memory-span like TV watchers, broadcasters invert some sentences in a clumsy and convoluted way, producing strange and ugly verbal pile-ups. Their - surely misguided - purpose is to ensure that a person's name comes at the *end* of an announcement: "Expected to be high on the agenda will be the Irish government's refusal to extradite Patrick Ryan". The most complicated inversions can be built up like verbal lego, e.g. "Following events at the scene of the Nottingham housing estate siege has been BBC Home Affairs Correspondent Chris Underhill"; or "Listening to this report from the disturbances on the border between Namibia and South Africa has been our African Affairs Correspondent, Cuthbert Ndebedele"; or "With me in the studio to hear what Minister of Agriculture David Furrows and food scientist Noel Wheatsheaf had to say on the vexed subject of food irradiation is Consumer Affairs Editor Veronica Salmon". The appearance of the name at the end may be an inbuilt cue for a reporter waiting to say his piece, but there must be cleverer ways of arranging private signals. On the other hand, news-editors might well consider rearranging the word-order to spare listeners needless fear and alarm. "A Boeing 737 with 158 passengers on board on a flight from Edinburgh to London made a crash-landing at Newcastle Airport after the pilot reported...." may pile detail upon detail and cause much anxious suspense before finally coming to "All the passengers escaped unhurt". Is it not better to start with "All 158 passengers on a Boeing 737 escaped when it made a crash-landing at Newcastle Airport..." etc? The same goes for news about persons, where a long litany of name, descriptions, qualifications, distinctions and honours may be recited before coming to the crucial part of the news - either "...has died in London at the age of 65" or "...has been awarded the Order of Merit". In the old days one could tell at once, because announcers knew how to use the *BLACK-EDGED VOICE*.

'NEW-KEE-LAR' "Nuclear" as said by some reporters, especially on ITV and local radio. I have also heard "binoc-lu-ar" and MOLE-CYULAR.

NEWS REPETITIONS A practice copied from newspapers, in which a headline brings a brief summary, followed by a "standfirst" paragraph, usually in slightly larger type than the main story, which is then told for the third time, in greater detail. In the papers this gives the reader the opportunity of scanning merely the headline (an opportunity usually thwarted because silly puns and word-games replace information - see *MediaWrite*), or reading only the summary of the "standfirst", before turning to something else. On radio and TV the practice works like this. Newsreader: "The raids are said to be in response to a whole series of violations of the ceasefire". Then the reporter's recording is heard: "The raids are said to be in response to a whole series of violations of the ceasefire". This is excusable only if the news editors had no time to hear the tape. Otherwise why can't they paraphrase?

NIZZEN HUT In spoken English an example of the genteelly *BUZZING S*-and in print a sign of the times. In the papers this piece of military equipment, a simple, tunnel-shaped building developed in about 1917 by Lieut. Col. Peter Nissen (1871-1930), is now frequently misspelt "Nissan Hut". Thus was the war in the Far East both won and lost!

'NODDADAWL' Like its positive brother ADDAWL, a trendy way of saying not at all and at all, common among interviewees - perhaps those who have seen too many American films and TV series, because the Americans like to make their *t*s sound like *d*s.

NODDIES Name for the manic nodding movements with which interviewers encourage their subjects to tell all, on TV as well as radio (where fortunately they cannot be seen). They mean, "Yes, I HEAR WHAT YOU SAY - please do go on". In the old days radio interviewers would interject exclamations like "Oh yes", and "You don't say!", and "Is it really?" or the odd confirmatory "Quite so!", or just "Uh-huh?" TV news reporters also nod a lot, but for emphasis, as they are taught not to indulge in gesticulation. Some nod so much that they look like farmyard chickens establishing a pecking-order. See also the Sideways LOOK of TV presenters.

NO THIS IS NOT... Teasing programme-opener, perhaps after a misleading *ACTUALITY* noise or the signature tune from another programme, e.g. when introducing a feature about tropical islands, "No, this is not *Desert Island Discs...*" Also "Yes this *is...*" and YES YOU'VE GUESSED.

NOW IF YOU'LL EXCUSE ME Play cliché, introduced for the purpose of changing scene. Usually followed by "I've got work to do". Real-life people are seldom so brutally frank but invent excuses.

NUGATORY Trifling, small, worthless. I include this useful but rare word because some, having never heard it spoken, pronounce if to rhyme with bug-a-tory or bug-a-tree. So it was pronounced on *Bookshelf* (Radio 4) by someone reading a passage from a novel by Kingsley Amis - who was also on the programme and spoke next. One could almost hear him biting his lip.

O

OF COURSE In impromptu speech a useful introductory noise of the BASICALLY kind. Also to express emphatic assent, like POSITIVELY.

OH As in Nineteen-oh-eight for "1908": perhaps, like "zero", better left to telephone-operators. Radio 3 prefers "nineteen-hundred and eight", which takes a little longer but sounds more authoritative.

OH (YES) AND ...! The phoney, scripted "after-thought". This works only if the speaker has the skill to read his script or autocue to give the impression he is speaking impromptu, or if the exclamation introduces a genuine last-moment idea. See also NO THIS IS NOT and YES YOU'VE GUESSED.

ON A DAILY BASIS A favourite with politicians and other longwinded interviewees who like to savour their own words or crave maximum exposure. Their Lord's Prayer would ask God to "Give us our bread on a daily basis"; and they do not put money on the collection-plate but "contribute on a cash basis".

ONE See ROYAL ONE.

ONE OF News cliché words that can usually be dispensed with, as in the common statement "The situation is *one of* utter chaos" (why not "There is utter chaos"?), and especially when they are combined with a *PLURAL CONFUSION*, e.g. "Their feelings are *one of* anger and dismay..."

ONE TO ONE Two persons talking to each other, e.g. in an interview.
'ON(G)-VELOPE' Now slightly-dated, ostensibly-posh, *RP* pronunciation of envelope (see also RESTAURA*N*TEUR). I suggest that as the word, meaning the cover of a letter, etc., has been in daily English use since 1704,

it has probably earned itself the English pronunciation "enn-velope". Town planners and architects prefer the English form when they speak of "*enveloping*" - a process of repairing or restoring all the houses in a whole street or neighbourhood; in spite of the fact that the verb previously got its stress on the second syllable, env*e*lop.

ON (HIS) HANDS See MAJOR HEADACHE.

ONLY Like ALSO, "most", and other qualifications, this word is often understressed: see *REVERSED STRESS*. "Oh Lord, who gavest thy only *Son*" might suggest that there was a daughter, too. "Only" is often misplaced, too: "He went to France only last year/he only went to France last year/he went only to France last year/he only went to France last year..." etc.

OUT THE ROOM As in "She went out the room". An American time-saving device based on the German, "*Sie ging aus dem Zimmer*" which saves a mere monosyllable of a preposition. Americans have similarly and imperfectly translated "Schreib uns" (which, because there are cases in German, has the preposition built into the verb) as "Write us", which sounds absurd in English. But see also HALF ONE.

OVERSTRESSED PREPOSITIONS Common affectation of reporters in search of stress-markers, though why hit the poor preposition? "Mr and Mrs Bush went *to* Buckingham Palace where they are having tea *with* the Queen". Presumably not *away* from the palace to have tea *against* her.

(THE) OVERSTRESSED T A fad by which the final *t* at the end of a word is given almost an *s* sound, perhaps for added emphasis, as in "Cricket*s*, AND in the Headingley Test..."

OVER-USE A dreaded word among freelance broadcasters who work for the BBC and tread the narrow path between popularity and over-popularity, when listeners and fear that viewers may begin to mutter, "Oh, not *him* again!" What often happens is that a new star (speaker, singer, player, writer or comedian) is discovered - is made a fuss of by a few critics, and then approached independently by many producers and programme-makers on all channels. All persuade him to work for them. Even "formats" may be devised specially for him. Only listeners and viewers get the full effect of this over-use, as they observe it all from the outside, whereas programme-makers usually see/hear only their own programmes. Then, suddenly, at a high-level meeting, someone cries "over-use" - and the star disappears as suddenly as he exploded, for he is RESTED. Musical performers, too, may enjoy (or suffer) over-use. When the delightful soprano Emma Kirkby was first discovered she seemed to be broadcasting almost daily, until her appearances settled down to more reasonable frequency. In the more distant past no oboist was heard on the BBC except Heinz Holliger, no flautist but James Galway. Talks and current-affairs presenters come and go with even more alarming speed. In this respect the BBC is in a difficult position. It provides an important - some say the only - showcase for musical performers, and often this very exposure earns them such acclaim that they turn into stars - whose agents increase their fees so much that the BBC can no longer afford to employ them.

P

PACE/PITCH VARIATIONS The need for relative changes in both speed and pitch utterance is often overlooked. No speaker who in ordinary daily life drones his conversation at a constant, unvarying pace will hold our attention. He will be shunned as a bore. Some words (or groups of words) are more important than others. Quotations can be delivered a little more slowly to emphasise that they are not the words of the speaker but of another person, or spoken with a slight drop in both pitch and/or volume. Parenthetic ideas, too, may be speeded up and given a pitch-difference, with a return to the "home key" after the bracket (see AND I QUOTE). A greater word-speed may indicate greater enthusiasm, whereas a slowing-down makes for solemnity. Peter Barker, Chief Announcer of Radio 3, says there are many other ways of varying delivery according to content: faster, slower, higher, lower, more precise, more slurred, etc. most of which are impossible to describe in print. The best way of learning these is by studying the work of the best speakers, like him and his colleagues: their teaching is available free at the touch of a switch. So why do so many speakers prefer a gearless, gormless, droning delivery, with the unvarying intonation and constant pace of an electric milk-float? See also *PUNCTUATION-BY-INTONATION*.

PARENTING Fashionable *VERB-MADE-FROM-NOUNS*. It often figures on *PHONE-INS* and appeals to women's rights enthusiasts, especially when it replaces "fathering" ("mothering" has slightly different connotations). But beware of condemning it as a neologism: the *OED* has a example from 1663, but calls it "rare".

'PENINSHOOLA(R)' *YOD-DROPPING*. The noun has no final *r*, contrary to common belief.

PERFUME/PERFUME

> To gild refined gold, to paint the lily,
> To throw a *per*fume on the violet...
>> Shakespeare: *King John*

> Sae bonny was their blooming
> Their scent the air perf*uming*...
>> A. Cockburn: *The Flowers of the Forest*

PERIOD OF TIME As one of the BBC weather forecasters from the London Weather Centre said, when accused on *Feedback* of making unclear statements, "We've got to put a lot of information across in a reasonably short period of time." See *REDUNDANCIES*.

PERSONALITY Nebulous description, as in "radio/TV personality". The same goes for the job-description of "broadcaster", which can mean, at one extreme, someone who has broadcast once or twice or, at the other, someone who is heard almost daily. (In the early days of broadcasting, incidentally, the past tense of the word was "broadcasted".) Personalities often wear attention-seeking dark glasses, "wishing to be recognised as persons not wishing to be recognised".

PFHHH This is the best representation I can devise to illustrate one of the more intrusive sounds of modern radio speech, i.e. the sharp, loud breath-intake, about which the BBC receives hundreds of letters. *Woman's Hour* is the oldest home of this noise, and I regret to say that female broadcasters make it more than men. It is somewhere between an inward sigh and an implosive breath-intake beginning with the mouth closed. The lips assume, first, a *p* position, turning to *f* as they open, which is then followed by the breath-intake itself. Starting with the lips already slightly apart, the sound is more like "ffhhh". When the mouth is opened even more as the breath is taken, a hissing "hhh" sound is heard as the air rushes into the broadcaster's cavities. Everyone has to take breath between phrases or sentences, but starting with closed lips will make for a greater implosion than with the lips already slightly parted. It also makes a broadcaster sound like someone affecting dislike of his job, like a teacher giving an exasperated sigh when confronted by a naughty pupil. Unfortunately the modern microphone over-emphasises the taking of breath.

PHONE-IN A cheap form of radio. Listeners - less often viewers - can participate and know that their views are valued, although they spend much of their time greeting the presenter and each of his guests ("Good morning, Sir James, Good morning Brian..."). One local-radio station had a phone-in on the subject of "Laziness and Lethargy". Nobody phoned.

PICK-POCKETING Should not the participle be pocket-picking, as pockets are picked, not picks pocketed?

PINPOINT To locate. As in "Divers have pinpointed the container to an area of fifteen square miles on the ocean-bed..."(!)

PLUNGE Like HURTLE, PLUMMET and other overdramatising terms (see *MediaWrite*) this is no improvement on the simpler and factual "fall" or "drop" - perhaps with the exception of necklines. If drama is called for it can be indicated with the voice, its inflexion and *PACE*.

PLURAL CONFUSIONS These are a constant source of confusion, complaints and attempts at formulating "rules". They seldom work. The only rule is that there are no rules. "A team of Soviet investigators *is* expected at Greenham..." But in subsequent references to this "team" (or a "group") it seems to be more natural to say "they" when one is obviously referring to the individual persons. Convention has it that one says "Liverpool *are* winning..." when talking about the Liverpool football *team*. But the club which employs the Liverpool team is singular; also the city itself ("Liverpool is winning its battle against unemployment"). One can only go by the "feel" of a sentence. Thus both "The city's speciality *is* Wet Nellies and Scouse", and "Wet Nellies and Scouse *are* what the city specialises in" would sound acceptable. "A number of" is also tricky: some say that because "a number" is singular one should say "A number of people has been hurt", but it *sounds* wrong. Yet there are many usages about which there is no doubt, and absurdities heard on radio and TV include: "There was more arrests on Saturday evening", and "Last year the balloonist Mr Lindstrand, with Mr Richard Branson, became the first people to cross the Atlantic..." In "The Cotswolds are a lovely part of Britain" the speaker felt uncomfortable about "the Cotswolds *is*..." but the verb referred to the "part", which is singular. If still worried he could have rephrased, e.g. "The area known as the Cotswolds is a lovely part of Britain..." Difficulties often occur in longer sentences, when the singular subject is much separated from the verb: "I believe that we shall be able to judge only when the truth about all the facts are known..."

PLUS In mediaspeak this means "and". Especially favoured in *MENUS*: "After the break we take a LOOK at childminders, we hear HOW MANY people are starving in Ethiopia, plus WEEBEE bringing you a report on..."

POISED See SET and *MediaWrite*.

POLIT BUREAU One of the earliest Russian *ACRONYMS*, made from the (Russian!) words for "politics" and "bureau". The BBC Pronunciation Unit oddly recommends a first-syllable stress, whereas the Russians stress the second: "po*lit*". A subconscious reference perhaps to Harry Pollitt, the 1930s English communist leader?

POSITIVELY See DEFINITELY and OF COURSE.

'PREE-DELICTION' Common confusion of ideas: Latin *dilectus*, beloved, gave us delight and pre*dilec*tion; and *delictum*, a crime, produced delinquents - but not "pre*delict*ion", which is a non-word. If it meant anything it would be a predisposition towards crime.

PRESENTER Usually a *FRONT MAN* who reads what RESEARCHERS have written for him: one of the deceits of radio and TV. Some programmes (e.g. natural history on Radio 4) use two presenters, who contrivedly alternate sentence-by-sentence when giving their *MENU*, ending with the obligatory BUT FIRST... Perhaps a variation of the BACKCHAT EFFECT.

PRESENTLY For a long time presently meant soon. When Jeeves is asked to bring a drink he says, "Presently, sir", meaning "soon, quickly". Today it is the lazy speaker's time-saving adverb (cf. CURRENTLY) for at present, though he can claim archaic and dialect precedents. See also AT THIS (VERY)(PRESENT) MOMENT IN TIME.

PROBE Investigate, examine - a headline word which looks and sounds foolish and clumsy everywhere else.

PRO*DUCE/PRO*DUCE A noun/verb stress difference some speakers are no longer observing. The same applies to

*PRO*GRESS/PRO*GRESS* "Our parliamentary reporter has been following the *pro*gress of the bill as it pro*gress*es through parliament..."

'PRON*O*UNCIATION' A common spelling/pronunciation error - and one for which no-one should feel ashamed. Blame the often senseless cussedness of the English language.

*PRO*TEST/PRO*TEST* The first is the noun, the second the verb. But those who protest are pro*test*ers: a heavy stress on the first syllable ("*Proe*-tester") makes it sound like an antonym of the imaginary "*anti*tester".

PUNCTUATION-BY-INTONATION Bad punctuation in radio and TV

scripts soon becomes audible, and its total absence (like *RIP AND READ* material) must be assumed when one listens to the perfunctory news bulletins given by local stations, especially junk radio. From the evidence of Radio 4 news alone, many writers treat full-stops and commas as interchangeable, as in "The driver is thought to have lost control at a bend, he is not seriously hurt", this could be a way of indicating urgency, if that is so it fails miserably, most listeners who think about these things are disturbed by it it certainly doesn't help the news-reader. Good punctuation in written material helps to make the writer's meaning clear. A reader should not be obliged to read a paragraph over and over again before he understands it. A newspaper reader is able do this, but radio listeners cannot say, "I beg your pardon, would you mind repeating that?" The skilled broadcaster should be able to make audible the difference between a comma and a semicolon, a colon and a full-stop. Material in quotation-marks must be made to sound like a quotation (without need for the interjection AND-I-QUOTE): see PACE/PITCH.

'PUR-CHEE' A pronunciation of poetry favoured even by one or two poets. It stems from the uneasy relationship many English English-speakers have with the letter *r*, which they seldom if ever roll, and often fake or omit (see FEBB-YOU-AIRY). (I myself have to fake it, being unable to roll my *r*, but refuse to make a JAMA out of it).

'P'ZHOOMABLY' Almost the standard form of "presumably" among habitual *YOD-DROPPERS*.

R

RAP Reprimand - but only in headlines, if there.

REBEL/REBEL

> Poor soul, the centre of my sinful earth,
> Fool'd by these *rebe*l powers that thee array,
> Why dost thou pine within and suffer dearth
> Painting thy outward walls so costly gay?
> Shakespeare: *Sonnet 146*

> Aspiring to be gods if angels fell,
> Aspiring to be angels men re*bel*.
> Alexander Pope: *An Essay on Man*.

'RECKERNISE' Produces many complaints from listeners: perhaps the pronunciation of bad spellers who believe it comes from "reckon".

REDUNDANCIES AND PLEONASMS "Pleonasm", the *OED* says, is "the use of more words in a sentence than are necessary to express the meaning..." - but it also writes, in its definition of "Celeriac" "The word does not appear to be known outside of English", which seems to be as good a pleonasm as any. An educationist on Radio 4 said, "Pictures can speak a language *equally as* powerful *as* words", and the general secretary of a teachers' union, "Teachers are finding it *increasingly more* difficult to..." A redundant "that" or "what" is often needlessly added: the famous song does not go, "The man that I love". And (a complaining teacher again!) "There is no doubt that in this country teachers are having a harder time than *what* they are abroad". "On the day *that* Concorde celebrated its 10th anniversary..." could also have been simplified. See also *HADNAVES* and the *OFFOFS* as exemplified by a distinguished and popular TV scientist and conservationist saint who said: "If we hadnave destroyed the peat blanket..." The dreaded *CAN'TARDLIES* double their negatives; as a correspondent reported from China: "You *couldn't hardly* see the road..." Other examples include, "They *don't none of them* want to miss Father Christmas" (a Radio 4 reporter in a scripted item about Christmas shopping); and "He now reads the seventh *out of* eleven episodes..." (*Woman's Hour*). A reporter on Radio 4: "If he had been arrested he would now *have had to have* been released..."

REMIT The dictionaries give the stress on the second syllable but many speakers (perhaps those who have never heard the word spoken?) say it like "*ream*-it". Or it could be a verb/noun stress difference.

REFUSE/REFUSE One of the MAJOR confusions for foreigners: "*Ref-*yooss" is put into sacks, unless the dustmen "reff-*ooze*" to collect it; whereas electricians "*ree*-fyooz" appliances when putting a new fuse in.

> What ailed us, O gods, to desert you
> For creeds that ref*use* and restrain?
> Come down and redeem us from virtue,
> Our Lady of Pain.
> Charles Algernon Swinburne: *Dolores*

REPORTEDLY As in "He is reportedly very ill". A clumsy, newfangled (and lazily applied) adverb that assuredly turns every sentence into an indefensibly clumsy one. Why not "He is reported to be very ill"? It takes no longer.

REPORTERS' SINGSONG Have you noticed that the way reporters speak to listeners and viewers bears little or no resemblance to how they speak, formally, face-to-face, to their fellow men, let alone in informal, normal conversation. (See also the Foreword of *MediaWrite*). Real people talking to each other adopt a natural rise-and-fall: some words pitched higher, some lower, louder or softer, according to the sense to be conveyed. But reporters who may be clear, lucid and intelligent-sounding when talking impromptu, suddenly sound like dyslectic adolescents when reading*their own scripted words*. It is the dreaded Reporters' Sing-song. Vocal range is reduced to three or four "notes", delivery flat as a dalek's; pitch undulations as monotonously regular as corrugated iron, the voice unnaturally raised (reminiscent of the nasal urgency of 1930s cinema newsreels or an old person on the telephone who can't believe the thing works). PACE is unvarying, deadpan, *staccato*; intonation remains the same whether they report a national triumph or 100 dead in a rail-crash (no sympathetic *BLACK-EDGED VOICE*). Many voice-simulating computers would sound better. Within this general awfulness there are individual variations. One man, for a time regularly heard on Radio 4, sounded like a cross between Calamity Jane in her final depression and an "I-speak-your-weight" machine. Yet unscripted (e.g. when interviewing) he spoke normally, fluently and with great authority. He was either untrained or untrainable, but it took many months before he was put to more suitable work. A Radio 4 *SPORTS REPORTER* has developed an idiosyncratic sing-song of his own: he turns *up* every phrase-ending so that each last word of his every clause or sub-clause comes to rest on the identical note: as if checking aloud items from a list of groceries. Yet he has a good voice, is a fluent and capable interviewer, and speaks excellent modified-*RP*. A reporter often heard from Westminster has a beautiful voice and fluent delivery, but at each last word of each and every phrase suddenly spreads the sound to an elongated *crescendo*. Many impromptu-speaking bores who recount endless stories, especially wartime reminiscences (and fail signally TO CUT A LONG STORY SHORT) also adopt this up-turn at the end of every clause and phrase, as if to say "Don't stop me, I haven't finished yet!" This goes back to the early days of radio, when people often recounted their experiences from World War One. The pubs are full of their heirs. *Most* radio/TV reporters now *habitually* land on every last word of every phrase or sentence with vehemence and force, as though triumphant at having successfully negotiated yet another short phrase (see *LAST-WORD STRESS*). Each last word is over-emphasised: an increase in volume combined with a rapid downturn in intonation, producing a kind of moo as from a sick cow. When these final sounds are cut from the tape and edited together they sound like a cross between a deranged Anglican priest's one-note chant and a milking-parlour, except that cows do not all moo the *same* note. In addition *to* all that, the average reporter goes for the *OVERSTRESSED PREPOSITION*, making the listener feel that he has no idea *of* the sense he is trying *to* convey *to* his listeners *for* whom he reports *from* the places *in* the news.

I suggest that the greatness of Alistair Cooke, James Cameron or René Cutforth lies/lay in their awareness that broadcasting is *talking to real people* (with such variations in pace, stress and inflexion that requires) not in reading a dead script to a microphone. Have you ever heard any of the *Today* presenters (as opposed to *reporters*), or the professionals on Radio 3, overstress a preposition or lapse into singsong? The inescapable fact, although unpalatable to egalitarians, is that "educated" speakers tend to be more fluent. People who have passed through the higher education system are more accustomed to *communicating* (which is why more financial reporters than sports reporters make sense of their despatches). A different type of singsong can be heard from some presenters of popular musical classics who through sheer habit (OVER-USE?) adopt a kind of "automatic pilot" inflexion, as mechanical and predictable as the classified football results, with a curiously undulating, pseudo-sympathetic, "bedside" manner:

RESCUE SERVICES WERE QUICKLY ON THE SCENE News formula, like TIGHT SECURITY and others to be found in both *MediaSpeak* and *MediaWrite*. For all I know this standard phrase in every news-editors' armoury has a computer reference number: "There's been a gas explosion in Stepney, lads. Call up No. 74 from the phrase memory..."

RESEARCHERS The back-room people who write the material for script-writers who re-write it and put the words into the PRESENTERS' or FRONT MEN'S mouths.

'RESTAURANTEUR' The superfluous *n* is heard in about 25 per cent of instances when the word "restaurateur" is said on radio or TV (or printed in the papers). Whether the final *t* in "restaurant" should be sounded is another matter: I tend to omit it, but as it has been an English word for at least a century it must sooner or later be anglicised. Many people do pronounce it "rest'runt". But see ON(G)VELOPE.

RESTED A broadcaster may be "rested", usually after a period of *OVER-USE*. This is really a euphemism for sacked: dropped down a deep metaphorical hole of oblivion from which he is unlikely to emerge, at any rate until he qualifies for the time-honoured BBC title THE DISTINGUISHED.

REVERSED STRESSES These come in several sorts: mis-stressed single words, mis-stressed compounds, and masculinised feminine endings. Some mis-stressed compounds have become almost standard, like Pry*minister*, *Santa*claus, *Guy*fawkes, Arch*bishop*, Head*master* - and even the BBC's own Reith *Lectures* and "Sound *Archives*". To my ears the *prime* minister is the first minister, the *arch*bishop different from a *suffragan* bishop; the

Reith Lectures are not the *Dimbleby* Lectures and the *Sound* Archives not the *Documents* Archives. Guy Fawkes was the *only* member of the Fawkes family who tried to blow up Parliament: there is no need to stress that it wasn't *Fred, Jim* or *Wally* Fawkes, by stressing *Guy*. The *head*master is at head of all the other masters (though unions have decreed that he must now be unsexed as HEAD). Masculinised feminine endings are found in many news reports from inadequately-trained news-reporters and LAST-WORD thumpers who fail to stress the qualifying word. In a report about swallows it is wrong to say "...most *swallows*" or "green *swallows*", or "dead *swallows*" (as though swallows had not been mentioned before): the words to stress are those which distinguish one kind of swallow from another. Reversed stressing is common also in WEATHERBABBLE, probably because weathermen imitate the *REPORTERS' SING-SONG* and *their* unerring way of stressing the wrong word, especially at the end of a clause, phrase or sentence. Thus, talking about winds, they keep saying "westerly *winds*", "northerly *winds*" and "southerly *winds*" - in stead of giving emphasis to the wind *direction*, e.g. "*westerly* winds", "*northerly* winds and *southerly* winds". They do this only when reading. Bill Green, arriving home after a hard day at the Weather Centre, is more likely to say to his wife, "Ooo-aarr, Beryl, DURBEE a stiff *northerly* wind blowin' tomorrow so get me *long*johns out..." Attention by script-writers to *HYPHENS* (See *MediaWrite*) also helps the reader to stress properly: e.g. "Hilliard was a *miniature*-painter, Lautrec a miniature *painter*". Word-stressing according to word-importance is so essential a part of communicators' technique that one marvels how so many broadcasters can get it so crassly and consistently wrong.

'REVOULVE(R)' Revolve and revolver, with a fashionable modification of the *o* sound.

RINGING OUT Whenever a shooting is reported news-editors recall Tennyson's wild bells: "...then a shot rang out and he took cover".

RIP-AND-READ Reading the news as it comes out of a tele-printer, fax, telex or similar machine, i.e. from a sheet of paper ripped out and passed to the news-reader. It is therefore raw, unedited, with little or no punctuation and often printed in capital letters only - all of which hinder the reader.

ROCKING See EXPLOSIONS.

'ROE-MANCE' Americans - and growing numbers of Britons who watch American TV and cinema *roe*mances - mis-stress this with a strong and elongated first syllable. English poetry proves them wrong, for in such things (as I try to show elsewhere in this book) there *is* often a right and a wrong way, otherwise the metre is ruined. The very lines that produced the over-used cliché "high romance", from Keats's *In a Drear-nighted December*, illustrate this:

> When I behold upon the night's starr'd face
> Huge cloudy symbols of a high ro*mance*.

It was also a favourite word in Kipling's poetry, and in every instance he stresses the second syllable.

(THE) ROYAL "ONE" Only after the rise of *CHAT SHOWS* on radio and TV was royalty seen and heard being interviewed. Until then it was an unwritten rule that when royals and commoners met, only the royal persons asked questions (and many people do not understand how great a strain this throws on them, as few normal conversational exchanges are possible). When Princess Margaret broke with tradition and appeared on Roy Plomley's *DESERT ISLAND DISCS*, the first attempt at recording the programme had to be abandoned: not used to being questioned she answered her host's questions with either "yes" or "no", which is not how the programme works. There is nothing peculiarly royal about "one": well-brought-up persons used to be told that it is immodest and selfish to reiterate the first person singular too often, so they varied "I" with "one", e.g. "One doesn't always think about the dangers", etc.

RP Much tendentious nonsense has been written about Received (Standard) Pronunciation. It has been dismissed as "upper-class", "Oxford English", "superior", "effete"(!), "class-conscious", "snobbish" or just "posh"; even absurdly as "BBC English". Yet in 1934 H.C.Wyld, Professor of English at Cambridge University, still felt able without selfconsciousness to define *RP* as "the best kind of English ... spoken by those often very properly called the best kind of people", and added that it was "most consistently heard among Officers of the British Regular Army (whose) utterance...is at once clear-cut and precise, yet free from affectation; at once downright and manly, yet in the highest degree refined and urbane." Anyone who dared write that today would be laughed out of court. Wyld's army officers probably sounded like present-day parodies of upper-class twits; but then they were *required* to make themselves understood - and *were* understood - by Scotsmen, Scousers, Geordies, Ghurkas and Sikhs, many of whom were perhaps unable to communicate with each other because of their respective native accents. Wyld's RP was also the language used by Neville Chamberlain, whose famous war announcement of 1939 is preserved on record: "Eh em spikking to you from the Cebbinet Room..." which, again, is not exactly what people would call Received Standard Pronunciation *now*. On the other hand, while there was an outcry when the Yorkshire comedian Wilfred Pickles read the BBC Home Service news in the 1940s, recordings show that his speech is very close to what is accepted as present-day RP. In truth, "standard" English is constantly changing, constantly enriched by multi-racial, multi-national influences and social attitudes. What has not changed, however, is the need for intelligibility, especially as English is now spoken by more people worldwide than any language: and an *accepted* (which is what is meant by *received*) standard form is therefore more necessary than ever before. (English, for example, is the language of international airline pilots, who must be able to make themselves clear in potentially life-or-death situations.) Yet the BBC is under constant pressure to abandon *RP* (and the BBC World Service, to its shame, has in some respects already done so), because critics claim RP to be "middle-class" and "elitist". This is not just plain nonsense but "divisive" nonsense (to use a favourite word from the egalitarian vocabulary), typical of British class obsessions. Speaking clearly should be the aim of all "classes" - especially as those who never get beyond the slovenly speech of pop stars and *DJ*s are more likely to find themselves relegated to an under-class, with lessened employment prospects - which cannot be what egalitarians intended. The BBC on the whole favours clear English, with the occasional inevitable aberration and deviation (some mentioned elsewhere in this book) from colourful eccentrics, a practice outlined in the foreword to its 1971 *Pronouncing Dictionary*. As a public service its first responsibility is to provide information that can be understood by everyone: by the hard-of-hearing, the elderly, the immigrant trying to grapple with the language - in short, Prof. Wyld's Scotsmen, Scousers, Geordies, Ghurkas and Sikhs. The self-conscious preservation of colourful urban or regional accents, while laudable, is a different matter altogether. It would be unthinkable in, say, Germany, to hear the national news spoken by an annnouncer with a strong Swabian accent, or for the French to broadcast nationwide in Marseillais dialectal sounds. British regional accents when coming from the BBC regional and local stations provide a useful perspective and sense of place, whereas emanating from the "London" BBC (as in the national news) they disorientate. This is borne out by the barrage of protests received when strongly Scottish-speaking *PRESENTERS* or news-readers are employed - who may appear to talk about "perils" when they mean "pearls", and fail to distinguish between "naughty" and "knotty" problems. It is a matter of clarity, not class. An Irish speaker's "working" sounds like RP "walking", the Yorkshireman's "staffing" like "stuffing", a Lancastrian's "mammoth task" like the tusk of a hairy prehistoric animal, an "aunt" like an "ant". The cockney-sparrer *DJ* who introduced a woman as a "sow singer from Wows" should have been sued for defamation by the *soul* singer from *Wales* he introduced; though the owners of the grocery chain Finefare would have been delighted when he announced "The Finefare

Trumpeters of the Brigade of Guards": sponsorship of the highest order. Viewers may recall a televised outburst by Sir Robin Day when he thought that a Midlands-accented politician had accused him of being "profane", when the man had merely said "profound". In short, the listener must not be misled - like the immigrant hospital patient who collapsed when she thought a London nurse was telling her, "We're sending you home to die". The nurse meant "today". As Samuel Daniel wrote in 1599:

> And who in time knows whither we may vent
> The treasure of our tongue? To what strange shores
> This gain of our best glory shall be sent
> T'enrich unknowing nations with our stores?
> What worlds in th' yet unforméd Occident
> May come refin'd with th' accents that are ours?

ANOTHER MISUNDERSTANDING.

'Arry (on a Northern Tour, with Cockney pronunciation). "THEN I 'LL 'AVE A BOTTLE OF AILE."

Hostess of the Village Inn. "ILE, SIR? WE 'VE NANE IN THE HOOSE, BUT CASTOR ILE OR PARAFFINE. WAD ONY O' THEM DAE, SIR?"

"RUDE" WORDS During the first few decades of the wireless age use of the word "bloody" on the air would have caused nationwide outrage. Then, in the 1950s, came the Lady Chatterley Trial, and the press started to bandy rude words about as if they had just been invented. Yet, at about the same time, when *Z-Cars* was televised live, one actor forgot himself and cursed with genuine pain when he was hit during a staged fight. The producers were deeply worried, and no-one noticed, but the word was excised from the filmed repeat. Then Kenneth Tynan's used "f**k" on live BBC TV in the 1960s and although there was a fuss, the rude-sound barrier was broken. Dramatists and their producers joined a headlong rush to out-curse and out-blaspheme each other, and if anyone complained (as they did about violence) the three-word formula "Valid Social Comment" was always trotted out. In the late 1970s and early 1980s the pendulum began to swing the other way, after an unsuccessful prosecution for obscene libel, although demands for banning this or that invariably increased viewing-figures. Meanwhile, milder rude words became accepted. "Cockups" and "balls-ups" are now universally (and thoughtlessly) used, in spite of obvious connotations of the male sex organs (where are the militant masculinists?). In 1988 Radio 4 broadcast a documentary about the British nuclear bomb with the title "A Bloody Union Jack on Top of It" (admittedly a quotation from Ernest Bevin, a somewhat uncouth politician) and in 1989 a German ex-Chancellor described something as "bullshit" on Radio 4. "Wanker" as a term of abuse is in the ascendancy, tossed off with gay abandon in *CHAT SHOWS* and comedy programmes, though many listeners find it offensive. The scare about Aids has lent respectability to "condom" (though not "French Letter" - in deference to the Common Market?) but any mention of the name "Willie" always produces gales of audience laughter.

S

'SACRELIGIOUS' A common mispronunciation/misunderstanding (hence often mis-spelling) of sa*crileg*ious - perhaps because sacrilege is a profanation of things religious. See also EX-PATRIOT and PREDELICTION .

(IN THE) SAME WAY 'THAT' "The viewer is taxed by the BBC in the same way *that* he is taxed by the state". Things are the same *as*... See DIFFERENT THAN/TO.

SATISFIED "Police are satisfied the woman was murdered" or "Are you satisfied it was not an accident?" seem to express the wrong sort of satisfaction. The word suggests pleasure, contentment or gratification (even sexual) so perhaps we should find better ways of expressing certainty about bad news.

'SAUL' A frequent broadcaster who never speaks but is constantly mentioned by those who do: "Goodbye from Saul here in the studio".

SCHEDULE See SCHISM, below.

SCHISM I include this word - which most people last uttered in history lessons at school - because of arguments about its pronunciation. When a schism developed in the Roman Catholic Church in 1988, BBC newsreaders said "sism" while ITV preferred "skism". The early *OED* recommended the first and gave no alternatives, although its listed spellings include several versions which indicate a *sk-* sound. If, like the Americans, you say "sked-yool"(and the BBC likes "shed-yool" better) you may prefer "skism". But the latest *OED* concedes that "sism", formerly "widely regarded as incorrect" is now "frequently used. ... both in the UK and in North America".

'SECK-A-CHEE' Common *SYNCOPATION* of secretary.

SCOTS/SCOTTISH/SCOTCH The *Scots* say they are *Scottish* but drink *Scotch*.

'SECK-SHOOL' Now almost universal way of pronouncing sexual, by *YOD-DROPPING*, current among speakers of all backgrounds. Also "seck-shlee" for sexually.

SEE YOU (NEXT TIME) *FRONT MEN'S* sign-off cliché. Absurd enough on TV (where they can at least *be* seen) but on *radio*?

'SEMM' I maintain that educated Scots and Welshmen speak clearer English than the English (as do some English-speakers from the Indian subcontinent); but why do so many Welshmen pronounce "seven" as if it were spelt "semm"?

SET "As a response to sanctions Iran is set to end diplomatic relations..." This *MEDIAWRITE* nonsense word saves a little space in headlines but makes *nonsense* in spoken English. Jellies and blancmanges set, and so - as the ultimate sanction against language-manglers - do concrete boots... Occasionally replaced by POISED - and *that* is better reserved for ballerinas.

SEXISM-AVOIDING PLURAL CONFUSIONS People are now so ter-
rified of being labelled "sexist" that they mangle the language, with utterances like, "After all, that person and that person alone has got to live with
themselves" (BBC TV presenter).

'SHAHS' As in "DURBEE winchy shahs o'er EYELAND": *WEATH-
ERBABBLE*.

SHALL WE SAY An hesitatory interpolation of the WHAT and IF YOU
LIKE groups, as in "We are going to need shall we say a hundred million".

SHAMBOLIC Must we really accept this, with GINORMOUS, LOOK-SEE
and other baby-talk, as real words uttered by grown-up communicators?

'SHEEBEE' Ingredient of many a *MENU*, as in "On *Woman's Hour* today
sheebee talking to rape victims who..." And "weebee LOOKING INTO ways
of saving money..." See also their declensions, AHBEE, HEEBEE, YOUBEE,
WEEBEE and THEYBEE. Also DURBEE and many other *SYNCOPATIONS*
scattered round this book.

'-SHEER' There is an old convention that the *-shire* element in county
names is either glided over with hardly any stress, as in "Che*sha*", "York-
sha", Worcester*sha*", or given more stress and pronounced "-shire" (to
rhyme with "wire") - the latter preferred by Scottish-English speakers. But
the newest trend among announcers is to stress and elongate the last syllable
and pronounce it "sheer", which I humbly suggest sounds better in traditional rustic speech ("Oi cum fra York*sheer*") than stuck in the middle of *RP*.
See also FITH.

SICK AND TIRED Twin condition that afflicts viewers and listeners who
make their opinions known to broadcasters. If their letters do not begin "I'm
sick and tired..." it is WHY (OH WHY) OH WHY?

SICK CELSIUS A mysterious illness, believed to be accompanied by a low
temperature, often mentioned in *WEATHERBABBLE*.

(THE) SICK SHARD BOX A white line marked on a soccer-pitch six
yards from the goal-line: *YOD-DROPPING*.

'SICK SHEARS' See DISHEER.

SING SONG See REPORTERS' SING SONG.

SITTING/SAT Common tense confusion, as in "We were sat there at the airport waiting for the minister..." (Radio 4 reporter). *Who* sat them there? Faulty toilet-training perhaps: not since his mum picked him up and *sat* him on his potty would he expect to be so treated. See also LAY/LIE.

SNEAK PREVIEW No *ordinary* preview is enough on radio and TV. It must be accompanied by its kneejerk twin, "sneak": "AND our reporter Carol South has been along for a sneak preview". It suggests that Miss South, tape-recorder in hand, climbed through a lavatory window to sneak an early view. "Sneak" is not only a cliché but one of many words beginning with "sn-" and "sl-" that have unpleasant connotations (see *The Joy of Words*).

(THE) SOFT-BOILED X/EGGS EFFECT New speech trend which makes exactly into eggs-actly, exile into eggs-ile, exuberant into egg-zooberant and customs people into egg-size officers. Also eggs-ecutives and eggs-c-cutioners. Indeed anyone who now says ecks-actly, eck-sile or ecks-yuberant (see also *YOD-DROPPING*), may get funny looks or be taken for a native of Wales, where pure vowels and crisp consonants still rule - SEMM apart. As Nelson never said, England egg-spects it will get worse. Explosives has undergone a double softening, to eggs-ploe-zives. Yet anxiety has long been pronounced angs-iety, perhaps subconsciously echoing the pseudo-German *Angst*. See also ABBZOULVE.

(THE) SOFTENED SH MODIFICATION According to this recent fad, the hard *sh* in "version", "aspersion", "aversion", "conversion" etc. turns into a kind of Hungarian *zs*, as in Zsa Zsa Gábor, or like the English "measure". See also *SOFT-BOILED EGGS* above, and *BUZZING Z*, as in Michael "Hezzletine".

SOLID Now also means non-stop: " He worked on his book for three months, solid" - and (a Radio 4 travel programme reporter): "While in Greece she had diarrhoea for a fortnight solid".

SORT OF Expletive widely used (like "kind of") until ousted by the IF-YOU-LIKE epidemic. See also YERKNOW.

'SOULVE' Like INVOULVE, REVOULVE, etc., examples of *(THE) GENTEEL O*. Some speak of "soul-vent sniffing youngsters".

'SPAY SHUTTLE' *SYNCOPATION* pronunciation of space shuttle.

SPECIAL See VERY SPECIAL.

SPECIAL APPEARANCE OF ... In TV *TITLES* (sometimes radio billings) this can be used for any well-known actor who has accepted a small supporting role, either because he is short of money or no longer able to memorise bigger ones.

SPECIAL GUEST As above, but a sop billing to placate a famous person willing to make a fool of himself by taking part in a GAME-SHOW.

SRI LANKA The pronunciation of this news-worthy place is in dispute: "Shree" or "Sri"? During a radio interview a Sri Lankan diplomat consistently said "Sri", whereas his English interviewer persisted in "Shree". I asked, in a letter to the *Radio Times*, how we should say it. A correspondence ensued, from which it emerged that both are "correct" and that variations occur in the country itself - just as the English word "station" has progressed from "stat-ee-on" and "stas-see-on" to the now standard "stay-shun". Given the choice I say "Sri" because "Shree" is reminiscent of the ISSHOO effect. Persia, formerly "purse-ee-ah", has long become "Purr Sha" - and anyway we are now supposed to call it Iran. Doctors who a generation ago would have pronounced dementia and nausea "day-ment-ee-uh" and "naw-see-ah" now opt for the easier "dee-men-shah" and "naw-sha" - though many Scottish English-speakers are valiantly maintaining the purer forms. But the process of modifying "s" into "sh" should be resisted for proper names, e.g. when speaking about the African politician Ndabaninghe Sithole.

STAGGERING Newspapers may get away with it, but when a newsreader tells us that there has been "a staggering rise in drunkenness" he may be misunderstood.

'STATCHERCHEE' *YOD-DROPPERS'* statutory.

STATISTIC Newly-singularised noun. Until a generation or so ago people spoke only of statistics, in the plural, as they did of acoustics (not "an acoustic") and of tactics (not "a tactic"). Ethics, too, always came in the plural but now we have only one, most commonly the work ethic. A pop song still has lyrics, not "a lyric", but tailors may soon be using a scissor for making a trouser.

STAY *WITH* US An injunction, generally uttered at the end of the *MENU*. The middle word, being a preposition, has to be *OVERSTRESSED*.

(A) STONE'S THROW A figure of speech which, in these days of universal protest, should be used with caution; as when the BBC news-reader said, "Sir Geoffrey drove to within a stone's throw of Winnie Mandela's house".

'STRAWD'N'RY' See under *SYNCOPATION*, below.

STRINGS ATTACHED News cliché meaning conditions. As a man said during the Cleveland Babies case: "The parents want their children to be returned to them without any strings attached".

*SUB*JECT/SUB*JECT* The same remarks apply as for SUSPECT, below.

SUBURB/SUBURBS The Latin word for city, is *urbs*, hence the idea that it is a plural noun - and the erroneous "singular" back-formation "suburb".

SUDDEN In *WEATHERBABBLE* indistinguishable from southern.

*SUS*PECT/SUS*PECT* "A *sus*pect left a passage sus*pect*ed of containing explosives".

*SUR*VEY/SUR*VEY* *Sur*vey for the noun, sur*vey* for the verb. We do not sing Isaac Watts's famous hymn, "When I *sur*vey the wondrous cross".

SYNCOPATION The musical sense of the word, often associated with jazz, has all but displaced the formerly more general meaning: "the contraction of a word by omission of one or more syllables or letters in the middle" (*OED*). Some of the commonest syncopations will be found scattered throughout this book. Many show the natural shifts of language: what one generation objects to is accepted and adopted as standard by the next. This has been so for centuries, especially with modified foreign loan-words, like *gubernator* into "governor", *procurator* into "proctor" and *jeu parti* into "jeopardy". Syncopation is by no means "bad" speech: few *RP*-speakers give "ex-tra-or-di-na-ry" its full six syllables: some even contract it to two: "strawd'n'ry". See also VUNNERABLE.

'SUSSINCT' To people of older generations, who carried a little Latin in their school satchels, "suck-sinct" came as naturally as "accident". It is no longer so. Fashion broadcasters speak of "assessories" and I have even heard a clothes-MODEL say "suss-sessful" on TV. But "flas-sid" is now more common than the *OED*-recommended "flak-sid".

T

TABLOID TITLES Also called "Attributive Pile-ups" (though I rudely call them "Yobs' Titles", for they betray the verbal yobbo lurking behind many accomplished speakers and broadcasters). This odious, slovenly practice is taken from the newsrooms of the papers, where information is received by cable, teleprinter and telex. On these machines time and money can be saved by piling-up all available or necessary information before a person's name. Thus a despatch reading, "International Russian concert pianist refusenik Yuri Popovsky was today..." *should* later be re-written and sub-edited into "Yuri Popovsky, the international concert pianist and refusenik, was today..." or "Recently sacked Personal Assistant to President Bush, balding bespectacled bachelor Hiram C Hittenrunner was yesterday..." into "Hiram C. Hittenrunner, a balding and bespectacled bachelor who was recently sacked by President Bush..." But that takes a little effort and some extra punctuation, so the lazy journalist changes as little as possible. The result *looks* bad enough in print, but is execrable in spoken English., destroying rhythm and making the words that emerge from speakers' mouths as exciting as toothpaste squeezed from a tube. And it can sound downright confusing, like "Oven-ready chicken producer John Williams..." (see A for ARTICLES); or "fellow compatriot Zoo Vet Naylor has been helping to raise the hippopotamus...", which to the unsuspecting ear sounds like some Asian name, "Zuvet Naylor". It may save the time of a writer or speaker, but wastes that of the reader or listener. See also *MISSING ARTICLES* and the *YOBS' POSSESSIVE*. Also *MediaWrite*.

'TACK SHEER' More *YOD-DROPPING*: "The current tack sheer ends at the beginning of April".

TAKEN FOR A RIDE Beware of too-literal applications (or sub-tabloid puns). As a presenter said on *You and Yours*, "Some people are being taken for a ride by funeral directors". Nearly always their last.

TAKE THAT! In radio plays, an explanation to the listener that the cracking noise that follows is the sound of a blow by a fist to the chin. "Take that!" comes from strip-cartoons and is part of the "Kerpow!" group of noises. In real life no-one about to strike an opponent would be so foolish as to give him verbal warning; and you will notice that TV drama, with all its violence, never has people telling each other that a blow is about to be delivered. They just get on with it.

TALKING HEADS On TV, when a speaker is shown looking the camera squarely in the lens and speaking to viewers without the help of pictorial illustrations, as if they were grown-ups talking together. Every effort is made to avoid this, even in news programmes, and usually with the help of still pictures, *GRAPHICS* and *LIBRARY FILM*.

TALKING IN TERMS OF... What the speaker usually means is "talking *about...*" In only few instances is "in terms of" really meant. See SHALL WE SAY and the interpolated WHAT.

TALKING TO... A confusing radio practice. When we hear "John Smith was talking to Jill Brown", who was the interviewer and who the interviewed? Standard practice is supposed to be that the last name mentioned is the interviewer's, but is so seldom observed that the listener is always in doubt. See *CONCEITS.*

TALKING AGAINST MUSIC It is easier to listen to music than to speech. Listening to music does not require the identification or naming of notes. Indeed, much music can be enjoyed when merely overheard, not listened-to with total concentration. The listener/hearer may miss a bar or two without seriously losing his understanding of it. In speech, on the other hand, one misheard consonant can completely alter the meaning. Anyone with the slightest hearing defect (which means more than 60% of the population, and about 85% of middle-aged or older persons, who lose upper frequencies) requires a higher volume to understand speech - that is, a level which is too loud for music. Yet when broadcast speech and music are mixed, the balance between the two is decided upon in the perfect conditions of a studio, by engineers chosen for their near-perfect hearing. In the home this mixture may be heard on a small transistor set, and against competing household sounds. The music is thus *invariably* too loud, the speech all but meaningless. Thousands of listeners complain that they are constantly turning the volume of music down and that of speech up, because they find the existing relative balance intolerable. The effect is even worse when producers add background music to speech for dramatic effect (a custom copied from the cinema: "It'll be OK when we put the music on!"). *MENUS* are often spoken against noisy signature-tunes that are faded up and down (never sufficiently down). Radio Four programmes intended for intelligent listeners, like *Medicine Now* and the science slots, announce their contents over inane disco-drumming. The transport programme *Going Places* announces its spoken menu in competition with both music *and* exaggerated traffic noises and an open-exhaust motorbike! Local radio offends most consistently, but TV news (and football results) are read over a carpet of continuous pop music. On *PM*, one of the main Radio Four daytime news programmes, the *PRESENTER* is obliged to speak the headlines against a signature tune full of jaunty jollity which punctuates news of death and disaster with repeated "brumms" on the drums and jolly, scrubbing staccato syncopations on the fiddles. And, as I write this, someone on Radio Four is reciting Gerard Manley Hopkins's *The Wreck of the Deutschland* against background music *and* the sloshing of waves.

'**TAW**' "The England cricket team on taw". Most English people deprive the word tour (and others like it) of the final *r* and even many Scottish English-speakers no longer sound it. But the *aw* sound in place of the *ou*, is a more recent quirk, a modification of very old-fashioned posh.

'**TEMCHAS**' Tem-pe-ra-tures at first had four syllables. *RP* speech by natural *SYNCOPATION* reduced it to three ("temp'ratures") and *WEATHER-BABBLE* has further shortened it to two.

'**TEMP'REE**' *SYNCOPATION* of temporary.

TERRORISTS See FREEDOM-FIGHTERS. The BBC uses the neutral FIGHTERS, and "guerillas" is almost neutral.

THANK-YOU (VERY MUCH [INDEED]) Radio and TV thanks formulae come in various combinations, full of "professional sincerity" and therefore meaningless. "Hello and thank you for joining us" is how one presenter always opens his programme - like a telephone receptionist told to sound brightly ingratiating ("Thank-you-for-calling-Grand-Hotel-can-I-help-you?"): in other words, he is a creep. The Hand-over Thank-you is used by presenters who have just come on the air. Following the words "And here's Bill Bloggs with the weather", Bill Bloggs will address the world at large with meaningless thanks - variable from a plain "Thank you" to an elided "Thank-you-very-much" or the even more falsely effusive "Tha'ya'va'much-*indeed*". *Who* is is being thanked and for *what*? Is he thanking his colleague merely for mentioning his name? Politeness is to be applauded, but if people spent all day thanking each other for doing the jobs they are paid to do they would have little time for broadcasting. There is also the "I've Finished" thank-you, copied from station announcements: "The train standing on platform five is not the one to Crawley as advertised but goes to Plymouth-thank-you". The final thanksgiving may be a "Thank you for being *with* me", which the great Radio 4 broadcaster John Ebdon charmingly satirised by self-deprecatingly signing off with: "If you *have* been - thank you for listening"; and Douglas Smith used to sign-off Round the Horne with "You have been listening to or have just missed..." See also GOOD TO BE BACK!, (AND) A VERY SPECIAL HELLO! - and THE END.

THE DISTINGUISHED... "Tonight's recital is given by the distinguished Italian violinist Arcangelo Portobello..." may be interpreted as code for elderly musical performers - a kind of SPECIAL APPEARANCE. The real meaning is something like: "We know he's past his best but he's got such a big and loyal following that we must continue to let him broadcast". Also applied to a performer who has emerged from a long period of being *RESTED* after *OVER-USE*.

-THERE Useless suffix tagged on to words in back-announcements, as in "That was the English Chamber Orchestra-there, playing Schubert's Symphony No. 3 ...", or "Haydn's Emperor Quartet-there, played by the Allegri Quartet", or "Jerry Logan-there, talking to Sir Geoffrey Crowe." One Christmas Day, may we expect to hear, "Her Majesty the Queen-there"? The listener may legitimately ask, "Where?"

THERE MUST BE... Always heralds some drama cliché, e.g. "There must be some *mistake*, officer", or "There must be *something* we can do!"

THERE'S NOTHING WORSE THAN... Unfortunately there are few things than which there is nothing worse: a useful, if meaningless, programme item opener. See also NO THIS IS NOT and YES YOU'VE GUESSED.

THE/THEE See *ARTICLES (PRONUNCIATION)*.

'THEYBEE' Trail and *MENU* ingredient, as in "On *Breakaway* today theybee talking to holidaymakers who..." See also its declensions, AHBEE, YOUBEE, HEEBEE, SHEEBEE and WEEBEE. In *WEATHERBABBLE* there is also DURBEE, as in "Durbee WINCHY SHAHS coming from EYELAND".

THIN ON THE GROUND The TV debater who said, "In Africa, fat women are thin on the ground" would probably have rephrased, given a little time.

THIS REPORT FROM... Many listeners object to this formula because it is a verbless sentence. A more valid complaint would be that it is a fixed formula and that news editors seem to lack the imagination to vary it occasionally. Perhaps by inserting a verb now and again?

'TICKLY' As in "A front of tickly high pressure is GRADGLY moving northwards..." See *SYNCOPATIONS* and *WEATHERBABBLE*.

TIGHT SECURITY News twin-term . Sometimes varied with "strict".

'TISSHOOS' See ISSHOOS.

TITIVATE/TITILLATE The first, the *OED* says, is really "tidyvate", which describes perfectly what women do in front of a looking-glass before they go out. The second, what The Sun tries to do on page three. But a

Reporter on BBC 1 *News* wanted to have it both ways: "Rapid titillation is under way in preparation for the visit of the Queen and the Duke of Edinburgh," he said.

TO COIN A PHRASE What the speaker *means* is "...to flog a boring old cliché." See also THE PROVERBIAL - which is no more a proverb than the "coined phrase" a new coinage. See also HE WOULD, WOULDN'T HE.

TO CUT A LONG STORY SHORT Interviewees' (and storytellers') cliché. They seldom do.

TONGUE-LASHING Better left to *MediaWrite* - or better still, banished altogether.

TONGUE-TWISTERS (UNINTENTIONAL) Over-familiarity with clichés makes for a kind of word-deafness, and those who write news bulletins or other reports sometimes fail to "hear" the words they write (as a musician invariably hears in his mind's ear what he puts down). Thus material often goes out that is absurd when said aloud: "If the Israeli offer is really serious..."; or "She objected to being subjected to these most objectionable methods of interrogation..."; or "The broadcast has been made available from our Maida Vale studios"; and the (probably fictitious) tongue-twister "Italian battalions scaled precipitous escarpments". A sports reporter said, "It's a worthy cause of course..." and "Rush was playing well as well..." A different reporter, quite unselfconsciously, said, "Another eyesore I saw(re)on the way to the airport..." (See *INTRUSIVE R*). In the House of Commons an MP is reported to have stated, "The Factories Act as a matter of fact is a most unsatisfactory act" - almost poetry, like TV commentator's "You've seen the scenes on your screens..." Another common phrase is "The black-led African National Congress...", which sounds more like pencils. And an interviewer on *Today* asked Sir Geoffrey Howe, "Sir Geoffrey, how are you going to...?" Punctuation may help; and attention to word-order, to avoid things like, "The cat will rub itself against you as you go to the fridge and meow".

TORMENT/TORMENT The noun is stressed *tor*ment, but the verb -
> He that first invented thee,
> May his joints tor*ment*ed be.
> Ben Jonson *On Lord Bacon's Birthday*.

'TORTUROUS' "After two years of torturous negotiations..." said a man on the *PM* programme, and numerous other reporters do the same. This could be for one of several reasons. Either they don't know how to spell *tortuous* or they think it has something to do with torture; or they cannot avoid the *INTRUSIVE R.*

TRAGICALLY WRONG Often used by unthinking news-editors in an attempt to explain a murder: "This may have been a mugging that went tragically wrong". A tendentious way of writing news, for the listener may ask whether the mugging would have "gone right" if the crime had been successful as originally intended.

TRANSFER/TRANSFER As with *TRANS*PORT/TRANS*PORT*, below, the noun/verb stress difference is being confused, perhaps because many football commentators fail to make the distinction. A player may get a free *trans*fer when his manager decides to trans*fer* him to another club.

TRANSITIVES "The meeting convenes once a year in Oxford..." "Talks resume this afternoon...", "The trial resumes on Tuesday...", "Parliament resumes on Monday" etc. Such events *are* convened or resumed, etc. They themselves have no power of convening or resuming.

TRANSPORT/TRANSPORT Both in the happiness sense and in what Americans prefer to call, needlessly, transportation (see -ATION) the stress in the noun is on the first syllable but shifts to the second for the verb. Goods are (and slaves were) trans*ported*.

> Oh *trans*port! how can this
> Be true to heaven's bliss?
> Anon.

> Trans*port*ed with celestial desire
> Of those fair forms, may lift themselves up higher.
> Edmund Spenser: *The Faerie Queen*

TRIFFICINNIT! Not a Cornish village but an all-purpose exclamation of sports commentators and others expressing enthusiasm.

U

UM See ER.

UNDER-PRODUCED This is a term of criticism (!) among radio producers, used with reference to feature programmes which are permitted to run their course with little or no interference from sound-effects, superfluous music faded up and down, ACTUALITY recordings, and other extraneous noises. In reality "under-produced" should be a form of praise, just as vegetables are better eaten under- than over-cooked. Some producers refuse to allow words like "sea", "fire", or "train" to pass a speaker's lips without superimposing the pre-recorded sounds of waves, the crackling of flames or the puffing of a choo-choo train; nor allow people to talk without having their words drowned with "point" music. But many *speakers* are regrettably underproduced - in the sense understood by actors, who welcome suggestions from *their* producers about word-stress, word-order and pronunciation.

U*N*DRESS/UND*RESS* "*Un*dress uniform will be worn by gentlemen" - but when they take their clothes off they un*dress*.

UNWARRANTED The twin-word for intrusion, risk, incursion, etc. See FULL ENQUIRY.

U*P*SET/UP*SET* We may suffer an *up*set, and be up*set* by it.

'URSHLA' *YOD-DROPPERS'* Ursula - like "inshlin".

USED/USED Creeping changes are affecting the English s sound, and beginning to extinguish the difference between the hard *s*, "yoosed" ("We used to go out together...") and the soft *s*, "yoozed" ("...but he only used me to feed his vanity").

'UZZ' *BUZZING S* way of saying us, in all accents, from *azz*, to *ozz* and *oozz*

V

'VATE' *NAY-LONGER RIND O* vote.

'VAY-VAY' As in "This is vay-vay important".

VERBS-FROM-NOUNS It is an ancient process. Although things have been "crafted" since the early 14th century purists take offence at each new coinage until it becomes part of the language. People have long been *alarmed*, but are now joined in their alarmed state by houses and cars: "This Car is Alarmed", warns the notice in the window. An alarm may *foil* intruders, but wrapped chocolates sold by Marks and Spencer are also described as "foiled". Words can be *honeyed*, almonds *sugared*; but to ask, "Is the coffee sugared?" is recent and may offend the stickler. Meetings have long been *hosted*, but "guesting" (i.e. at a concert) is a novelty from the USA (because Americans are more tolerant of, and adept at, new coinages). Children are *fathered*, men may be *mothered*; but "parenting" is still a neologism chiefly confined to social-workers - who also complain of being insufficiently "resourced" (with an unreasonable stress on the *re-*) . Bad parenting may lead to "truanting". Culprits may be "scapegoated" (a recognised word in the jargon of psychologists), footballers "cautioned" or even "stretchered" off, after which they may be "ambulanced", "hospitalised" and "medicated" (though not, one hopes, doctored); and "sidelined" until fit. If necessary they will be "toilet(t)ed" by nurse - though people were never "privied" in days of more primitive sanitation. Unemployed actresses may go "waitressing", but waitresses do not go actressing. In 1989 the National Curriculum Council (and educational body!) called for more "storeying"- doubtless asking that this should be "prioritised". This book (which I "authored" and *researched* on my own) was also "keyboarded" by me (though keyboarding could be a useful word for musicians who play the piano, organ, harpsichord, etc.) As the sexologist from Harvard, lecturing at a British university, said, "She orgasmed in a non-coital situation". He could have said "She came unscrewed".

'VERGER' *YOD-DROPPERS* "verdure", formerly *RP* "verd-yoor".

(A) VERY PRIVATE PERSON In biographical feature programmes means "I was unable to find out much about him". The same as a LONER in *MEDIAWRITE*.

(AND A) VERY SPECIAL HELLO! This "very special" greeting is enjoyed by a select group of several million viewers and we can count ourselves really lucky to be singled out. "A very good night to you" used to be confined to *WEATHERBABBLE* but is spreading.

'VERZSHON' See *SOFTENED SH*.

VOLUNTARY Now often means *unpaid*, as in "I had to work voluntar(il)y for a church" (i.e. as part of her probation).

'VUNNERABLE' Common *SYNCOPATION* which offends many listeners. Perhaps some fail to perceive the *l* because of hearing-loss.

W

WAIL/WHALE "The International Wailing Commission" is a body which bewails the suffering of the whale, and has much to wail about. But see the remarks under WERE/WHERE, below.

WAIT FOR IT! Borrowed from the army parade-ground: presenters' facetious interjection of the NO THIS IS NOT and YES YOU'VE GUESSED group. It can have various shades of meaning, from "Listen carefully to what I'm going to say" to "Now *this* is *really* funny!!!" or take the place of an exclamation-mark: "His salary will be - wait for it - a million pounds a year!" See AND I QUOTE.

WALKING A TIGHTROPE An activity not unlike being BALANCED ON A KNIFE EDGE.

WALKING FEET TV directors like to show people walking but in such a way that we see their legs only from the knees downwards: almost as much-flogged a cliché as people in romantic situations running (or hair in shampoo advertisements bouncing) in slow motion.

WATER-SIPPING In TV *TALK-SHOWS* people take a sip of water not when they are thirsty but when acknowledging applause. They tell some well-rehearsed anecdote, the audience laughs - and they reach for their water-glass. Pavlov's dog was less predictable. Chat-show hosts, on the other hand, develop a nervous twitch of pretending to remove an imaginary speck of something from the outside of the nose by delicately brushing a forefinger down the side.

WE ASK... *MENU* opener, as in, "And we ask are the election prospects of Labour being harmed by Militant...", perhaps followed by a pat answer: "Yes says Mr Kinnock, no says Mr Skinner". See also WE HEAR HOW...

WEATHER CONDITIONS As in "The North can expect bad weather *conditions*..." The last word is a mere makeweight, like "situation".

WEATHERBABBLE Like most professionals, the clever meteorologists who try to predict our weather have their own jargon. It is no more eccentric than that of other trades, but (like sports commentators) they seem to annoy listeners more than others. This is particularly so when weathermen, who are scientists, use language that is not only unscientific but meaningless, like "beefy showers" and "lumpsa cloud". When they make even quite small mistakes (not to mention big ones, like flatly denying that the Great 1987 Hurricane was imminent) the whole nation is up in arms. Some critics go so far as to suggest that weathermen are chosen more for their showbiz eccentricities than the usual qualities expected of broadcasters, such as clear speech (though some, of course, are excellent). For myself, I would sooner have the information prepared for and presented by professional speakers. To offer an analogy: the skilled engineers and labourers who build our motorways are not the best people to paint the road-signs. Like TV newsreaders weathermen may become PERSONALITIES, famous for being famous: even their dress can be a matter for public debate. Unfortunately many listeners and viewers find that after a weatherman has done his stint they find they are no wiser - having been so distracted by the eccentricities that they completely forgot to notice what they were saying.

'WEEBEE' An ingredient of many a programme *MENU*, as in "On the *PM* programme today weebee LOOKING at..." See also its declensions, AHBEE, HEEBEE, YOUBEE, SHEEBEE and THEYBEE.

WE HEAR HOW... See MENU.

WE'LL MEET AGAIN Presenters' meaningless parting formula. It suggests phoney mateyness, for it merely means "I'll be sitting here doing my job while you are listening to me or possibly ignoring me". See SEE YOU.

WERE/WAS Shakespeare has Macbeth say, "If it were done when 'tis done, then 'twere well it were done quickly". Most journalists today have little use for this mode of contingency, doubt or future time. They prefer, "If it *was* done ... 'twould be well if it *was* done quickly". This leads to such time-absurdities as, "If he *was* there by three he would be too late". Was he there or wasn't he? Another waswolf, presenting a music programme on Radio Four, said, "Here's John McCormack singing a version of the *Londonderry Air* with words beginning *Would God I* was *a tender apple blossom*". John McCormack then started to sing and, with his wonderfully clear diction, sang, *Would God I* were *a tender apple blossom*.

WHAT An Interpolation used for numerical or time estimates, as in " We shall need, what, a million pounds", or "I'll be arriving, what, in an hour's time." SHALL WE SAY can also be interjected in this manner. And see the now ubiquitous IF YOU LIKE.

WHERE DO WE/YOU GO FROM HERE? The final question in many an interview, after the interviewer has attempted to make his subject quantify an opinion with JUST HOW questions and probably asked him whether he was living in CLOUD CUCKOO LAND.

'WHOOBEE' See WEEBEE.

WHO/WHOM The trend in *informal* speech is towards using *who* where *whom* would be "correct" i.e. "who d'you mean?" As a result, the proper way, "whom do you mean?" may sound affected or stilted; and "Whom are you kidding" puts a pedantic horse before a colloquial cart. Unfortunately many speakers, in *trying* to be correct at all costs, commit the greater sin of pretentiousness, using *whom* because they think it is posher - and nowhere is a lack of grammar more in evidence than among who/whom mis-users. Almost daily one hears on radio and TV, and reads in newspapers, statements like, "Police want to interview a man whom they say is armed..." The best way of avoiding these solecisms is to isolate the elements with appropriate punctuation, and then mentally replace *whom* with *him* and *who* with *he*. Thus "Police want to interview a man *whom*, they say, is armed..." sounds and looks absurd: was *him* really armed? Conversely, ask yourself when you read, "An armed man who police want to interview..." - do they want to interview *he*? (The same applies to the I/ME, HE/HIM and LAY/LIE con-fusions). Getting it wrong betrays a lack of reading/listening experience of the best writers/speakers. According to this pseudo-posh way the Psalmist (and Handel in his *Messiah*) would have sung, "He trusted in God that He would deliver He, let He deliver He if He delights in He". On the other hand - let him who is without sin cast the first stone...

WHY (OHWHY) OH WHY...? Traditional opening of letters of complaint, especially from women writing to *Woman's Hour*. They may also be SICK AND TIRED or "absolutely disgusted".

WIN OUT An extension of the equally illogical "losing out", though this has acquired meanings of disadvantage as well as of "losing".

'WITH-DRORAL' (For withdrawal) - is heard almost daily on every channel from Radio Four downwards (though seldom on Radio Three), but especially on TV and pop-and-pap radio and Independent Radio News. See INTRUSIVES.

WOULD HAVE LIKED TO HAVE... *REDUNDANCY*, as in "I would have liked to have been there" or "I would have liked to be there". You can't have it both ways without muddling your tenses.

Y

YE OLDE I.e. mis-pronounced "yee oldie": traditional for facetiously-spurious suggestions of antiquity, as in Ye Olde Tea Shoppe. For one thing, the final *e* would not have been pronounced (at any rate in the 1600-1800 period); and for another, the *Y* was a "thorn" which, in old handwriting as well as type, simply represented the *th* sound: they also wrote "yis ying" and "Yomas". Thus however you write it it remains - The Old Tea Shop.

'YER-KNOW' Expletive of hesitation. The difference between it and IF YOU-LIKE is one of class/education. The equally meaningless interjection "don-cherknow" is still sometimes heard from the very old. SORT OF is also on the wane, but the least articulate are irredeemably hooked on the suffix -LIKE .

YES See INDEED.

YES YOU'VE GUESSED Introductory cliché of the NO THIS IS NOT group.

YOBS' POSSESSIVE This can be geographical, political or organisational: "In London's St Paul's Cathedral yesterday..." or "In a speech by Labour's Tony Benn..." and "British Petroleum's Sir Kenneth Sweet..." or "On BBC's *Breakfast Time* today..." Such unnatural, angular and awkward utterances are copied from tabloid prose, where style is sacrificed to save space and time and which is not meant to be read aloud (at least by those who can read without moving their lips) - see TABLOID TITLES. Transferred to spoken English it is the hallmark of the verbal yobbo who would not recognise good style if he fell over it. The time saved is infinitesimal, the loss of rhythm and balance calamitous. Yet it infests all areas of broadcasting, even Radio Three ("The Midday Concert today comes from Manchester's Free Trade Hall...") and arts programmes like *Kaleidoscope* on Radio Four ("One of neo-surrealism's brightest votaries..." or "Birmingham's City Art Gallery"); and, of course, the Yobs' Possessive is used relentlessly in news on all channels of radio and TV. You might expect it from sports reporters, most of whom speak in tabloid language anyway ("British Boxing's Board of Control") although no human beings would talk *to each other* like that (least of all punch-drunk boxers, because it is in fact more difficult, because less natural). Yet some of the most respected presenters and announcers, whether trailing, introducing or back-announcing programmes, are happy to impersonate Hissing Sid with nonsense like "One of today's *Medicine Now's* topics is..." (Why *not* of "One of the topics in

Medicine Now today is..."?) or Labour's spokesman's Dave Blair's speech..." The more sibilant the words the worse the Yobs' Possessive sounds: "The hostages are expected to FLY INTO Paris's Orly Airport"; "Manchester's Piccadilly Radio's disc-jockeys..."; "Essex's fast bowlers failed to stop Middlesex's batsmen..." and even a Triple Yobs' Possessive: "Labour's Liverpool's Walton's MP Eric Heffer".

YOD-DROPPING Name given by phonetics experts to the omission of the *y* sound in words like assume, for until about the middle of the present century standard RP pronunciation was *ass-yoom*. Pursue *pur-syoo*, resume *rez-yoom*, tune *t-yoon* and suit *s-yoot*. Now almost everybody (on radio, TV and in real life) says *soot, rezzoom , assoom* and *pur-soo*. The *s* sound preceding a dropped yod is also often modified into *shw-* like Jesuit *(Jez-you-it)* /Jesh-woo-it. WEATHERBABBLE soothsayers greet us with *Morning chew*, reporters quote *Scotlan-chard*; and a preacher in the *Daily Service* invites God to "look graciously on *ush-oor* children". Stature, formerley *stat-yoor*, is made to rhyme with Thatcher, and Radio 3 occasionally offers Puccini's *Chew-randot* or poetry by *Ted Shoes*. More southern-dialect speakers drop their yods than Scottish and Wessh English-speakers, who still largely cherish them. Americans drop them "routinely" (as they like to say). One or two Radio Three announcers tell us that "Bach was fond of the loot" (aren't we all)?) and before long may start announcing "toons"and reading the" noos" Education has become *edgication*, and enthusiasm anything from *enthoosiasm* to *entheesiasm.* . (See also *NAY LONGER RIND O*).

YOU ARE... Interviewers' trick of introducing interviewees to viewers and listeners by telling their *subject* what they already know - their names, jobs etc: "Andrew Mitford,you are editor of the *Sunday Beast* and were closely connected with the Gubbins takeover battle. You knew Pam Bordella well - did you ever... (followed by the first question)?"

YOU BETTER COME IN Said in plays whenever someone comes to the door. See I'LL SEE MYSELF OUT and DRINK THIS IT'LL DO YOU GOOD.

YOU NAME IT This means "I could say a lot more if only I could remember it". See also ECKSETTERA and BLAH BLAH BLAHH.

'YOU'N'JAWS' YOD-DROPPING pronunciation of the BBC programme for CONSHOOMERS, *You and Yours*.

Z

ZERO See OH.

THE END
or
THAT'S JUST ABOUT IT FOR TODAY
or
THANK YOU FOR BEING WITH US
or
IT'S BEEN GOOD TALKING TO YOU
or
AND THERE I'M AFRAID WE'LL HAVE TO LEAVE IT
and
OH YES AND KEEP THOSE LETTERS COMING IN!

but

If you turn this book upside down you can start again, for

WE SHALL BE LOOKING AT

MediaWrite

MediaWrite

By the same author:

The Joy of Words
InWords and OutWords
Music through the Looking Glass
Keep taking the Tabloids
A Small Book of Grave Humour
Dead Funny
Lern Yerself Scouse (Ed.)
Scally Scouse (Ed.)

Typeset on an Apple Macintosh II with Microsoft Word 3.00 /4.00 and Aldus Pagemaker
by the author, who therefore takes full responsibility for *all* errors.
Acknowledgements to Sharon Quayle and Ian Jones of the AppleCentre Liverpool.

The Unchanging Clichés of Newspaper English

MediaWrite

**A hilarious tongue lashing expose
speling out the highl-
ights of journalists prose'n'cons**

With a Free Supplement on MediaSpeak

Fritz Spiegl

FRAM, Dus. Moc.

Elm Tree Books · London

ELM TREE BOOKS

Published by the Penguin Group
27 Wrights Lane, London W8 5TZ, England

Viking Penguin Inc, 40 West 23rd Street, New York, New York 10010, U.S.A.
Penguin Books Australia Ltd, Ringwood, Victoria, Australia
Penguin Books Canada Ltd, 2801 John Street, Markham, Ontario, Canada L3R
1B4

Penguin Books Ltd, Registered Offices: Harmondsworth, Middlesex, England

First published in Great Britain 1989 by
Elm Tree Books

British Library Cataloguing in Publication Data
CIP data for this book is (!) available from the British Library

ISBN 0-241-12704-1

This book is dedicated to wife,
petite blonde vivacious artist, stunning Ingrid Spiegl (39)
with all my love
(see *ATTRIBUTIVE QUEUE*, *AGEISM*, STUNNING)

INTRODUCTION

Here are two books for the price of one: *MediaWrite* and *MediaSpeak* - both titles satirical of the current typographical fad of running words together and sticking a capital letter in the middle. To get your second book free, all you have to do is turn the volume upside-down and start again. The contents occasionally overlap, but you may find cross-references drawing attention to this. Some of the entries presented me with a quandary. Should I, for the sake of the kind of completeness even a light-hearted reference-book must strive for, include subjects I had already touched upon in my previous books, *The Joy of Words* and *In-Words and Out-Words*? I decided to compromise by putting in, on the whole, only those about which I felt I had something new to say. That applies to both sections. Some of the more obvious idiocies of newspaper English have appeared in my *Keep taking the Tabloids* (Pan Books, 1983, now out of print); and that title, too, was ironic, but in those days I did not know that irony is the last thing readers and writers of our smudgier prints understand.

Britain has what is probably the most free press in the world, which is something to be very proud of. Unfortunately a section of it blatantly abuses that freedom by publishing half-truths, lies, manufactured quotations and "interviews" that never took place. This book, however, examines only the extraordinary *manner* in which newsmen communicate with their readers. For newsmen employ stilted, unnatural and out-dated forms of English, with a vocabulary they would never ordinarily use when talking to each other or to their families. Every situation has a stock phrase or cliché which comes out almost by reflex action - hence my frequent use in these pages of the word "kneejerk". Obviously this applies more to the tabloids than the broadsheets, but not a day goes by when we do not read - in *all* the papers - of a "stamp of approval" for a post office scheme; of "up, up and away" reactions (or "turbulence") relating to aviation; of doctors with "a bitter pill to swallow"or "getting a taste of their own medicine"; of railways coming to "the end of the line" (and it's not "just the ticket"when commuters "get a rough ride"); of musicians hitting "high notes" (or low and sour ones); of the mortally sick "fighting for their lives"; of axes, bids, blows, dashes, thuds, storms and moves...the list of appalling clichés is inexhaustible. But I try to list them.

It comes as a shock to discover, when one buys some of the foreign papers, that in technical quality even our "good" papers lag far behind that of their counterparts in Europe and North America. If you look at the *International Herald Tribune*, the *Wall Street Journal* or, in Switzerland, the *Neue Zürcher Zeitung*, (to take only three quality papers), the first thing you will notice is that they all have a great dignity about them. The headlines do not scream. They are big enough to be easily readable on a news-stand, but not disproportionate to the page. Instead of making foolish puns they inform (as headlines used to in this country until a generation or two ago) giving the reader a brief outline of the text below. In a few carefully-chosen words, sometimes in double- or triple-decker headlines (abandoned in this country in the 1950s) they summarise the story and offer the reader the choice of reading on or moving to another report.

In those European papers you will find no unnecessary photographs (and to some extent *The Independent* has revived this practice, as it has several other long-abandoned practices of good journalism) though occasionally topical pictures are printed for illustrative or artistic reasons. Paper and print, too, are better abroad, although the collapse of the British print unions' stranglehold has brought an improvement in quality here, too. Since the advent of the new technology some of our papers are at last able to do justice to the work of their photographers. But the British newspaper designer has a mania for "breaking up the text" with all manner of tricks, including that curious device, the single-word "cross-head" which no-one reads. More than six inches of continuous bodymatter (which the reader of books is able to negotiate quite comfortably) is considered too great an expanse of "grey". Therefore text is arbitrarily cut into short paragraphs. Every time the prime minister is mentioned, out comes a scratched old stock photograph, probably cropped so that little more is shown than eyes, nose and mouth - as if we didn't know what the prime minister looked like (local papers thus overexpose the mayor or council leader). Foreign papers do not automatically use "flashback" pictures to remind readers of past disasters they already know about from over-exposure at the time they happened. You will find no insensitive or sensational pictures in the good foreign press. By contrast, after the Hillsborough football disaster the London *Evening Standard* not only printed an horrific picture of the face of an apparently suffocating young woman pressed against the wire but made it into a recurring vignette which decorated the beginning of each paragraph! Just to break up the text! *The Liverpool Echo*, a noted local crime-fighter, recently crowed that it was printing exclusive pictures of a bank-robber, taken by security cameras, and asked its readers to identify him. The (unintentional) joke was that lousy printing (such as Gutenberg would have disowned) made the pictures into an over-inked mess, with show-through from the other side of the newsprint making the man unrecognisable as a man, let alone showing his features.

I did not spot a single misprint in any of the foreign papers I saw, let alone surnames spelt in three different ways during the course of a single column, as we see daily in the British press. Indeed, some papers, like the Swiss and German ones, make it a practice to *italicise* every person's name when it is first mentioned, reverting to ordinary type for subsequent occurrences: probably a throw-back to hand-setting, when the compositor would have been obliged to stop and go to a different type-case for a name, thus ensuring that he concentrated on it. In the Swiss and German papers the language is that used by people in everyday intercourse: no journalese or stock clichés.

American papers do have their own forms of (often imaginative) news jargon English, but it is more inventive and witty than the foolish, repetitive puns and archaisms you see in our papers. For whereas *spoken* English is constantly changing (as the other end of this book tries to show), British-English news language is fossilised in a kind of self-parodying time-warp..

Of course, just as one cannot lump together carefully trained BBC announcers and distinguished presenters with the rough trade of some semi-articulate radio and television reporters, so must one distinguish between the aristocrats of British print journalism and the yobboes, which once again means chiefly (though not exclusively) between the broadsheets and the small-format tabloids. It is tempting to say that the latter are written by idiots for idiots. This is not so. They are written by extremely clever, manipulative (and vastly overpaid) print-workers who cynically exploit - and at the same time despise - the idiot readers who keep them in business. The worst joke they play on the customer (or "punter" as they call him) is to make their product more expensive than the bigger papers: for an extra eight or ten pence the broadsheets offer about ten times as much reading-matter, and (within the reservations expressed in the following pages) prose of a better quality and readability than the tabloids.

However, all papers share most of the foibles outlined in this book, though some, like *The Daily Telegraph, The Times* and *The Independent*, have been reducing the number of journalistic kneejerks of late. *The Guardian*, in spite of a relaunch (and redesign that makes the whole paper look like its own Supplement) merrily continues to spell talk "torque", right or write "rite", plane/plain, soul/sole and peddle/pedal (and vice-versa), though headlines have lately become more factual and less teasing. Instead of informing the reader, British journalists like to play jokey punning- and guessing-games. But as the jokes are the same, day after day, it is not so much a game as a daily irritation. Perhaps they do it because they are embarrassed at printing news which the reader saw on the television the previous night, and therefore they feel they must hide their embarrassment by turning every story into a joke. In fact they are playing games not with the reader but with each other; or worse, playing with themselves (certainly no-one else gets any pleasure from it). Once again, as with semi-articulate sound-reporters (see *MEDIA-SPEAK*), we must blame the education(al)ists: it is hard to credit, but *much of the nonsense you will read in the following pages* (and the foretaste below) *is actually taught in faculties and colleges of journalism*, or copied by those who wish to keep up with their peer-group. Movement between papers merely spreads the blight. And *The Times* now has *The Sun* as a stable-mate - the word "stable" being in some respects not out of place.

Maybe there is, somewhere, a well-written British tabloid without silly puns, kneejerk quips, giant, pseudo-cryptic headlines and "broken up" text. If so I have yet to come across it. Since most newspapers went tabloid the cynical rule has been "the smaller the paper the bigger the headline" - which of course deprives the reader of news he would expect from a newspaper. Buy any local evening paper and you will feel you have been swindled of 20 pence (or more), with little real news among the acres of classified advertisements and leaden, angular prose - reminiscent of John Aubrey's description of a classical writer's style: "Seneca writes as a Boar doth pisse, by jerkes".

Imagine a couple of reporters who live together ("common-law", no doubt, with their "love child") at breakfast, discussing life as they would in print:

"That was flame-haired temptress, raunchy cycling postlady mother-of-four Sarah (aka Sally) Johnson (38-40-44) riding high, peddling her post bag with a letter from Mum, shapely blonde thrice married divorcee mother-of-six, Rita Grunge (61) which has just landed on the doormat. Does it have your stamp of approval?"

"Er - just a minute. Haven't you forgotten something?"

"Sorry, luv, the letter landed *with a sickening thud*. Silly of me. I think I must be slipping! She's long vowed she's coming to see us".

"So a visit from Battling Granny is looming. I suppose she's adamant? Fancy dropping that bombshell on us. I can see a rumpus ensuing."

"Wants to take a stroll down memory lane. It's potential dynamite. I can see you're chuffed! A visit's been on the cards since Xmas."

"Yes, The Smile that Says it All! She's got her pensioner's railcard so she can get a cheap ticket to ride. Hoping to make tracks on Thursday. Last Christmas it was a nightmare dash for her, and Easter was a carbon copy. It's a blueprint for an ongoing saga. The trip's balanced on a knife edge but she'd like to go on a shopping spree".

"Shock horror in store! And she'll bring boyfriend, portly balding bowler-hatted bespectacled retired bricklayer, battling pensioner Ron Glubb (84). I suppose he'll be quaffing all our bubbly and puffing my smokes. Last time I clashed with him over it. I very much fear a fracas may ensue."

"How many times have I underlined to you that smoking may damage your health! Only last week Health Minister Nigel Hoppers (56) slammed it."

"I suppose we could take them for flied lice."

"No, heartless takeaway thieves yesterday ransacked Chinee restauranteur Johnny Lo's city-centre eaterie. They assailed him with a wok and he sustained a serious fracture, he did. Police are expected to swoop any moment now and detain a man expected to help them with their enquiries."

"Let's curry flavour at the Taj Mahal instead. They've cooked themselves up a real fortune following rocketing prices, but Ron can pick up the tab."

"How *is* mum's office Romeo then? Has he unveiled his plans yet? "

"Oh, alive and well and living in Manchester's Didsbury. He hasn't popped the question yet after their whirlwind courtship so it's unlikely they'll walk down the aisle. He doesn't seem to want to wed her she chuckled, though their names have been linked for 30 years. He alleges he bowed out of his job but I think he was really axed."

"Tell them not to bring the cat - whenever it sees the budgie..."

"The fur and feathers fly: fowl play!"

"Darling, you read my mind. Just purr-fect! I suppose we'll have to give them the green light."

"Look! Chubby bouncing baby Darren (2) is making a bid to grab the pinta. If he's not careful it'll hurtle to the floor and he'll plummet after it".

"Then he'll come down to earth with a bump, won't he. Yesterday he nearly plunged headlong when he was on a collision course with the grate and, deplorably, played with matches risking a towering inferno."

"He was weeping openly. Dicing with death, that tot is. I sometimes feel I could slay him. I've spelt out a warning to him over it, loud and clear. When he goes to school he'll be a handful for sir."

"Why can't the love child chomp his Krispibrek and tuck into his toast?"

"Importantly, he'll have to munch his breakfast amid tight security, or we'll have egg on our faces."

"He's losing his nappy. I can see the bare facts - in fact he's baring all. Why don't you whisk him along to the bathroom and make a mercy dash for a big cover up? Red faces! And put his potty under him. Strategically placed."

"Well, I'm off."

"Don your hat and don't drag your feet. And call in on famed singing butcher Ted Jones (60) who's been hitting the high notes lately. He's set to sing at Nottingham's town hall next week. But his prices have soared so much I'm thinking in terms of..."

Both in unison: "Giving him the chop!"

"And another thing. On your way back don't wend your way to the hostelry to sample the local brew with mine host. It would be a bitter blow and I'd call time on our relationship."

A

ABUSE See BEAST, INTERFERED WITH, MONSTER.

ADAMANT Obstinate (from Greek/Latin *adamas*, hard); one of the SMILED group indicating the *mood* in which something is ALLEGED to have been said: "He was adamant he was not there..."

AFFAIR OF STATE Politician's alleged love-affair, as surely as a sportsman's marriage is his MATCH OF THE DAY.

AFRO-CARIBBEAN Black: "The wanted man is of Afro-Caribbean appearance." "Negro(id)", "half-caste" and "coloured" are taboo.

AGEISM Discrimination on grounds of age, analogous to sexism, raci(al)ism, etc., e.g. needlessly mentioning a person's age. *The Washington Post Desk Book on Style* says: "Mention [it] in stories when it is relevant, particularly if it helps to identify or describe a person. But do not mention a person's age simply because you know it or to pad out a short headline". Thus "Nun raped by Sex Beast, 98" is news, "Nun raped by Sex Beast, 23" nothing unusual. So if ever a journalist asks, "May I ask how old you are?", reply "You may ask but I won't tell you because it's not relevant to the story". Unless, of course, you are a 98-year-old sex BEAST.

AGONY Headline eye-catcher, like HORROR, TERROR, etc. "Agony of GYMSLIP MUM in drugs HEARTBREAK".

AGONY COLUMNS Advice columns written by Agony *Aunts*, though some of these are men, who enjoy concocting answers and sometimes questions (see also HOROSCOPES) . The term was invented by *Fun*, a Victorian contemporary of *Punch*, which in the issue of 3 October 1863 announced "Our own agony column". *The Times* personal column is also known as an agony column because of its coded messages between secret lovers.

AKA Abbreviation of "also known as", but the typographical affectation of abandoning full-stops causes it to be pronounced "acka". Why not *alias*? See DUB.

ALADDIN'S CAVE Hyperbole for even the smallest hoard of stolen goods. The tiniest CACHE of arms is an ARSENAL.

ALIENS Used to mean foreigners, tourists or immigrants. Now that Britons are more familiar with foreigners (and have discovered that *they* are foreigners in *other* countries) "aliens" usually means alleged visitors from outer space.

ALL AT SEA "Sailors of the Royal Navy, on shore leave in Gibraltar, were all at sea yesterday as..." Also SCUPPERED, TORPEDOED, SUNK, UP THE CREEK, etc.

ALLEGED Legal safeguard ("the alleged thief") though carrying innuendo. Quotation-marks also help: HUBBY IS "RAPIST".

AMPUTEE The *-ee* suffix is of legal origin, from Old French *-é*, as in "lessee", "legatee", "garnishee", etc. later applied humorously to what the *OED* calls nonce-words, e.g. "sendee", "educatee" and "devotee", denoting that something has been done to, or suffered by, persons with an -ee suffix. Yesterday's nonce-words become today's standard, and *-ee* words are useful *MEDIA UGLIES*. Transport correspondents without facetiousness refer to standing passengers as "standees", and after World War II we all got used to "evacuees". Employ*ees* of the National Health Service also love words ending in *-ee*. Indeed the *OED* gives a 1910 reference in verse from the *St Bartholomew's Hospital Journal*: "Please put the patients both (!) to bed/and then, perhaps, we'll see/ which is the amputated part/ and which the amputee". (See HOPPING MAD). But "escapee" is no improvement on "escaper".

AND THAT'S OFFICIAL Cliché to lend weight to what might otherwise be read as speculation. And *that's* a fact.

ANGER See FURY.

ANNIVERSARIES The celebration of anniversaries of previous violence often encourages more. The media also reopen old hurts, e.g. send out camera crews and photographers to picture relatives of Zeebrugge victims dropping wreaths into the sea - so they can show them WEEPING OPENLY all over again. Before TV no-one would have even organised such a trip. Sensational terms like "Bloody Sunday" and "Black Monday" etc. also cause further misery.

ANTI- A prefix which, like EX-, confuses when a double concept is mentioned, e.g. "He belonged to the anti-white paper camp" (a paper camp of anti-whites?) "as an anti-blood sports writer" (a sports-writer who can't stand blood?) or an "anti-hare coursing" event (as if the poor hares hadn't enough to contend with). Why not re-phrase, or dispense with *HYPHENS* to even out the qualifications? See also POST-.

ARCHAISMS Newsmen must have their CHAIN REACTION jokes when writing about defecation although they flush lavatories with a lever; write about BLUEPRINTS for the future when this form of plan-reproduction is 25 years in the past; and decades after the invention of the electronic flash insist that FLASHBULBS POPPED. See also HASTENING (THITHER) and cross-references: SPED, WED, WENDING, whither, hie, proceed, QUOTH, etc. Unable to bring the news as fast as TV and radio, they try to entertain; and archaisms are part of this ALLEGED entertainment. Or so "methinks".

ARISE SIR - ! Stock headline for the newly-knighted (in one glorious tabloid malapropism *benighted*). Especially suitable when the man to be so honoured has a nickname, e.g. "Arise Sir Nobby!" When the overweight Liberal MP Cyril Smith was knighted several papers independently hit upon "Arise Sir Cyril - if you can!"

ARSENAL Illegal CACHE of arms, however small. And see ALADDIN'S CAVE.

ASSAILANT *ARCHAISM* for an attacker - and never used in ordinary conversation ("Me mum-in-law assailed me with a rolling-pin").

AT LAST/FINALLY The first may be opinionated ("At last!"), the second is non-committal. Thus "Support for the Chinese students is at last waning" *appears* to be taking the side of the government.

ATTRIBUTIVE QUEUE See A for ARTICLES in *MediaSpeak* but meanwhile you may wish to study these written examples.

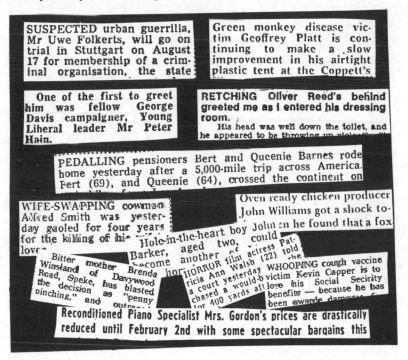

SUSPECTED urban guerrilla, Mr Uwe Folkerts, will go on trial in Stuttgart on August 17 for membership of a criminal organisation, the state

Green monkey disease victim Geoffrey Platt is continuing to make a slow improvement in his airtight plastic tent at the Coppett's

One of the first to greet him was fellow George Davis campaigner, Young Liberal leader Mr Peter Hain.

RETCHING Oliver Reed's behind greeted me as I entered his dressing room.
His head was well down the toilet, and he appeared to be throwing up violently

PEDALLING pensioners Bert and Queenie Barnes rode home yesterday after a 5,000-mile trip across America. Bert (69), and Queenie (64), crossed the continent on

WIFE-SWAPPING cowman Alfred Smith was yesterday gaoled for four years for the killing of his love-

Oven ready chicken producer John Williams got a shock today when he found that a fox

Hole-in-the-heart boy John Barker, aged two, could

Bitter mother Brenda Winsland of Davywood Road, Speke, has blasted the decision as "penny pinching," and out-

another actress Patricia Ann Walsh (22) told a court yesterday the chased a would-b for 400 yards all

HORROR film victim Kevin Capper is to

WHOOPING cough vaccine victim Kevin Capper is to lose his Social Security benefits — because he has been awarded damages

Reconditioned Piano Specialist Mrs. Gordon's prices are drastically reduced until February 2nd with some spectacular bargains this

(THE) AWARD-WINNING... Media and showbiz people give themselves prizes at bogus award ceremonies preceded by SLAP UP dinners:

preceded by "nominations" - so even those who are not declared somebody's something OF THE YEAR can proclaim that they were at any rate *nominated* for the honour. Thus, as in children's and chimpanzees' tea-parties, even the loser gets a going-home prize. To the cynical these "nominations" sound like the Indian student who returns home from England with printed visiting-cards: "R. G. Bharjee, B.Sc. Oxford University (failed)".

AXE (verb) Grants axed, funds axed, hospitals axed, even boss axed. Tree-fellers (and sometimes criminals) also wield axes but the maddest axemen are journalists.

B

BABE (IN ARMS) A TOT younger than a TODDLER, perhaps a BUNDLE OF JOY and, if sick, invariably BRAVE.

BACCY See SMOKES.

BAREFACED CHEEK/CHEEKY Belong to the NUDE group of words. See also COLD SHOULDER and, of course, "Baring All"..

BARGAIN BASEMENT Originally a place where cheap goods were sold, not necessarily below ground ("For Bargain Basement follow the signs to the second floor" - in the old Whiteley's store!). Also used adjectivally:

BAR WARS Like OH BROTHER! this served a dual purpose during the late 1980s, when there were, simultaneously, disputes among barristers and a much publicised DAWN RAID on a chocolate-manufacturer. Even the normally staid BBC news joined in the fun, describing *both* negotiations as "the so-called bar wars" - though some news-readers managed to invest "so-called" with audible distaste. The allusion to STAR WARS will not have escaped you. All popular film, book or SOAP titles are eventually annnexed by the punning funsters of the press, however inappropriately - e.g. GOOD LIFE.

BATTLER/BATTLING "Battler Nora (62) Routs Mugger". The description is set before a person's name in such a way that it almost suggests he was so christened ("I name this child Battling Bill Lonegan"); "Battling GRANNY" for *any* old lady who has lifted an umbrella against a YOUNGSTER, or refuses to be bullied by bureaucrats. See PENSIONER.

BEAST A sex offender or MONSTER.

BELEAGUERED Medieval cities were beleaguered; in the Boer War Mafeking, and Stalingrad in World War II. Now a mere *ARCHAISM*, e.g. "beleaguered Neil Kinnock".

BEST/WORST DRESSERS (etc.) Part of the OF THE YEAR craze. A firm or trade association "votes" for/against well-known people and their alleged dress-sense (or lack of it) and issues a "statement". Year after year the papers fall for it, presenting "votes" as fact (see also AWARD-WINNING) although it is nothing but a publicity stunt, starting with a bogus "Pipeman/Tieman/ Shirtman (and for all I know Mad AXEman) of the Year" declaration. A firm of opticians now commissions an annual Gallup poll for the "Sexiest Spectacle Wearer". Nationwide free publicity is given by newspapers that have nothing better to print.

BID Headline word for "attempt" or "try", also now heard even in spoken news, like SET.

BIGAMIST Strictly a man who has married *two* wives, the second unlawfully (see also MASS MURDERER). As the anonymous limerick has it

> There was a young fellow from Lyme,
> Who married three wives at a time.
> When asked, "Why the third?"
> He replied, "One's absurd,
> And bigamy, sir, is a crime."

BIG-HEARTED Generous.

BIG SHAKE-UP A small reorganisation.

BILLION Most people know that a million is a thousand times a thousand, i.e. 1,000,000. But a billion is confusing because the British and Americans cannot agree about it. A USA billion is 1,000,000,000, that is, a thousand millions, which the English call a milliard (as do the Germans and the French) and a million millions (1,000,000,000,000) a billion. Hence a trillion is the third power of a million, or a million billions. Then again, in France and *parts* of the United States, it is a thousand billions, i.e. an English billion. This terminology goes back to ca.1484 and can be adapted almost indefinitely, from quadrillions to nonillions and even zillions. The confusion described so far is made worse by the fact that many British newsmen use the American form, either because they do not know there *is* a difference or think that the Americans must be right because they have more money. For this if no other reason the American way will eventually prevail. Meanwhile why not specify the amount in numerals, however many noughts it takes, or enumerate the *number* of millions in words? Or, if all else fails, restrict millions to "millyins" as in Liverpool Scouse hyperbole: "There was millyins of rats runnin' all over the kitchen..." meaning "rather more than I was able to count".

BILLS The happy accident that parliamentary legislation may result in a bill, which is also a man's name, can create ambiguities (see next page).

BIMBO After an American politico-erotic scandal in 1987-8 the British press took to this word meaning a pretty but empty-headed young woman. In America it has been an insult since the 1920s: usually but not necessarily a whore (as the scouse word "tart" is not always derogatory in Liverpool). It also has an alcoholic meaning: a Bimbo is a cocktail shaken by barmen

(American bartenders): "... made nearly in the same way as Arrack punch, except that Cognac brandy is substituted for Arrack"; and Bumbo is "a liquor composed of rum, sugar, water and nutmeg".

BITCHED See SMILED, SIGHED, QUIPPED, LAUGHED, GRUFFED, CHUCKLED, ENTHUSED, etc.

BITTER For any adverse-news *STORY* about publicans and barmen - e.g. when a STORM IS BREWING. Also, more rarely, MILD; and, of course, "The government is *calling time* on tied houses".

(A) BITTER PILL (TO SWALLOW) Anything doctors or pharmacists find unacceptable. In extreme cases it may mean GETTING A TASTE OF THEIR OWN MEDICINE. Dentists, on the other hand, KNOW THE DRILL.

BLACK See CARBON COPY. For other connotations of black see the *Colour Supplement* in my *In-Words and Out-Words*, Elm Tree Books, 1987; and in this book under COWBOYS.

BLACK MARK Like CANING and SIR, the schools cliché: "Liverpool teachers were given a black mark yesterday as their exam-ination results were caned..." etc. *Black* marks seldom figure in teachers' marking: most mark in red.

BLANKET BAN As in "NHS workers have imposed a blanket ban from today..." See also the equally ill-fitting OVERALLS.

BLAST Strictly the *result* of an explosion, not the explosion itself, but who worries about meaning when a word has five letters instead of nine?

BLASTED Supposedly time-saving description, like SMILED, SIGHED, BITCHED, QUIPPED, GRUFFED, CHUCKLED, ENTHUSED, all intended to convey the *manner* in which something was said, e.g. **I QUIT BLASTS DENZIL.** In this instance, "Denzil" simply resigned: certainly in anger, but he neither "blasted" nor STORMED OUT.

BLAZE A fire, even a very small one, reported in the news - not big enough to be likened to Dante's INFERNO. Blazes and infernos usually "rage", possibly "out of control": ordinary fires just boringly burn.

BLIMEY! See COR!

BLONDE For some reason light-coloured head-hair on a woman is supposed to titillate readers; also her age and "vital" statistics (see *AGEISM*). Many papers make blond and blonde, fiancé and fiancée, interchangeable.

BLOW Although even Shakespeare used this word in the sense of a setback, disadvantage or disaster, it has been devalued by constant headline misuse. Often preceded by DEVASTATING.

BLUE In the papers generally denotes obscenity, not Tory politics: "Blue Comic Rapped by BBC" (usually making someone SEE RED). Wartime British censors used a heavy blue pencil, hence to "blue-pencil" (see *Colour Supplement* in *In-Words and Out-Words*).

(THE) BLUES A mild form of depression. From jazz-singers' usage ("Ah feel sow blue") though it has been the colour of despair since the middle ages. The *Liverpool Daily Post* reported the mental breakdown and committal to an asylum of an internationally-acclaimed classical pianist - under the tasteless headline **PIANO BLUES.**

BOFFIN A scientist (World War II slang for "back-room boys"). See also MANDARIN, DON, GURU, PUNDIT.

BOMBSHELLS Archaic weaponry (full of political DYNAMITE?) which are always clumsily (metaphorically) "dropped". Real ones were fired.

BONANZA Spanish word meaning fair weather at sea, adopted into USA speech in about 1840. More recently a press cliché for any promised abundance, usually financial or commercial.

BOUNCE BACK Sportsmen or politicians do this when COMING IN FROM THE COLD or returning after absence or sickness.

BOWING OUT *ARCHAISM* of retirement or resignation, suggesting some ancient ceremony, a respectful backward departure accompanied by a low obeisance and sweep of the hat. Would even the most hardnosed hack say

to his colleagues, "After 30 years on the *Echo* I'm bowing out of my job..."?
Like so many journalistic terms "bowing out" has been dragged KICKING
AND SCREAMING into radio and television news-talk, where it sounds even
sillier than it looks on paper - like VOWS.

BOYFRIEND When mentioning LOVE TANGLES outside marriage the
press describes men and women as boyfriends or girlfriends until they die
of old age. In horse-racing, too, people remain girls and LADS for ever, as
in "Mrs Bumphrey-Davenport's head lad retires aged 87". See also
GRANNY and PENSIONER.

BRAVE *Any* sick (even comatose) small child, BUNDLE OF JOY, TOD-
DLER, etc. (though GYMSLIP MUMS are never brave). As meaningless as
FIGHTING FOR (HIS) LIFE and BATTLING.

(GETTING A) BREAK One of the snooker clichés: see ON/OFF CUE.

BREAKTHROUGH Any advance, achievement or discovery, e.g. medical or scientific (often coupled with MAJOR); or the promise of a successful
end to negotiations. It might be appropriate for, say, the Channel Tunnel; but
"a major breakthrough in surgery" implies that the surgeon and his assistants
shook hands through a hole in the patient. In a letter to *The Times* (15 August
1988) a reader reported finding four breakthroughs in a single issue of the
paper and assumed that there must a lot of holes somewhere. (Another
suggested they might have been caused by all the "tips of icebergs" he kept
reading about.) They came from World War I, when breaking through the
enemy's lines was something to be accomplished in a real sense. The word
is not even English, merely naturalised, a clumsy wartime translation of the
German military term *Durchbruch,* and unknown before that war.

BRILLIANT Vogue-adjective of approval (chiefly among the young)
over-used in the writings of women journalists who, especially in the fashion
pages, describe nearly everything they like (also good-looking people) as
STUNNING. Until recently it would have been FABULOUS.

BROUHAHA One of the *MEDIA UGLIES*, like GLITZ(Y), KERFUFFLE,
PIZZAZZ, RAZZMATAZZ, TOHU(WA)BOHU, ZIZZ, etc. From 15th-century
French meaning "commotion, uproar, etc." Hence perhaps HOO-HAA.

BROWNIE POINTS Suddenly fashionable cliché for praise or credit
given to, or looked for by, a person.

BRRR! The tabloids' favourite cold-weather headline. See also PHEW
WHAT A SCORCHER!

BRUSH WITH... Painters, decorators, roadsweepers and artists have a
Brush with the Law, Fame, Destiny and in extreme cases Death (though
death traditionally engages people in a DICE game). If a broom is involved,
the Clean Sweep *PICTURE CLICHÉ* will be contrived. In the North of
England a "brush" means a broom with a *long* handle whereas a South-

erner's brush has a short one or none at all.

BUBBLY Hacks' champagne, SIPPED or QUAFFED, after "Corks popped". When TUCKING INTO food (a SLAP UP meal?) bubbly WASHES DOWN or is DOWNED ("They downed bubbly at a fearsome rate..."). Yet *PICTURE CLICHÉS* usually show bubbly not quaffed but shaken-and-sprayed: a disgusting showbiz/sporting habit dating from the 1950s and the song *The Night they invented Champagne* (in the film *Gigi*) - wasteful tricks unthinkable to a generation brought up on wartime shortages. Even Champagne Charlie drank the stuff because he liked it, not because he could afford to splash it about.

BUMP INTO Gossip columnists and DIARISTS never look where they are going. "The other day I bumped into novelist Amnesia Randy" actually means "I met Amnesia Randy in response to an invitation from her press agent who wants to publicise her". See also I HEAR...

BUMPY RIDE One of the traffic clichés, e.g. "The rail bill is expected to be given a bumpy ride". See RIDING HIGH, TURBULENCE, etc.

BUNDLED AWAY What happens to WANTED MEN after they are arrested, perhaps following a DAWN RAID. Famous people, or wanted men after acquittal, are WHISKED AWAY.

BUNDLE OF JOY A very young baby. Unless unsuccessfully FIGHTING FOR HIS LIFE (BATTLING or BRAVE) he grows into a TOT or TODDLER, progressing by stages, perhaps into a LATCH KEY KID or GYM SLIP MUM, all the way to PENSIONER or BATTLING GRANNY, sans dignity, sans everything, so far as the hack is concerned.

BUNKERED Kneejerk for a golfer's REVERSAL or disadvantage, i.e. "Sevvy was bunkered by a duck yesterday after it wandered on the course..."

BUXOM Used to describe a woman (in former times "wench") with big breasts. See BLONDE, SHAPELY, WELL BUILT.

C

CACHE See *MEDIASPEAK*.

CALLING TIME See BITTER.

CALLOUS See HEARTLESS.

CANCER An emotionally charged word debased by news usage, like CRUCIFY, SPASTIC (to a lesser extent GERIATRIC). The original allusion was probably to "a cancer in the body politic", usually ascribed - wrongly - to Shakespeare, who used the word only once, preferred the English "canker", and never applied it to politics.

CANING See GETTING A CANING and SIR.

CAN REVEAL THAT... Hint that what follows is an EXCLUSIVE: *The Observer* can reveal that..."

CAPSIZE See SUNK.

CARBON COPY In newspaper offices a carbon copy of typewritten matter is known as a "black" - though this word has been banned by the National Union of Journalists. It is in any case an *ARCHAISM* as copies are either computer- or xerox-printed. Will future newsmen write about xerox copy murders and xerox copy accidents? And see COPYCAT.

CARBUNCLE William the Conqueror, Ethelread the Unready, Henry the Navigator, etc... are convenient regal nicknames. Perhaps the present Prince of Wales should be named (no, canonised as) Charles the Environmentalist, protecting his future subjects from the self-aggrandising designs and modish fads of architects, from their clichés, which are every bit as laughable as those of the press though infinitely more obtrusive (at present they are sticking "atriums" everywhere - greenhouses with inverted-U-shaped windows, even in the monstrous Lloyds building in London!) and making vague environmentalist noises. The famous speech in which he compared a proposed extension to the classical National Gallery in London to "a carbuncle on the face of a much-loved friend" not only gave a new meaning to an old word but also helped to speed "post-modernism", another fad-word, meaning "traditional-but-acceptable" design. A similar turn-around can be observed in music, but that is another subject.

CARD-CARRYING (Though the luxury of a *HYPHEN* is seldom offered) - obligatory prefix to membership of a left-wing political party, e.g. "Card carrying communist". Tories, fascists and flat-earthers apparently never carry their cards. See also PRACTISING.

CAREER *ARCHAISM*. "Smith said he was driving at 25 mph when the Rolls careered into him..." My guess is that this was *FALSE VERBATIM*: real people do not speak about "careering".

CARNAGE Dramatising word for bloodshed, cynically used for the SHOCK/HORROR value it can give to a STORY.

CASANOVA See ROMEO.

CASH REGISTERS TINKLED Like CHAIN REACTION, an *ARCHAISM*. Modern cash registers give an electronic bleep.

CATERING TO... Catering *for* somebody or something has been the accepted form for centuries. "Catering to..." is suddenly enjoying an unexplained vogue, like the epidemic MAY for "might". See also DIFFERENT THAN.

CENTURION Sports reporters have annexed this word (for a Roman commander of 100 men) to describe a cricketer who has scored a century!

CHAIN REACTION Joint cliché for mayors and lavatories - in spite of the fact that both are now losing their chains: mayors, because LOONY Labourites loathe tradition; lavatories, because of the lever-flush. When the 800-year-old office of Lord Mayor of Liverpool was discontinued the *Liverpool Daily Post* headline was "Chain Reaction". The *Guardian's* headline? "Chain Reaction". And the *Independent's*? The same. These were the only papers I saw that day. No doubt the rest did the same.

CHALK UP To amass or collect, e.g. victories, perhaps by SOARING/ SAILING/RUNNING etc. into the RECORD BOOKS; also CLOCKING/NOTCHING UP.

CHEEK(Y) NUDITY word, like BAREFACED and COLD SHOULDER.

CHEQUE BOOK JOURNALISM Even those who survive some harrowing experience that MIGHT have had the nation praying for their safe deliverance have become wise to the fiscal possibilities. As they are helped to safety by rescuers they may just find the strength to whisper "NO COMMENT" - and await the best offer from a TABLOID. That deal concluded, they are WHISKED AWAY by the successful bidder, pursued by the *RATPACK* of losers, who must content themselves with a snatched photograph before turning their attention to SPOILERS. See also *DUSTBIN JOURNALISM* and *GHOST*.

CHEWING (ON) Reflecting: one of the food kneejerks, used even in the most inappropriate context, though dentists are also often saddled with it.

CHOMPING Eating, but please see also MUNCHING and TUCKING INTO.

> By John Tanner
> A new calorie-enriched famine biscuit is saving the lives of thousands of children in drought-stricken Ethiopia and is giving international relief agencies something to chew on. The "energy biscuit," as it has been described, was developed recently by Oxfam, Britain's largest overseas aid charity.

CHORUS (Verb) To say something in alleged agreement with another person or persons. A peculiarly journalese formation, as in "'It's great', they chorus(s)ed". In ordinary speech people never "chorus"; indeed most people are unaware that such a verb exists.

CHORUS OF DISAPPROVAL/CRITICISM Critics always ALLEGEDLY burst into united song, never songs of praise.

CHUCKLED See SMILED.

CITY Has several meanings, depending on which newspaper uses it and where. In local papers it means the town (though a "City Father" could be either a respected citizen, e.g. councillor, or merely a father who lives in the locality). Elsewhere the City means financial institutions, formerly concentrated in the INNER CITY of London.

CLASH A quarrel or a disagreement, however slight or a sports contest. And when during the cultural revolution some Chinese students surrounded a car the papers could not resist an adaptation:

CHINESE IN CAR CLASH

CLASSIFIED Short for "classified as secret"and, more absurdly, "unclassified" means *not* secret. Not a serious abuse of the language but nevertheless deplorable, like the suborning of fine old words like "intercourse" and "gay" for sexual purposes. Also short for Classified Advertisements.

CLASS OF... Suddenly modish way of referring to generations, i.e. "Class of 67". Probably from a television schools SOAP.

CLEAN SWEEP See BRUSH WITH.

CLOCKING UP A CENTURY See CHALKING/NOTCHING UP, MATCH OF THE DAY, NOT OUT, THROWING IN THE TOWEL and WEIGHING IN.

CLOSE FRIEND Variation on the ubiquitous, absurd, "Common Law Wife/Husband" euphemism (see *In-Words and Out-Words*). As the *Evening Standard DIARIST* wrote "...pianist Helena Bachkirev, with whom he has been close friends for four years, and by whom he has two small children". Presumably they needed to get fairly close to produce offspring.

(THE) COLD SHOULDER Essential ingredient of reports about NUDITY. For exposed buttocks see BAREFACED CHEEK.

COLLIDING WITH... When some (possibly drunken) driver's car hits a lamp-post or knocks down a PENSIONER who was walking on the pavement minding his own business, the papers say that they "collided". Latin *collidere* means to strike or clash *together*, so the lamp-post (or old person) would have had to leap out at the motorist. Journalists use the malapropism so as not to be thought to apportion blame.

COLONIC IRRITATION: Even in the best newspapers there are subeditors who feel the need to jollify picture captions with a contrived tabloid quip or pun followed by a colon (which is why, taking a leaf out of their book, I call it "colonic irritation"). Do they really think "Stringing Along" added anything more than bad taste to a picture of the Amadeus Quartet after the death of one of its members? Or "Making a Meal of it" under a representation of Leonardo da Vinci's *Last Supper* (both in *The Independent*, of all papers)? More obscurely, the same paper had a workman crouching on the roof of Ely Cathedral, captioned "Casting Crouch". In the *Times* an old man, a grieving World War I veteran, is shown WEEPING OPENLY. Caption: "War cry: Comfort is provided by Lyn Macdonald, author of *Somme*, after the wreath-laying." During anniversary celebrations (celebrations?) of the Battle of the Somme, headline writers in more than one newspaper joked about the CARNAGE with "Somme like it Hot". The *Guardian* printed an article under the headline "Turkish Mine Deaths Toll rises to 97". The accompanying photograph of the search for survivors was captioned "In the Blackstuff: Miners carry injured colleagues..." - a reference to a television SOAP. In one of the TABLOIDS a photograph of the raising of the Zeebrugge disaster ferry, still with corpses of victims aboard, was captioned "Up She Rises" (for song titles or refrains, like names of books and TV programmes, are an unfailing source for headline "jokes"): only lack of space made the SUB omit "Hooray". In the *Daily Express*, a picture showing the rear view of the body of an IRA terrorist shot at Gibraltar was captioned "Dead End". Perhaps writers of such captions were TIRED AND EMOTIONAL after sustained QUAFFING, of which much goes on in the HOSTELRIES near newspaper offices.

COME OFF IT ...! Tabloid cry of simulated indignation, dots representing the name or abbreviated NICKNAME of the person exhorted to come off. FROGS are exhorted to HOP OFF.

COMING DOWN TO EARTH WITH A BUMP What happens to a project not FLYING HIGH, e.g. "The President's STAR WARS project has run into TURBULENCE and came down to earth with a bang yesterday as..." Also SICKENING THUD.

COMING IN FROM THE COLD Returning to favour, office, political popularity, or a former way of life after an enforced absence, perhaps IN THE WILDERNESS. Those who fail to come in are "left out in the cold". But HOPEFULLY they will BOUNCE BACK. From John le Carré's book, *The Spy who came in from the Cold* (1963).

CONFIRMED BACHELOR Euphemism/innuendo for a male homosexual. Calling someone TIRED AND EMOTIONAL has resulted in successful litigation, but allegations of homosexuality have yet to be tested, perhaps because this is now legalised among adult males. According to hacks there are no heterosexual confirmed bachelors nor anyone chaste or celibate by choice. See SPINSTER.

CONTROVERSIAL Generally meaningless description fitted to names, e.g. "Controversial artist Thomas Gainsborough..." or "Controversial dog-lover Minnie Barkworth..." It may be noticed that while the Central American "Contras" were fighting their war many words like "controversial" began to be mis-spelt "contraversial".

(A) COOL For some reason objects UP FOR GRABS with a big PRICE TAG are usually thought to have a low temperature, e.g. "... at a cool £1m". See also the invariably CRISP FIVERS - though ONCERS, alas, are no more, except in Scotland.

CONVERSATION PIECE Established meaning: a kind of painting, e.g. of two or more subjects or a family posing as though engaged in some domestic pursuit. Press meaning, usually in articles on antiques and "collectables": any unusual or interesting object likely to start a conversation(!) See *PICTURE CLICHÉS*.

COPY In the outside world a *copy* is a transcription (now also xerox or photograph) of an original. For journalists it means the original work or composition (handwritten, typed or word-processed) submitted for publication (whereas an author of books speaks of his MS). This usage goes back to Caxton, who wrote in 1485: "And I accordyng to my copye haue doon sette it in enprynte" - so he also gave us *setting* for typesetting.

COPYCAT The cat is a proud, independent creature and does not imitate humans. Journalistic clichés like "Copycat Murder", "Copycat Theft", etc., are probably derived from an early photo-copying system trade-named "Copycat". See BLACK, CARBON COPY.

COPYTAKER A person who sits by a telephone whose receiver is wired to earphones so that his hands are free to type the words journalists and contributors dictate to him: one of the most important jobs on a daily paper but a dying craft. More and more *COPY* is now sent either by facsimile-machine or goes direct into the central computer, saving the misunderstood writer much frustration and depriving the reader of innocent sport: e.g. "aperitif" for imperative, "white elephant" for quite elegant and "the loneliest monk" for Thelonius Monk.

COR! Euphemism for "God!", sometimes followed by "blimey" (bless me): in tabloid headlines simulates astonishment. Since a former tabloid editor turned disc jockey the word has become a stock BBC word.

CORKS POPPED AS... Stock opening for reports of celebrations at which wine or BUBBLY are served, SIPPED, QUAFFED or DOWNED, and if food is MUNCHED, this is WASHED DOWN. I have *never* seen a press description of *any* SLAP UP celebration or feast, even in the best papers, in which one or more of the above clichés failed to appear.

COSMIC PREDICTIONS Always sensational but never verifiable, and probably as old as newspapers themselves. Now favoured especially by Sunday papers, printed on Saturday and consequently short of up-to-the-minute news. The earliest I have seen was a Victorian assertion that by the year 1935 London streets would be submerged under 14 ft of horse-manure

- so the invention of the motor-car must have deprived Londoners of loads of valuable fertilizer for their window-boxes. Others are "By 2047 the Great Barrier Reef will have been eroded", there are frequent, conflicting, but definitive statements of when the Leaning Tower of Pisa will fall down, and that by the year 2030 we shall all have died of AIDS. For myself, I am not totally convinced - yet - even by the - now almost visible - holes in the ozone layers and the promise that Brighton will soon have a delightfully sub-tropical climate.

COST A PACKET See FUMING. For the Spanish-holiday cliché (Costa Lotta, Costa Topless, Costa CUPPA, etc.) see *In-Words*.

COUPE See LIMO.

CRACK What people are said to do to bottles before QUAFFING, etc. Crack is also criminals' slang for a form of heroin.

CRACK DOWN (ON) To take strong measures (against), as in "Thatcher VOWED to crack down on football hooligans..." and "Judge cracks down on Prostitutes".

CRACK/CRACKER Denote alleged excellence or beauty, "cracker" often preceded by "a real": "Navy's crack ship sinks in Atlantic". (Crack is also a deadly heroin-derived illegal drug).

CRESCENDO One of many musical terms misused by journalists. See UPBEAT (and *In-Words*).

CRISP Adjective for "fivers" (i.e. five-pound notes) even when limp and dirty after years of passing from hand to grubby hand. Formerly also crisp "oncers" - an absurd word the press invented but which never entered ordinary speech. Since superseded by a coin the "oncer" has disappeared.

CRITICAL/SERIOUS "Bishop Critical", "Actress Improving", "TV Comic Serious", the papers write and newsreaders absurdly say (though in more measured tones). The suggestion is that the bishop is being critical (probably of the government, as most bishops seem to be these days) and that the actress is at last getting better at acting (which some are). The bishop and the actress may well both be critical of the persons or circumstances that made them ill; and the TV comedian may for once be in no mood for jokes. What is meant, and could be said with only a little extra effort, is that their *condition* is whatever it is. Like FIGHTING FOR (HIS) LIFE, a silly formula. See STABLE.

CRUCIFYING Cruel death-punishment invented and used widely by the ancient Romans - though (as usual) the Jews got the blame for the most publicised crucifixion, although they never used that form of punishment.

During the Roman occupations many Britons, too, were crucified - but nothing like as many as have since been "crucified" by the media. There is no better indication of the insensitivity of much news prose - both to religious feelings and the meaning of words. See also CANCER, GERIATRIC, SPASTIC.

CRUNCH For the last decade or two, many and various "things" have been "coming to a crunch" when reaching some sort of critical (noisy?) moment of decision. The expression must have been amusing at first, but should now be consigned with a SICKENING THUD to the limbo of old clichés. The crunch SITUATION can produce beautiful noun/verb misunderstandings, e.g. "Women Priests Crunch Looms".

CRYING FOUL "Police cried foul yesterday as retired soccer referee Bill took the law into his own hands..." They could also have blown the WHISTLE, "shown him the red card", or he could have been KICKED INTO TOUCH. The ingenuity of journalists...

CUDDLE As in KISS AND CUDDLE. News yobs have robbed a fine old word of its comforting innocence and made it sexual. The "little boys" in Charles Kingsley's *The Water Babies* "who have kind mammas to cuddle them" would today probably be made wards-of-court on suspicion of child ABUSE. See HANKY PANKY, HORSEPLAY, SLAP AND TICKLE, etc.

CUE See ON CUE.

CUPPA See PINTA.

CURRYING F(L)AVOUR Even in these race-conscious days papers are full of pungent curry "jokes". Nor are the days of "flied lice" over. Any burglary in a Chinese restaurant is inevitably described as a (CHINESE) TAKEAWAY. Indian food news-items are always DISHED UP curried, however foolish and incongruous the effect, e.g. "India Curries Favour with I.M.F." And when Mrs Edwina Currie revealed the existence of poisoned eggs the headline-writers were beside themselves with ingenious quips. Unfortunately they all made the same ones.

CURVACEOUS Of a woman with a feminine figure, probably BUXOM or SHAPELY and certainly WELL BUILT.

CUT-AND-THRUST Fencing term. In the media boringly twinned with "of politics".

D

DAD See MUM.

DARBY AND JOAN From an 18th-century song, "Old Darby, with Joan at his side": a loving old couple, mutually devoted and living in humble circumstances. In media jargon, *any* pair of PENSIONERS, even those who spent their whole lives at each others' throats. "Police are treating the death of a Darby and Joan couple as murder and suicide ..." See THE GOOD LIFE.

DASH Any journey, however slow and leisurely, reported in the papers. If at the end of it some service, however small, is rendered, it becomes a "mercy dash" (sometimes, echoing military operations, "mercy mission"). A mercy dash may RAISE hopes, but they can FADE and be finally - dashed.

DAWN RAID Unexpected CITY take-over BID. From the practice in totalitarian states of taking people by surprise when arresting them. British police have now also adopted this method of catching WANTED MEN, hoping to find them at home, unwary, undressed and probably unarmed. When they are BUNDLED AWAY and photographed (press photographers may accompany police) it will be observed that British criminals habitually sleep in vest and underpants. The traditional blanket draped over their heads is for legal purposes, not to keep them snug on the way to the police-station.

DAY Drama-seeking headline cliché, as in DAY THE VICAR CALLED ON BLONDE.

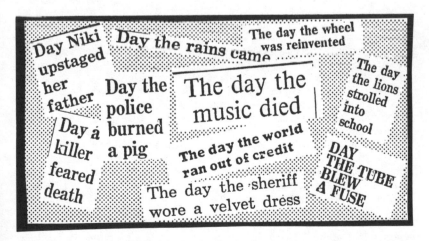

DEADLY (or LETHAL) COCK-TAIL A strong mixture, e.g. of drugs. See WASHING DOWN.

DEAD MEN They may not be able to tell tales but in newspaper reports they can do all manner of things long after death, e.g. "The dead man spent six weeks living with his sister..." or

> Mr Henry Weathersfield of Rock Ferry, who died last month, left £25 in his will so that his old drinking companions at the Crown would be able to drink his health. His brother William

"The dead woman was taken shopping in Marks & Spencers shortly before she disappeared..." Didn't the other shoppers *mind*? Also **DEAD MAN WAS UNFIT TO DRIVE** (hardly surprising!) ; and stranger still, dead men apparently even expect us to drink their health:see cutting, above.

DEMOLISHING Eating, as in "He demolished a steak..." See MUNCH-ING, CHOMPING and TUCKING IN. And if you are by then not too disgusted, also QUAFFING and WASHING DOWN.

DEMONSTRATORS See HOOLIGANS.

DEVASTATING Generally kneejerk-twinned with BLOW.

DIALOGUE Talks ("meaningful"?), generally of the political/trades-union kind, from a Greek word for two people speaking to each other. Why not, for a change, "Me and my members are not prepared to sit down for a meaningful *colloquy* until there's something on the table..."? The heavens would probably fall in.

DIARISTS These (really gossip columnists) have come a long way since Samuel Pepys ended his daily journal with "So to bed." In newspapers they are fed by contributions from informants, publicity-seekers and their PR agents; from readers in general; and, in the tabloids, from scandal-sniffing freelances; also from disaffected employees and MOLES selling stolen secrets. Hoaxers sometimes feed diarists false information - then sit back to watch the RED FACES or the WRITS FLY. Gossip columnists are necessarily FREELOADERS. People with something to sell (or socialites merely hoping for publicity) invite them to parties, where diarists BUMP INTO celebrities. In all but the smallest papers diaries are the combined work of several reporters, although the person whose name heads the column takes both responsibility and credit. They assume a quaint corporate personality ("This column wishes him a speedy recovery...") and the present incumbent of "Atticus", a long-running political gossip-column in the *Sunday Times*, refers to himself in the pseudonymous third person, "Atticus hears that..." Since the advent of the *Independent* the diary scene in the quality papers has changed. At first it, too, had a gossip-column diary but it was far from independent and followed the tee-hee, egg-on-face *Schadenfreude* line, usually ending items with the traditional diarists' three-word quip, e.g.

"Watch this space"; or "We shall see"; or "Time will tell", etc. It was soon replaced by a real diary, called "My Week", in which different writers claim to relate what befell them during the previous seven days. *The Times* followed this trend, abolished its staff-written daily diary and handed it to what appears to be a rota of notabilities. Mr Pepys would be pleased. But he would probably now call his diary an ORGANISER.

DICING WITH DEATH Taking a risk, as reported in the news. Even a TODDLER can play this gambling-game although he wouldn't know a die, or set of dice, when he saw one.

DISHED UP The catering "joke", as in "Restauranteur [sic] Neville has dished up a new entertainment for his customers..." etc. See also CURRY-ING F(L)AVOUR.

DOCTOR News shorthand: "Dr Death", "Dr Sex", "Dr Slimming", etc. Most medical men are in fact "only" *Bachelors* of Medicine: "doctor" is a courtesy title until they pass a special examination few take. Political doctorates, especially African ones, are questionable for a different reason: they may be either self-awarded or obtained from strange institutions. Some writers have cast - possibly unfair - doubts on the provenance of *both* the titles of The Reverend Doctor Ian Paisley, perhaps because he often behaves like neither a REVEREND nor a doctor. His doctorate comes from the Bob Jones University in the USA. For other titles see DON, GURU, MANDARIN, BOFFIN, SUPREMO.

DOFF Usually applied only to hats. Press *ARCHAISM* and, like DON², a contraction.

DOGS OF WAR Mercenaries. Shakespeare in *Julius Caesar* let them *slip*, but journalists prefer to UNLEASH them, like bullets.

DON¹ (noun) Spanish for "mister" but used in English for a university teacher (lecturer or professor). Female dons don't seem to have noticed this, and so the equality industry has yet to insist on "donna". See also BOFFIN, GURU, MANDARIN, SIR.

DON² (verb) Press *ARCHAISM* for putting on an article of clothing, a contraction of "do on" (as DOFF is "do off"). As long ago as 1933 the first edition of the *Oxford English Dictionary* described it as archaic. Even the hardest-boiled hack would be taken aback if his wife said to him: "Don't forget to don a tie before going out." Doffing, curiously enough, is slightly less old-fashioned, but applied only to hats.

DOORSTEPPING Media euphemism for laying siege to and harassing supposedly newsworthy people, e.g. HEARTBREAK MUMS.

DOUBLE TROUBLE Stock cliché for news about twins. From an old film.

DOWN¹ (verb) See TO UP.

DOWN² (verb) How journalists think people consume drinks, when CORKS POP and champagne is QUAFFED.

DOWNBEAT See UPBEAT.

DRAMA Any STORY reported in the papers. With a FOLLOW-UP it may become a SAGA, possibly ONGOING.

DREAMING SPIRES Brought out at the merest mention of Oxford or other universities. If a NIGHTMARE can be discovered that disturbs the dreams, so much the better for the *STORY*. The words come from *Thyrsis* by Matthew Arnold (1822-1888):

> And that sweet City with her dreaming spires,
> She needs not June for beauty's heightening.

(KNOWING THE) DRILL Cliché for dentists. See also (A) BITTER PILL.

DRAGGED See KICKING AND SCREAMING.

DRAGGING FEET Delay or inaction, e.g. "The Government have [!] been dragging its [!] feet". Plural confusions may vary the implied number of feet.

DRIVING AMBITION For motorists, especially young or ambitious ones - probably IN THE DRIVING SEAT or "moving into" the FAST LANE.

DUB Medieval word meaning "to invest in a dignity or title", as when the Queen ceremonially touches her new knight's shoulder with the flat part of a sword (though some of the more eccentric recommendations from previous governments MIGHT have tempted her to turn it 90 degrees). Like DON², seldom if ever used by ordinary people, but survives as one of the sillier press *ARCHAISMS* - an affected way of saying "called" or "named". And AKA.

DUOS/TRIOS Musical terms for up to four people. There are no quintets and sextets for hacks: they use instead the *FAMOUS FIVE CLICHÉ*. Radio and TV news editors also admit duos and trios, although Radio 3 understandably reserves them for musical use.

DUSTBIN JOURNALISM Americans have dignified this with the name of "Garbology" and even made it into a university faculty - the study of a person's life-style and personal habits by examining the garbage he discards. Also a kind of back-DOORSTEPPING, cheaper than CHEQUE BOOK JOURNALISM. Journalists in search of a STORY go dustbin-grubbing, e.g. at Gordonstoun School, where an enterprising HACK stole Prince Charles's essays and sold them to the international press. The resulting new Mercedes was the envy of this garbologist's colleagues, but he put the earnings to good use, became a media MOGUL and provided many with employment. Eventually the WHEEL OF FORTUNE slowly but sweetly turned full-circle. At an artistic function which the ex-journalist's now prospering firm had generously sponsored, the Prince of Wales was guest of honour. Special Branch detectives did their best to keep the two apart.

DYNAMITE Journalist's ARSENALS contain armoury like BOMBSHELLS and MINEFIELDS - "political", "potential", "veritable", etc.

E

EATERIES Where DIARISTS go FREELOADING before dancing the night away at NITERIES.

ELEMENTS People. Whenever there is a demonstration at a university, "*outside* elements" are blamed; and policemen speak of *unruly* ones. In a modern *Messiah* the first tenor recitative might be "Comfort ye, my elements" (and it would fit better to Handel's music than the original "pee-hee-ple").

(THE) END OF THE LINE One of the railway clichés, like MAKING TRACKS, JUST THE TICKET, SIGNALLED, etc.

ENGULFED *ARCHAISM* usually followed by "in flames".

ENTHUSED See SMILED.

EQUATION Mathematical term misused as a fancy substitute for "problem", "question", "position", or other simple words; and see PARAMETERS and QUANTUM LEAP. Also on radio and TV - see *MediaSpeak*.

-ER or -OR? A generation ago it would have been rare to see in print "protestor" for protester or "imposter" for impostor, but endings are now often confused: writers seem to rely on a fifty-fifty chance of getting it right. There is no useful rule about *-er/-or* endings but in general a *person* is*er* (protest*er*, supervis*er*, play*er* and snapp*er*-up of unconsidered trifles), while *inanimates* take *-or* : (motor, rotor, carburettor, etc.). There are inevitable exceptions: impostor (above), dictator, assessor, professor and propeller. Good spelling is not a matter of *learning* but of *reading* and getting used to the "look" of words. This requires eye-experience; but alas, in this age of television, the young get little reading-practice, and if they don't often come face-to-face with a word they can hardly be expected to remember what it *looks* like - just as they would not recognise their first cousin if they never came face-to-face with him.

ESCALATION Fashionable since the late 1950s for anything already bad but thought to be getting worse - violence, inflation, etc. The *OED* included it only in 1972, dating the first use 1938, when the *Kansas City Star* explained, *"Escalation means the building of bigger battleships when other nations do so."* Previously the word had been applied only to travelling on escalators, which of course go down as well as up.

ESCORT Innuendo/euphemism for a woman's male lover, their NAMES LINKED. See also LIFE-LONG COMPANION, CLOSE FRIEND.

ESTRANGED Usually applied by newsmen to a wife or a husband - an *ARCHAISM* seldom used elsewhere.

-ETER* or *-ETRE? The *-eter* ending generally applies to a measuring instrument or appliance: gasometer, speedometer, voltmeter and clap-o-meter (for measuring television applause, not diagnosing SOCIAL DIS-EASE); and the *-etre* to the distance: metre, centimetre, kilometre. For the "wrong" pronunciation "ki*lom*eter" see *MediaSpeak*.

EX- Prefix of confusion, as in "Ex-silent film pianist Francis King...", who is presumably no longer silent, and "Ex-Labour minister..." who has left the Labour Party but is still a minister (though in 1978/9 the Conservatives did have an "ex-Labour Minister" - Mr Reginald Prentice, who resigned from Labour to become a Conservative minister!). Try "the former ..." See also ANTI- and *HYPHENS,* whose absence can destroy sense.

EXCLUSIVE Often followed by "tag". When applied to a *STORY,* the claim to exclusivity is often dubious. A very ordinary picture of a woman sitting informally in a perfectly ordinary manner, was captioned: "Sue Lawley, posing exclusively for the *Sunday Times* yesterday". When one paper is about to RUN an exclusive, others are sure to have a SPOILER to discredit or pre-empt it.

EXECUTION "Terrorists have executed an Italian businessman": the correct word is *murder.* In spite of widespread complaints from readers and listeners some newsmen are still reluctant to take the side of the law.

EXPATRIOT Common mis-spelling of "expatriate" brought about by the almost universal mispronunciation "ex-pat-ree-ot" (see *MediaSpeak*). One day perhaps a patriotic expatriate will sue.

EXPLICIT Euphemism for "sexually explicit", or "adult".

EXPOSE Phoney-French for exposure, like EXTRAORDINAIRE. Al-though the final *e* never gets its acute accent, the word is pronounced pidgin-French "ex-*poe*-say". See *MediaSpeak*.

EXPOSED! As in "Exposed! The Ayatollah's Mistress!" Eye-catching gimmick word, like EXCLUSIVE!

EXTRAORDINAIRE Phoney-French, used in pseudo-French style *after* the noun: "flautist extraordinaire". Extraordinary is just as good. See also IRREPRESSIBLE.

F

FABULOUS Originally of a fable, i.e. a tale of imagination. Now alleged excellence (also "fabled", on the model of FAMED). See BRILLIANT, FANTASTIC, STUNNING.

FACE (verb) To expect or confront: used with such frequency and abandon that the meaning of the noun is forgotten. Hence "Villa Face Cream of Italy", "Tories Face Split Over Europe", "Gillette Workers Face Cuts", etc.

FACELIFT Cosmetic plastic surgery to remove wrinkles and "lift" sagging skin, but annexed to mean the repair, restoration or improvement of buildings and surrounding areas: "Face Lift for Dowager's Bottom" (a village in the South of England).

FACT CHECKERS Employed by a few enlightened publications - which save much money by avoiding litigation.

FACTS OF LIFE When I was young, knowing these meant one was aware of how babies were made. Today's facts of life are generally economic, political, harsh or realistic.

FADE What hopes do: first raised and then perhaps DASHED. Where headline space is short, hopes can absurdly and untransitively "lift".

FALKLANDS HERO *Any* member of the armed forces who merely *took part* in the Falklands War ("Falklands Hero on Fraud Charge"). Veterans of previous wars had to win a bravery medal to qualify.

FALLING FLAT What cyclists - sometimes balloonists - do when their efforts at RIDING (or FLYING) HIGH fail or are PUNCTURED.

FALL OUT Hair-and-baldness cliché, uneasily leaning on the nuclear threat. But there is another kind of fall-out: waste paper loosely stuffed into magazines. Bookstall floors are littered with fallen-out junk advertising. Some come with reply-paid envelopes, so that one can post the rubbish back (with suitable comments - yes, even to charities) - for litter-louts should be made to pay.

FALSE SINGULARS/PLURALS The commonest is the media "itself", while "agenda" and "propaganda" are the most commonly-cited examples of eventual acceptability - the latter wrongly, as it has a singular origin. Misuse eventually wins, although those who do not wish to be taken for ignoramuses (not "ignorami") are free to use the proper form. Many mistaken singulars are spread by technicians and scientists. e.g. "this data is..." But when a doctor says, "This bacteria is..." prospective patients should interpret it as a warning: if he doesn't know *that* there may be a great deal more he is ignorant of. The singular of "criteria" is "criterion": the London restaurant of that name was intended to be the *one and only* criterion ("a test ... or standard by which anything is judged" - *OED*), not a profusion of standards. But spiritualist mediums are not "media".

FALSE VERBATIM An answer rewritten to suit the interviewer's purpose. Thus when he asks, "Do you think this show is an outrage?" and the reply is something like, "Well, yes, um, er, I suppose so", the resulting report may read, "GRUFFED father of six Ron (65), This show is an absolute outrage!" Question: "Will you be seeing your former wife while you're in London?" Real answer: "No, she's away somewhere on the continent". Printed answer: " SIGHED Frank, 84, 'I will definitely not be seeing estranged wife Rosie, 35, while I'm London'". To some extent manufactured quotations are unavoidable because they remove the interviewee's hesitations and repetitions, and combine several replies into one ALLEGED statement. But the papers carry things too far: some journalists even manufacture entire interviews with people they have never met. One, embarrassingly exposed after concocting an interview with a Falklands War widow, was universally BLASTED for her dishonesty - and then made editor of a tabloid paper. See also SMILED, SIGHED, QUIPPED, CHUCKLED, etc.

FAMED Preferred by newsmen to "famous". It suggests some sort of artificial process (like rice and coconuts are "creamed") and, when used of a media-created PERSONALITY, perhaps rightly. I wonder whether the children of some famous columnist say, "Daddy, when I grow up will I be famed like you?" See also FABULOUS.

'FAMOUS FIVE' CLICHÉ From a book-title by Enid Blyton, for any news STORY involving more than one person, usually miscreants - from the "Bradford Eleven", the "Cheltenham Ten" and the "Sharpeville Six" to the "Shrewsbury Two" - at any rate until one of these was released. Not even the silliest tabloid could then bring itself to refer to the remaining prisoner as the "Shrewsbury One". If the press had been present at the TROUBLES in Israel 2,000 years ago the Apostles would doubtless have been DUBBED the "Gethsemane Twelve". See also DUOS/TRIOS.

FAN Often used in headlines as well as the accompanying STORY when "hooligan" (or the full form of "fan", *fanatic*) would be more accurate. See also FOOTBALL SPECIAL and SQUAD.

FAST LANE "Jackie Stewart lives in the fast lane..." - an almost actionable thing to write about a professional driver. Or "After years of stagnation the British motor industry is at last moving into the fast lane, AND THAT'S OF-FICIAL..." Writers of such clichés would fail their driving-test, for there is no "fast" lane. In Britain, as police and road safety experts keep reminding us, we drive on the *left*, and move into *an outside* lane only for overtaking - after which we return to the left-hand-most lane available. And that *is* official. See also TOP GEAR and FIRMLY IN THE DRIVING SEAT.

FAVOURITE TIPPLE See WASHING DOWN, QUAFFING, etc.

FEATHERS FLY During FOWL PLAY, no doubt, when there is FURY among bird-fanciers, bird-watchers, aviarists, etc., and they get RUFFLED or IN A FLAP. With other creatures FUR FLIES, or there is HORSEPLAY. Kangaroo-fanciers and FROGS get HOPPING MAD.

FIANCÉE A female betrothed. *Her* intended is her fiancé, but journalists usually unisex them (like BLONDES) and forget the acute accent.

FIENDS In the newspapers these can be all things to all HACKS and come in two sorts: one, a kind of devilish figure, enemy or evil-doer (as in FIEND KILLS SIX ON TRAIN, or WALDHEIM NAZI FIEND?) the other an enthusiast, e.g. fresh air fiend, cricket fiend, etc.

FIGHTING FOR (HIS) LIFE Little more, alas, than a cheap dramatising cliché. The notion that a person *in extremis*, unconscious and probably wired up to all kinds of medico-technological equipment, is doing any *fighting* is absurd. See also CRITICAL.

FIRE See BLAZE and INFERNO.

FISHY TAILS The cliché for angling, anglers and, of course, the "mermaid" publicity stunt - see *PICTURE CLICHÉS*.

FIXED ABODE *ARCHAISM* used in newspapers and legal talk but not everyday speech.

FLAK Seven decades after World War I people still "take the flak" (*ACRONYM* for a German anti-aircraft gun), are STRAFED (from German *strafen*, to punish) but the terms have now been trivialised, like SHELL SHOCK. Some wrongly spell it "flack" (which is the USA word for a HACK).

FLAMBOYANT Chiefly applied to people in the public eye who affect some eccentricity of dress, even men who wear bow-ties ("Flamboyant Peer Lord Wyatt"). Every British Parliament has one or two members whose dress qualifies them for flamboyance, although LOONY exhibitionist MPs who dress aggressively "working-class" (which the House considers inappropriate) are not so described. The *OED* definition is "flamingly or gorgeously coloured".

FLASHBULBS POPPED AS... News *ARCHAISM*. Years ago newsmen's flashbulbs not only "popped" but occasionally exploded. They have been superseded by electronic flash devices for at least two decades.

FLEET STREET Originally the site of a stinking open sewer, the River Fleet; later, and until recently, the home of the London and national press (and therefore its metonymous name). But during the 1980s and after the defeat of the print unions it was discovered that newspapers could be produced from smaller premises with fewer people, hence the exodus to less expensive areas of London.

FLIED LICE See SWEET AND SOUR. Also CURRYING F(L)AVOUR.

FLIGHT(S) OF FANCY Stock pun and *COLONIC IRRITATION* for anything aeronautical, like FLYING HIGH.

FLOOR According to ancient usage the *floor* is indoors, made of flag-stones, tiles, wooden boards, etc., whereas the *ground* is outside and usually earth or stone. In the media this is no longer so. Had the Bible been written by a journalist (see STRATEGIC PLACES) the first murderer (*Genesis* 3,10) would have heard God say, "The voice of thy brother cryeth unto me from the floor" - and on the *floor* Onan, too, would have spilt his seed, the BEAST.

FLUSHED With pride, success, etc.- the standard lavatorial cliché, like CHAIN REACTIONS.

FLYER News word, never heard from ordinary lips, for someone who pilots aircraft. Sometimes twinned with LONE (and see below). In USA English a flyer is a throwaway printed leaflet (from the German *Flugblatt* = "flying leaf").

FLYING HIGH *The Observer* once printed a memorable photograph of a ballooning meeting. None of the aircraft was more than about ten feet from the FLOOR, and one or two had failed to GET OFF THE GROUND at all. But the kneejerk caption was (YES YOU' VE GUESSED - see *MediaSpeak* - WAIT FOR IT) "Flying High". Perhaps it is all the fault of Icarus, the FABULOUS first man to fly high (doubtless ON A WING AND A PRAYER) though he only succeeded in FALLING FLAT. See also FLIGHTS OF FANCY, RIDING HIGH, MAKING TRACKS, JUST THE TICKET and the rest.

FOLLOW-UP A sequel to a STORY which itself is probably a LIFT from another paper. Few news-items remain EXCLUSIVE for long. Newspaper journalists avidly watch the television news; conversely, radio and televi-sion editors scan the first copies of the morning papers. Most news items on breakfast television, on the *Today* programme, on *The World at One*, *PM* and *The World Tonight* (to name only a few) will also have appeared in the papers or will be followed up by them if radio/TV got to the *STORY* first. The student of the media can usually trace a news-item back to its source. For example, a Sunday paper carried an article by its medical correspondent which had itself been lifted from one of the specialist medical journals. It was based on a researcher's findings that in a named English village no boys had been born during a certain period. This was printed under the headline "Girls and Girls come out to Play". A few days later the Radio 4 programme *You and Yours* not only lifted the story without mentioning either source but also made verbal sport with the headline the paper had used. Yet on many occasions when a follow-up in the same paper *would* be welcome there is none. A little old lady knocked down in the street makes news, but the fact that she is recovering does not.

FOOT-IN-DOOR REPORTING *DOORSTEPPING* reporters in pursuit of a *STORY*, especially an *EXCLUSIVE*, are taught to be persistent (and if necessary, unpleasant): never more so than when harassing bereaved persons. Whenever you read "The victim's parents were too upset to talk" you can be sure that a *RATPACK* had insensitively besieged them.

FORCED TO As in "After the withdrawal of the bus service children have been forced to walk home in the dark along a narrow lane..." Perhaps Shakespeare's "whining schoolboy, with his satchel and shining morning face, creeping like snail unwillingly to school" had occasionally to be taken by the scruff of the neck and *forced* to make his way there. The children in the news report above were not "forced" to walk to school. They "had to" (or were "obliged to") walk, the only force being that of circumstances.

FOREVER No: two separate words; and Rupert Brooke's corner of a foreign field is *for ever* England. As the poet C. S. Calverly wrote:

> Never more must printer do
> As men did long ago; but run
> *For* into *ever*, bidding two be one.

FORMICA Every time someone calls a washable plastic material for table-tops "formica", he or she will receive a stern and rather ill-humoured letter from its manufacturers. They point out that it is a registered trade name which is entirely their property, requires a capital F and must not be applied to any other product purporting to have similar qualities. The firm is fighting a losing battle, as aspirin, vaseline, Y-FRONTS, hoover and others did before them; and should feel flattered to be in such grand company. At present "Perrier" is becoming the generic name for any kind of fizzy, bottled drinking-water - which is deplorable, because England, Scotland and Wales can bottle and aerate water equal (or superior) to the French stuff (though Perrier is naturally-fizzed). If only British exporters could achieve similar

BREAKTHROUGHS, "Margate" could one day be the generic name for sand exported to Bahrain.

FORTE Contrary to common belief this does not mean *loud* in Italian but *strong*. Although it is not incorrect to speak of someone's forte it might be better to speak of his *strength*.

FOUL PLAY As in "foul play is not suspected". *Play*? See also INTERFERED WITH.

FOWL PLAY When FEATHERS FLY.

FREEBIES and **FREELOADING** Reviewers and critics receive books, records and tickets to concerts free of charge, but do not always review them favourably. This is not always so with *TRAVEL WRITERS'* facility trips, which may be free holidays given in exchange for publicity.

FROGS Tabloids' name for the French, especially when some nasty foreign habit displeases a paper. See HOPPING MAD and KRAUTS.

FULL STEAM AHEAD Some fifty years after the disappearance of steamships, maritime projects not SUNK or SCUPPERED are still said to Go Full Steam Ahead. Sometimes, even more absurdly, SAILING HIGH.

FUMING What cigarette manufacturers and tobacconists do when things go against them. Some anti-smoking measures may even COST A PACKET.

(THE) FUR FLIES A disagreement, however mild and amiable, among breeders, exhibitors or lovers of dogs or cats. With bird-fanciers FOWL PLAY is suspected (or generated, with FURY) - and FEATHERS FLY. Truly there is no end to the witty ingenuity and inventiveness of the papers!

FURY SHOCK/HORROR word. Anything from slight disapproval to a dispute. Fury and anger always "erupt" - like boils and volcanoes. See also HITTING OUT.

G

GARBOLOGY See DUSTBIN JOURNALISM.

-GATE The corruption or political embarrassment cliché suffix. It began with Watergate (named after the burgled hotel) and although done to death shows no sign of waning.

GERIATRIC Sounds impressively scientific but in fact a newish word: the *OED* did not list it before 1972 because the proper word for things to do with old age was, and still is, "gerontic" (from Greek *gerontos*, an old man). "Geriatric" came into fashion with the welfare state and soon crossed over into industrial and general use, for worn-out machinery, etc. The word contains the *-iatric* suffix (from *iatros*, a doctor), and should really refer to persons who are both old and sick. Like other medical words, e.g. CANCER and SPASTIC, it is best left to doctors.

GETTING A CANING What happens to SIR if he is reprimanded, disadvantaged or SLAMMED.

GETTING A TASTE OF THEIR OWN MEDICINE Doctors or pharmacists suffering a setback: perhaps (A) BITTER PILL TO SWALLOW.

GETTING OFF THE GROUND Ludicrous aeronautical cliché used for any venture, however earth-bound ("Liverpool Airport started to get off the ground in the 1970s...").

GETTING SHIRTY A 1930s colloquialism preserved only in media clichés, e.g. "Customers are getting shirty with West End tailors..."

GIVING/GETTING THE PIP The apples/oranges/lemons cliché.

GIVING/GETTING THE CHOP The butchers' cliché - and see (PUT) THROUGH THE MINCER.

GLITTERATI Made from "glitter" and "literati", i.e. famous literary persons, usually when attending some publicity function, at which no doubt FLASHBULBS POP. And see also, below -

GLITZ(Y) *DIARISTS'* favourite word meaning full of showbiz PIZZAZZ and RAZZMATAZZ. See *MEDIA UGLIES*.

GLOBE TROTTER An old-fashioned word for a traveller. Now seldom heard but frequently seen in the papers, e.g. about a LONE traveller.

(THE) GLORY OF THE GARDEN Ready-made horticultural cliché, also useful for Covent Garden Opera House. From a poem by Kipling.

GOING MISSING I have ranted against this foolish cliché elsewhere, but to no avail. People go walking, hiking, shopping, fishing or pub-crawling, but there is no such action as "*going* missing". Some unfortunate person who after having gone on an expedition is never seen again might have *disappeared*, but he did not "go missing" - though the fictional Reginald Perrin who, like a former government minister, faked his disappearance, might have done so intentionally. If newsmen had anything to do with it, Janacek's opera *The Man who Disappeared* would have been named in English "The Man who Went Missing".

GOLDEN GIRL Any winning female athlete or swimmer, etc., not necessarily one who gets an OLYMPIC gold medal. Golden boys are rarer, and silver or bronze boys/girls unknown. But hyperbole is rife, as in "Anna Bolyk-Steroidova yesterday became the fastest woman on earth..." (as if there were extra-terrestrial athletes).

GOOD CIGAR All media-mentioned cigars are invariably "good", just as binoculars are always POWERFUL, and battles always PITCHED.

(THE) GOOD TURN HEADLINE Hardly a week passes when the once-great *Liverpool Daily Post* or *Echo* do not print stories like "Pensioner's Good Turn Leads to Tragedy".

GRAB Dramatising word: "state grab" for nationalisation, "tax grab" for a tax bill, etc. See also UP FOR GRABS.

GRANNY Any female person over sixty (or thereabouts) who figures in the news. The description is applied without inquiry into her status: whether she is single, married, has had children, or if these also had issue and so made her into a grandmother. Grannyhood is indiscriminately thrust on the elderly, including SPINSTERS. "Grand-dad" (often confusingly "Grand Dad") is used more rarely.

GRAPHICS Imaginative diagrams purporting to show what happened in, or brought about, some newsworthy event which inconveniently provided no *PHOTO OPPORTUNITY,* e.g. a hijack, siege or terrorist attack. Graphics have proliferated with the spread of computer-generated drawings: over-dramatised and over-simplified, with emblems borrowed from strip cartoons, e.g. big, jagged-edged hollow stars ("Explosion Here") and flashes coming out of guns ("First shot fired here"); or sinister figures ("Intruders entered by roof light"). Only "Wha-a-a-m" and "Ker-pow" are missing. All papers use graphics - and comparisons show how conjectural they are. See also *GRAPHICS* in *MediaSpeak.*

GREEN LIGHT "Getting (or giving) the green light": one of the traffic and transport clichés. RED LIGHT, however, can be misunderstood.

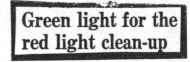

Green light for the red light clean-up

GRIM SHOCK-HORROR adjective, often associated with corpses: when these are recovered or examined it is always a "grim task".

GRISLY Applied, like GRIM, to human remains, usually of murder victims, e.g. "Stolen Van Reveals Grisly Secret".

GROUP Often a euphemism for "gang". The media are nervously evenhanded when reporting TERRORIST crimes. Thus the gang thought to have been responsible for the Pan Am bomb outrage was described by most papers as "Abu Nidal and his group", like some foolishly harmless pop band.

GRUFFED See SMILED.

GUIDELINES Guide-ropes and guide-lines (i.e. actual ropes) have existed in specialist applications since the 19th century, but figurative guidelines, now so common, were imported from the German *Richtlinien* only since the last war.

GURU The Hindustani word for a teacher or mentor, and (though by implication only) a priest, like the Hebrew *rabbi*. See also BOFFIN, DON, SIR, MANDARIN, SUPREMO, etc.

GYMSLIP MUM A schoolgirl (too young to be a COMMON LAW WIFE) who gives birth to a BUNDLE OF JOY. See also BRAVE, TODDLER and cross-references.

H

HACK *OED* definitions include (and I have chosen them with careful discrimination): "a sorry or worn-out horse...let out for hire", "a literary drudge who hires himself out to do any and every kind of literary work; hence, a poor writer, a mere scribbler"; "a prostitute, a bawd"; "hackneyed, trite, commonplace"; "to mangle or make a hash of'"; "to make rough cuts" (see *SUBS*); etc. No wonder journalists in need of a self-description reach for their large stock of *ARCHAISMS* and facetiously call themselves SCRIBES.

HAMMERING Britain may no longer be a manufacturing nation, but wages and other agreements are "hammered out".

HANDING DOWN What judges are said to do with their sentences. If the accused is acquitted he always WALKS FREE.

HANDS-ON New media and business jargon-term, usually combined with other words, e.g. "hands-on management", in which, say, a boss takes personal charge of things others may delegate to their subordinates. (As - perhaps rather unfortunately - in "Cleveland social services bosses have VOWED to initiate a hands on policy on detecting child abuse". (More rarely "hands-off", for a more relaxed approach). Although I HYPHENate the term, newspapers usually don't bother.

HANKY PANKY Originally meant harmless trickery or deceit, a gently jocular word which, with its jingling, juvenile reduplication, was used by *Punch* in 1841 in a satirical mock court-case involving the Lords Melbourne and Russell, in which the former says to the latter: "Oh! Johnny, this is your work - with your confounded hanky-panky." It now always refers to sexual misdemeanours, like KISS AND CUDDLE, KISS AND TELL, "slap and tickle" and, to a lesser extent, HORSEPLAY. (The "and" can always be abbreviated, e.g. KISS 'N' TELL).

HASTENING (THITHER) Favoured in stilted *DIARY* prose. Some diarists do not *see*, they SPY (with or without their little eye); never *come from* or *go to* anywhere but go "hither" or "thither" and "whither"; and (like policemen) do not *go* but "proceed" open sentences with "methinks" and write facetious drivel like: "...so I hied me along". More *ARCHAISMS* will

> All the same, spying two policemen outside the bank, I hastened to tell them of the theft; all they did was to pester me for the name of my employer. I had taken out another £150 and, in dumb show, proceeded to demonstrate how difficult it was to nick a bundle of fivers not bound by a lassy band. The sight of the notes almost got me arrested.

be found elsewhere in this book, e.g. *QUOTH HE.*. The cutting shown here, by a columnist on a London evening paper, is a good example of facetiously-archaic usage. It seems to flow more naturally from female writers than males. Notice also the word "lassy", which in that spelling may have puzzled readers. What was meant was "lazzy", a recent abbreviation of "elastic bands" - which have been part of everyday life ever since the Post Office started buying them in billions to discard on our doorsteps.

HATS Play an important part in *PICTURE CLICHÉS*. In prose they are largely confined to being "thrown into the ring" - by politicians announcing their candidature for election. (Some later throw car-keys into swimming-pools, but that's another kind of "ballgame" - see *IN-WORDS*).

HAVE A GO A person who fights off a burglar, robber, mugger, etc. - e.g. "have a go granny" or "have a go pensioner". Also BATTLING.

HEADACHES Come in various sizes, ranging from giant to MAJOR.

HEADS, BODIES, ARMS and LEGS See cuttings opposite.

HEARTACHE An often-diagnosed pain which can culminate in a -

HEARTBREAK In the view of SCRIBES, hearts are easily broken, and "Heartbreak" can be followed by any of the other media words the press gives to us: i.e. "Heartbreak Mum".

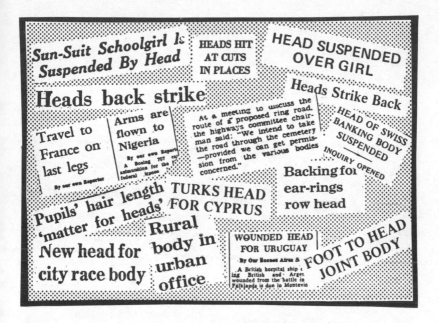

Sun-Suit Schoolgirl Is Suspended By Head

HEADS HIT AT CUTS IN PLACES

HEAD SUSPENDED OVER GIRL

Heads back strike

Heads Strike Back

Travel to France on last legs

Arms are flown to Nigeria

At a meeting to discuss the route of a proposed ring road. the highways committee chairman said: "We intend to take the road through the cemetery —provided we can get permission from the various bodies concerned."

HEAD OF SWISS BANKING BODY SUSPENDED

INQUIRY OPENED

Backing for ear-rings row head

Pupils' hair length matter for heads'

TURKS HEAD FOR CYPRUS

New head for city race body

Rural body in urban office

WOUNDED HEAD FOR URUGUAY

FOOT TO HEAD JOINT BODY

HEARTLESS Usually coupled with "thieves", as in "Heartless thieves yesterday robbed BATTLING pensioner Annie of £97.00, representing her LIFE SAVINGS". The word CALLOUS is also sometimes used for such reports. But journalists who camp outside an afflicted or bereaved person's house, *DOORSTEPPING* in the hope of a STORY and pictures, are never described as either callous or heartless.

HEIR Used more precisely than HEIRESS (below), e.g. when referring to an English hereditary title succession. It has only two punning possibilities, and they are endlessly flogged: "Heir Today", "Heirs and Graces", etc. Open any copy of *The Guardian* and Heirs will be sprouting somewhere.

HEIRESS Any woman whose father is assumed to be rich: and a fine example of the thoughtlessness that characterises tabloid prose; journalists are seldom if ever acquainted with testamentary provisions, if any, her father might have made; for all they know daddy might have left his millions to his dog, and the dog to his mistress. Qualifications are common, e.g. "Gold Heiress" for a female whose father owns a goldmine; and "Turkey Heiress" for a Miss Matthews, whose father made a fortune slaughtering turkeys.

HERALDIC MOTTOES Whenever a member of the aristocracy is in the news (preferably because of some kind of scandal) the practised SCRIBE will look for the family motto in *Debrett*. This is generally in Latin, but he will try to twist a translation that suits his *STORY*. See also *TITLES*.

HIGH NOTES "Hitting" or "striking" these is the most common music cliché in the papers, from the way the naively non-musical are immensely impressed when a singer "hits a high note". This may be a tremendous feat for a soprano, but if the singer happens to be a low bass, singing the role of Osmin in Mozart's *Die Entführung*, he will impress by his ability to hit *low* notes. Disagreement in a musical context heralds the inevitable SOUR NOTE. See also STRINGS ATTACHED.

HIT Available in various feebly-punning combinations with "Miss" or "myth". See also THIGHFUL and other stalwarts.

HIT FOR SIX What happens to a cricketer when he meets a setback, or is STUMPED, e. g. "Visa Ban Hits Trinidadian cricketer's hopes for six" (*The Daily Telegraph*) - just as a boxer's hopes are KO'd, golfers "stymied" or BUNKERED, etc., *ad nauseam*. But anyone, male or female, cricketer or not, who qualifies for that centenary "telemessage" from the Queen, is always 100 NOT OUT.

HITTING OUT Complaining about, or attacking, something or somebody. See also TONGUE LASHING, and cuttings opposite.

HO HUM A meaningless facetious rider to a sentence - a sort of verbal shrug of the shoulders - now enjoying a vogue among DIARISTS.

HOPEFULLY See *MediaSpeak*.

HOPPING MAD Cliché for FROGS, etc. (e.g. the headline "HOP OFF YOU FROGS" when the *Sun* expressed disapproval of some French action).

The Hacks' Bible, Exodus 10, would have written "Egyptian farmers were hopping mad yesterday as fields were HIT by a plague of locusts MAKING A MEAL of all things that remained..." etc). But in these more prosaic times we have to make do with reports like "Scientists at a Merseyside frog research laboratory were hopping mad YESTERDAY when they discovered that animal liberationists..." Every kangaroo *STORY*, too, has its quota of uncontrolled hopping insanity. One reporter even described an AMPUTEE as hopping mad, for which he was duly sacked, I hope. (See also HITTING OUT.) And when a marsupial escapes from a zoo, the keepers are sure to have been "caught on the hop".

HOROSCOPES Confidence tricks played on readers by the publishers of downmarket newspapers. The idea that the world is divided into twelve kinds of people who share a common destiny according to their "sign" proves only one thing: there's a fool born every minute. Other foolish horoscopes claiming to be Chinese allege that the *year* of one's birth separates the sheep from the goats, the tigers from the pigs. Many horoscopes are expensively syndicated on a wide scale, snapped up by cynical editors for their gullible readers, but some are really the work of local hacks who enjoy concocting them (as they do for *AGONY COLUMNS*), planting silly jokes for each others' amusement.

HORROR See SHOCK.

HORSEPLAY In Middleton's play *The Mayor of Queenborough* (1627) a character says: "Fellows, you use no horse-play in my house". What he meant was the slightly boisterous behaviour men engage in when perhaps a little drunk. Horseplay today is one of the sexually-suggestive SAUCY words, along with the unlovely KISS AND CUDDLE and HANKY PANKY twins. But stories featuring a horse or horses may also have journalistic horseplay in it. And, if at all possible, something about the horse's mouth. Straight from it, with or without "horse sense".

LIBRA (September 24—October 22): Good day for business planning; also for handling anything which is especially private to you.

SCORPIO (October 23 to November 22). — A time when it shows how necessary it is for the true Scorpio male to take himself in hand. If this is done correctly there will be a real burst of activity and pleasure.

GEMINI (May 21—June 21) LAY the foundations now for what is intended add to future security. Very important day if you're trying to get a mortgage. Uranus adds a touch of novelty to what you're doing this evening.

SCORPIO (October 23-November 21): Lot of family planning going on during the week-end, and, if you are a parent, you

HOSTELRY Newsmen's mock-facetious *ARCHAISM* for a pub. The landlord is "mine host".

HOTLY REFUTED The two go together like birds of a feather: things are apparently never "refuted" in a calm or cool manner - though the writer in any case usually means not refuted but *denied*.

HOT UNDER THE COLLAR What clergymen get when they are annoyed, perturbed, or express mildly contentious views.

HUBBY Seldom used by ordinary people: a space-saving newspaper abbreviation for "husband".

HUMAN CHAIN Two or more people linking hands.

HUMAN TORCH Any person on fire - which "engulfs" - an *ARCHAISM*.

HURTLE Like PLUNGE and PLUMMET, a dramatising news word (really archaic English seldom seen or heard elsewhere) for things that fall. Things that go upwards always SOAR.

HUSTLED AWAY Whereas celebrities and other newsworthy people are WHISKED AWAY by journalists who have bought their story, anyone making a nuisance of himself, e.g. a protester in the public gallery of the House of Commons, is "quickly *hustled* away".

HYPE Artificial publicity, generated by Public Relations men who hope to present their GLITZY product (usually an artificially produced PERSONAL-ITY) as full of PIZZAZZ, RAZZMATAZZ and other MEDIA UGLIES grate-fully accepted by *DIARISTS*.

HYPHENS "The primary function of the hyphen is to indicate that two or more words are to be read together as a single word with its own meaning". So say the textbooks. In reality, not only hyphens but most other punctua-tion-marks have fallen victim to careless English-teaching. Semicolons and colons are seldom encountered, even in the literary journals: most writers are unaware of their subtle function. Because the crude prose of tabloids seems to get along without them, the better papers shun them, too. Hyphens, however, are essential to meaning. If the reader is obliged to read a sentence twice, or three times, before he understands it then the writer has failed him. Are they boring tools or boring-tools? Is a guinea pig cheap at the price, like a tuppenny bun? What is superfluous about the superfluous hair remover? Was he the best Russian speaker or the best Russian-speaker? Is the headline BRIDE TO BE MURDERED a report or a threat? And when a writer asks "Do You Want a Woman Vicar?" is he offering to procure sex for the incum-bent? Can you tell the difference between a pedestrian-crossing and a pedestrian crossing? Can the walking stick walk? Do they mean a light house keeper, a light-house keeper, or a light house-keeper? If the king had six foot soldiers and ten cross bow men, how tall were the soldiers and what made the bowmen cross? A fellow-feeling in the bosom is not the same as a fellow feeling in the bosom; my great-uncle was, alas, not a great uncle. Did she go on a record buying-spree or a record-buying spree? It was the latter, in the report of a murder-case, but neither the papers nor the BBC news made it clear. In both written and spoken English a hyphen would make it clear: in print, to the eye, by joining what belongs together; and in sound, because the joining determines the required word-stress: "a *record*-buying spree" or "a record *buying*-spree". Omitting a hyphen could even cost you money: the well-known Mr Wiesenthal is a nazi-hunter. Call him a nazi hunter and he could sue. The more information a clumsy writer tries to convey the worse the confusion, like a stained glass designer or hot dog sales man. A murder-victim is confusingly described as a homosexual Turkish bath attendant. Was he a homosexual Turk who attended bathers,

Sheep worrying: appeal to dog owners

A hot dog salesman was led away with an eye gashed and bleeding after about 50 youths overturned his stall.

DO YOU WANT A WOMAN VICAR?

INTERESTING TALL BOYS AT JAMES ADAM'S SALE

The King had five foot soldiers and six cross bow men with him wherever he travelled.

ZAIRE'S flamboyant, currently troubled President Mobuto, took Mr Huang Hua, Chinese Foreign Minister for a ride in his leopard skin-seated helicopter yesterday to her arrival was greeted by a fly past of the islands' three Dakotas and the hoots and sirens of a small armada of yachts who went out to meet Britannia and her escort ship HMS Antrim.

Giant pay out bid to beat court

HORSE BACK UP SNOWDON

DOCTORS REVIEW BODY

ANTI-PAY BED BOARD IS TO BE ABOLISHED

Approved School-master IVOR COOK: "I was snubbed by my colleagues."

AWARD FOR ANTI-SNAKE BITE RESEARCH

vigilantes would take the law into their own hands over the murder of a homosexual Turkish bath attendant.

When he returned, he said there had been clear evidence of sheep rustling on the mountainside.

The Carl Davis-William Rushton musical thriller, "Sir Harry North's Last Case", won its laughs, though heaven help anyone who has to hear this undergraduate-type pastiche a

New help on sick notes

Whilst appreciating that large new organisations will have settling in problems, this flooring defect is an obvious danger

Charles Rupert Moore, stained glass designer and aeronautical artist, died on July 21. He was 77.

Delight on the faces of Dirk Treber, chairman of the Hesse environmental party, and his running mate, Priska Hinz, after the election results were announced.

From his sick bed at Wigan Infirmary Andy, his body a mass of bumps and bruises, said: "I don't remember the accident it happened so quickly.

and among the assembled guests were the mayor and many other big wigs who seemed to enjoy a

THE 500 francs costs imposed on Olympic athlete Sebastian Coe after a Lakeside punch up in Switzerland will be paid by the organisers of the Zurich athletics meeting.

UNIVERSITY OF MANCHESTER DEPARTMENT OF EXTRA MURAL STUDIES

or merely an attendant in a steam-bath who happened to be "gay"? One journalist claimed to have been given a ride by President Mobuto "in his leopard skin-seated helicopter" - and when we read, "Queen Juliana, with a leg in plaster yesterday swore in the Dutch parliament", we do not know whether the Dutch Queen administered an oath or uttered one.

I

I HEAR THAT... *DIARISTS'* code for "I was tipped off by an informant" or "I read in a public-relations PR press release that ..." See also BUMP INTO.

IMPORTANTLY As in "...and more importantly, I feel this is wrong..." The appropriate word in 999 instances out of a thousand is "important". I have yet to come across a satisfactory use of "importantly" - almost a non-word - but so fashionable! See HOPEFULLY, LARGELY and REPORTEDLY.

IN A FLAP What bird-fanciers, -breeders, etc., are when "ruffled" or FEATHERS FLY. "Solar Flare leaves Pigeon Fanciers in a Flap" (in *The Times* [!]) And see below.

IN A (FLAT) SPIN *ARCHAISM.* Pilots in the early days of fixed-wing flying dreaded a flat spin because it could lead to loss of control of their low-powered plane. The phenomenon has survived only in the imagination of mediamen, who have turned it into a cliché for anyone IN A FLAP. Non-flat spins, however, are for disc-jockeys - because they "spin" discs when they put records on the turntable: "Spoof chats get DJ in a spin".

IN A STEW Discomfited about food, as in "Fords canteen workers were in a stew YESTERDAY as..." and "Kangaroo Meat puts Australian MPs in a Stew; and "Hedgehog Crisps put Publicans in a Stew".

INFERNO See BLAZE.

INNER CITY A code for any deprived urban area, not necessarily inner or even in a city.

INSPIRED LEAK Intentional disclosure to journalists of supposedly secret information. Uninspired dislosures come from MOLES.

INSTANT VALUATIONS A journalist, as Oscar Wilde nearly said, "knows the price of everything and the value of nothing": "The victim, an £85,000 a year oil executive, was found in the lounge of his £135,000 house in Purley by his wife, a £40,000 a year fashion director. The intruders made off in his £90,000 Aston Martin, in which he had just taken the couple's son to his £3,500 a term public school after attending a £200 a head dinner ..."

and so on, *ad nauseam*. Figures stated are of course guesswork, for the purpose of such nonsense is merely to give some idea of a person's life-style.

IN STITCHES For any STORY about surgeons and their patients. Laugh? They nearly died.

INTERFERED WITH "Interference" is often a euphemism for *sexual* interference (just as "intercourse" was by implication "sexual"- though in the mid-1980s the catch-all word became "abuse": even tennis stars are now penalised for "racket abuse"!) The classic news-item reported

> the young woman's dismembered body was found by police in three separate shallow graves at the edge of the golf course. She had not been interfered with.

the discovery of the corpse of a young woman who had been horribly mutilated, dismembered and buried in several places - but, said the report, "she had not been interfered with". See also FOUL PLAY and VIOLATION.

IN TERMS OF... Mediawrite/speak for "about", e.g. "The Iraqis are talking in terms of a major victory".

INTERRELATIONSHIPS People do not usually have relationships with *themselves*, so "inter-" would appear to be superfluous.

IN THE DOGHOUSE A dog-owner in trouble or "dog-ged" by misfortune. See flying FUR and FEATHERS. WRITS also fly.

IN THE DRIVING SEAT Usually coupled with "firmly", e.g. "Mrs Thatcher was once again firmly in the driving seat when the Cabinet met yesterday..." Also used for motoring stories, of course.

IN THE WILDERNESS Biblical-sounding place where politicians, sportsmen, showbiz people and others wait before BOUNCING BACK, or else COMING IN FROM THE COLD.

INTRUSION Usually "unwarranted".

(NEWS) INVERSIONS Another form of the ATTRIBUTIVE PILE-UP, by which a list of a person's attributes etc. is dangled in front of his name.

> Indisputedly upper class and a formidable and resourceful opponent if crossed, she was born in 1907, second of three daughters of a colourful actor-manager Sir Gerald du Maurier. She took a

> Balding and bespectacled and just over five feet tall, Elton John was born plain Reginald Dwight in 1947, which makes

IRONING OUT See TEETHING TROUBLES.

IRREPRESSIBLE Double-edged journalistic description of people in the news: "Janet Kidd, the irrepressible only daughter of the 1st Lord Beaverbrook, has died aged eighty..." (a real example). This is like calling the vanquished invincible: death, alas, effectively repressed her.

-ISE/-IZE? Until 40 or 50 years ago many older people still wrote "surprize" as their fathers and grandfathers had done before them if they had a classical education. But the-*ize* ending has waned in recent decades and now only *The Times* prints "advertize" (perhaps following it with "advertising" in the next line). Even letter-writers who put "televise" may find that zealous sub-editors change it to "televize". But there are signs that even this paper, now part of a tabloids group, has begun to waver.

IRREVERSIBLE (BRAIN) DAMAGE A modish but nonsensical twin term. Damage can sometimes be *repaired*, never "reversed".

I THEN MADE AN EXCUSE AND LEFT This phrase figures in every journalist's report after he has investigated a massage parlour, brothel, pornography shop, etc., to indicate that he himself would never, but *never*, avail himself of such services. Not even in the course of duty - so he makes an excuse (which is never specified or described) and leaves.

J

JACK UP See (TO) UP.

JEEVES Generic media name for a man-servant, butler or valet, perhaps in an UPSTAIRS DOWNSTAIRS situation.

JEKYLL AND HYDE As in "My client is a Jekyll and Hyde character whose character completely changes when he has had a drink". The "client" is unlikely to have heard of R. L. Stevenson's strange tale, though he may have seen Danny Kaye as WALTER MITTY.

JOBLESS Shorter word for UNEMPLOYED.

JOY RIDING Car-stealing. There is no joy in it when innocent people get hurt or killed (too seldom the miscreants themselves). See COLLIDING.

JUST THE TICKET Railway and METER MAIDS cliché.

K

KERFUFFLE One of the *MEDIA UGLIES* group. This is actually a respectable old Scottish dialect word, properly *carfuffle*, to throw into chaos, confusion or disorder, from Gaelic *car* = a twist or turn + *fuffle* = dishevel, ruffle, disarrange (Robinson: *The Concise Scots Dictionary*).

KEY(S) See NOTE(S).

KICKED INTO TOUCH The bad-news cliché for footballers or their clubs, e.g. "Plans by Liverpool Football Club to extend their stand into Kemlyn Road were kicked into touch by the City Council as ..." They may also be RULED OFFSIDE, SHOWN THE RED CARD, the council might CRY FOUL or (BLOW THE) WHISTLE.

KICKING AND SCREAMING Over-used facetious cliché: "I was dragged kicking and screaming to his favourite NITERIE".

KID A child bigger than a TODDLER but perhaps younger than a teenager. "Kid" is a centuries-old nickname for a child, kept alive by papers because of its brevity. Many readers and listeners - and kids - hate the word and like to point out to adults that kids are the offspring of goats.

KISS-AND-CUDDLE Suggestive euphemism for illicit sexual activity, probably taking place in some other place than in a bed: perhaps a car, behind a filing-cabinet, or in some public or semi-public place. The media suggestion is that there was more than just kissing and cuddling. See also HANKY PANKY and HORSEPLAY. After the kiss-and-cuddle may come

KISS AND TELL The SAUCY memoirs of someone who (possibly induced by CHEQUE BOOK JOURNALISM) claims to reveal that HANKY PANKY/HORSEPLAY took place between her and a famous person.

KRAUT Tabloid word for Germans, even "friendly" ones, e.g. sportsmen. If these are bad-tempered, or at least not as magnanimous (in defeat or victory) as a hack expects them to be, they become "Sour Krauts". A SIEG HEIL or two (usually mis-spelt) may not be far behind. See FROGS, OLÉ.

L

LAD See BOYFRIEND and PENSIONER.

LAND (verb) In newspapers, jobs and contracts are always "landed", like fish, and if an *INSTANT VALUATION* is possible (e.g. "Wendy has landed a £30,000 a year job in America..."), so much the better.

LASHING OUT Condemning or HITTING OUT at something.

LASHINGS Plenty, especially of food or drink. See WASHING DOWN and cross-references, e.g. FAVOURITE TIPPLE, MUNCHING, QUAFFING, etc.

LATCH KEY KID A child of working parents; a neglected but self-reliant one, is implied.

LAY/LIE The next-most-common confusion after WHO/WHOM. "Lay" is a transitive verb: you lay something or somebody. "Now I lay me down to sleep", or "When Father laid the Carpet on the Stairs". That

> CRICKETER Ian Botham, bored with laying flat out in bed after his back operation, has been cheered by a visit from his close friend Elton John.

which has been laid lies. (Perhaps some people prefer the mock-genteel "lay" and "laid" because they remember that lying is a sin, or are simply afraid of being misunderstood). The confusion is compounded by old-established dialect and rustic usage, but jars when it occurs in the over-elaborate, stiltedly mock-archaic writing so often found in the papers.

LEITMOTIF (also often leitmotiv or leitmotive - but not "light locomotive"): in Wagner's operas, a theme associated with a particular character, thing or situation. In the journalistic cliché, a persistent thread or continuing argument. See also NOTE(S) and its cross-references pointing to other misuses of musical, scientific, medical and technical terms.

-LESS IN GAZA "Clueless in Gaza", "Homeless..." "Tieless..." etc. From John Milton, via Aldous Huxley's novel, *Eyeless in Gaza*.

LETHAL/DEADLY COCKTAIL See WASHING DOWN.

LICENCE TO ... A James Bond-based cliché: from *Licence to Kill*.

LICKING In disputes the losing side always "gets a licking" (especially in an "ice cream war") but the word dates from 1567, when it was defined "lycke - to beate"; so it has been around long enough for writers to pause and remember the more literal meaning.

> "NOBODY but a millionaire can afford to have arthritis," says Dr O. C. Wenger, the famed doctor, who licked venereal disease in the army during World War II.

LIFE SAVINGS Any sum, however small, stolen from a PENSIONER, however rich.

> **Our women lick male sportsmen**

LIFE-LONG COMPANION Either a COMMON-LAW partner or, more likely, a CLOSE FRIEND, or homosexual partner of long standing, e.g. "Peter Pears, Britten's life-long companion".

LIFT Euphemism for journalistic theft or plagiarism, as when one paper's STORY, perhaps an *EXCLUSIVE*, is lifted by another. Some call it a "rewrite" or *FOLLOW-UP*.

LIFT THE LID To investigate, or PROBE.

LIMO A usually disapproving abbreviation, e.g. when left-wing politicians are driven in limousines at their electors' expense. The word looks misleading, as literates tend to read it as "lye-moe", but newsmen say "limmoe".

LIMP WRISTED Offensive euphemism for homosexual. But it (or at least the accompanying gesture) seems to have been in use ever since Gilbert and Sullivan made fun of Oscar Wilde in *Patience* in 1881. This picture appeared on the title-page of one of the songs from the opera.

LIVE-IN (Noun) A person sharing another's residence. The implication is that (THEIR) NAMES ARE LINKED.

LONE *ARCHAISM* perhaps kept alive by the Lone Ranger : lone FLYER, lone climber, walker, yachtsman, etc.

THE LONELINESS OF ... From *The Loneliness of the Long Distance Runner* by Alan Sillitoe (1959).

LONER Usually a convicted man about whom the reporter was unable to find any information. So, "he was a loner" adds an air of mystery but little else.

LOOM Only unpleasant events seem to "loom". From sailors' slang, an object, perhaps a ship or a ROCK, coming slowly into view.

LOONIES Formerly amiable abbreviation of "lunatics" but now usually extreme left-wing politicians who force costly, unpopular or far-fetched measures on their electors, especially in education and sex/race equality. The best place to read about loonies' antics is on PAGE THREE of *The Daily Telegraph*, which specialises in exposing them.

LOUD AND CLEAR Media twins, often associated with the SPELLING OUT of warnings.

LOVE CHILD Tabloid hack's bastard child, probably conceived in a

LOVE NEST A place shared by an unmarried male-female couple (perhaps in the middle of a "Love Tangle"). Their "Love Child" (see above) may later turn into a TUG OF LOVE CHILD.

LOVERS' LANE *Any* secluded semi-rural place where a body has been found. The murderer, if caught, will probably be a LONER.

M

M'NAGHTEN RULES Rules under English law governing criminal insanity. These were formulated after the acquittal, in 1843, of a political assassin on the grounds that he was insane when he shot Sir Robert Peel's private secretary. I have included the term here in support of those who write "McNaghten" and are "corrected" by SUBS, correspondents or clever-dicks who say that it should be "M'Naghten". But in 18th- and 19th-century typography McDonald, McGregor and other Mc names were often printed (and indeed written) with a c-shaped apostrophe in place of a raised, small letter "c". Mr M'Naghten or McNaghten was joined by Mr M'Guinness and Mr M'Gregor.

THE MAD AXEMEN OF "FLEET STREET" With CUTS always in the

news, writers dramatise the repetitive *STORIES* with suggestions of violence: "giant" axes "hanging over" industries, people and places.

Crisp giant to axe 265 at Widnes factory

About fifty students broke into the college, smashing a pane of glass and chanting: "No cuts, no cuts." A porter had his hand injured. The police

PEER 'AXED' FROM PARK COMMITTEE

The Tory peer, Viscount ,gleby, has been "aed" from the North Yorkshire Nati~ Park Committee after 14 y·

Big cuts to be made at hospital

POLYTECHNICS THREATENED BY £80m AXE

Threat to axe teachers dropped

City primary schools face cuts axe

Grant axe will hit ratepayer

Hospital axe hits patients—doctor

DINNER LADIES TO GET CHOP

MISSILE FACES AXE

Ex-alderman dies
ONE OF EIGHT AXED BY TORIES

Jobs cut rocks brakes workers

"The firm (Gillette Safety Razor Co.) were very happy to be associated in the effort to send the team to Sofia. Without their help we would have had to cut the team and this would have been a great disappointment to everyone."

Strike may cut meat in London

MAKING A MEAL The food and eating cliché, e.g. "Environmental health inspectors were making a meal out of recent reports of cockroaches in a FAMED London club..."

MAKING TRACKS Until the END OF THE LINE or coming OFF THE RAILS. It's JUST THE TICKET (also used for METER MAIDS) or, thanks to the Beatles song, a TICKET TO RIDE.

MANDARINS High-ranking British civil servants, e.g. "Whitehall mandarins"; scientists are BOFFINS. Pseudo-foreign titles abound: university teachers are DONS; mentors or advisers GURUS ("Rod Hackney, Prince Charles's architectural guru"); bosses SUPREMOS; and experts - often self-appointed - PUNDITS.

MANHOLE COVER Now banned by (surely dirty-minded) sex-equality LOONIES, who insist on "inspection cover".

MASS MURDERER Murder two persons and you are a double murderer; three, a "triple killer"; but four or more victims make a "mass murderer".

MATA HARI Generic name for a female spy.

MATCH OF THE DAY A sportsman's wedding. See also CLOCKING UP A CENTURY and NOT OUT. A snooker star gets married ON CUE, of course.

(THE) MATING GAME Not a match of the day but a cliché for stories about animals, e.g. pandas or members of other rare species brought together for mating. Probably after a play or film title. The press also has us playing "waiting games".

MAY/MIGHT After a lifeboat disaster at Penlee in which the entire crew drowned, a headline read "Swift Launch May Have Saved Lives". And *The Times* stated (in a *STORY* about the King's Cross Underground disaster), "There may well have been no loss of life if measures had been taken to allow the proper movement of emergency vehicles". According to the old-established usage, "may" in the first context means that there *was* a swift launch, that lives *were* saved and it was *this* that was thought to be the cause for their saving; and in the second example, that there *may* have been no loss of lives. In fact the launching of rescue-services was not swift, and none was saved; and many people did die at King's Cross. "Swift Launch *might* have Saved Lives" and "There *might* have been no loss of lives" is the correct way of making this clear. There are no two ways about this and reporters should get it right!

MEANINGFUL See DIALOGUE.

MEDIA UGLIES Some journalists love ugly words, which they fall upon and flog to death: BROUHAHA, GLITZ (by 1988 not yet in the *OED*), KER-FUFFLE, PIZZAZZ, RAZ(Z)(A)MATAZ(Z) and sometimes TOHU(WA)BOHU, which comes from the Bible but sounds none the prettier for it, HO HUM!

MEMORY LANE An unadopted road found in every journalist's street-directory. People revisiting old haunts, whether on a bicycle, by car or taxi, or even just by watching television without stirring from their armchair, are invariably said to be "taking a stroll down Memory Lane." Also a favourite picture caption cliché of the *COLONIC IRRITATION* type. Steve Race says it probably comes from a song by De Silva, *Down Memory Lane* (ca.1930).

METER MAIDS See MAKING TRACKS.

MIGHT See MAY.

MILD See BITTER and (A) STORM IS BREWING.

MILESTONE *ARCHAISM*: "Our Motoring Correspondent describes the new Ford Sierra as a milestone." And when did you last see a milestone on the M1? Especially one shaped like a Sierra..

MINEFIELDS Usually prefixed by "political" or "legal" "absolute", "potential" or "veritable". See DYNAMITE and BOMBSHELL.

MINE HOST The landlord of a HOSTELRY - where one QUAFFS "imbibes" or "partakes of" one's FAVOURITE TIPPLE: all silly *ARCHAISMS* related to newsmen's consumption of alcohol.

MIRACLE BABY A BATTLING infant that overcomes a serious illness by FIGHTING, and who may grow, successively, into a TODDLER, TOT, TUG OF LOVE child or GYM SLIP MUM, etc. finishing up as a GRANNY or OAP.

MODEL A respectable word given salacious undertones. Sometimes a clear euphemism for a whore - probably because NUDE artists' models have always provided newsmen with an endless source of speculation.

MOLE A person, usually an employee, who steals company or national secrets and reveals them to the press or competitors. See INSPIRED LEAK.

MON(N)I(C)KER Facetious *ARCHAISM* for a name or nickname which *DIARISTS* like to use but cannot agree on its spelling.

MONKEY BUSINESS The simian cliché, probably from a Marx Brothers film. Almost obligatory for zoo stories.

MONSTER Also BEAST. Often prefixed by "sex". Can be either a known, convicted sex offender or an anonymous suspect who, if caught, will doubtless turn out to be a LONER.

MOTHBALLED Kept UNDER WRAPS - perhaps in anticipation of a SNEAK PREVIEW (See *MediaSpeak*) before being UNVEILED.

MOVE Headline word indicating that something is thought to be about to happen: a frequent verb/noun confusion for the reader. As in "Roman Skeletons Move" - indicating that a decision was to be taken about these.

MUGGING This used to have an old, friendly meaning: "I'll mug yer", i.e. "I will treat you (perhaps to a drink)" and especially in Liverpool (See *Lern Yerself Scouse*, Scouse Press). But in 1949 *Fortune* defined it as "the vicious American art of 'mugging' by which a Negro thug grabs the victim around the neck from behind while two others, with knives, clean out his pockets." However, blacks can point to an English origin: "To receive a muggin' is to be beaten" (*Cheshire Dialect Glossary*, 1877). In recent years it has become an English street crime, usually committed by the young against the elderly or old; and the slightly facetious sound of the word does not hide its nastiness. See also TRAGICALLY WRONG in *MediaSpeak*.

MUM Any woman who has borne children; prefixable by a range of other media-words: GYMSLIP, TRAGEDY, FURY Mum, Heart Swap Mum, HORROR, etc. DAD is rarely used in this way. See GRANNY.

MUNCHING What journalists - and not only in the tabloids - think people do when they eat, e.g. when they DEMOLISH a steak, etc. See also QUAFFING, NOSH, WASHING DOWN, etc.

MYSTERY BUG Dramatising word for any illness whose cause is unknown to the writer.

N

NAMES, TITLES AND NICKNAMES With the TV satire wave of the 1960s politeness towards public figures declined in the press, too. "Mr" or "the Right Honourable" for ministers became rarer, as did "M(onsieur)" and "Herr" for foreign politicians. Mrs Barbara Castle, a Transport Minister, was immediately "Babs", Mrs Thatcher "Maggie" and President Gorbachev "Gorby" (Mr Harold Wilson never "Harry", nor Sir Alec Douglas Home "Alec" or "Douggie" - and Chinese politicians' names are too short for further abbreviation). Members of the royal family are freely first-named ("Anne to open School", "Charles to visit City" - not to mention "Fergie" and "Di") - which would have been unthinkable to older journalists. *RATPACK* photographers shout "Give 'er a kiss, Andy!" and other "instructions" - boorish *en masse* but awed and tongue-tied if confronted with royalty. The Queen and the Duke of Edinburgh are still spared the worst impertinences, but that, too seems to be changing as *Spitting Image* (TV again!) lowers the tone by degrees. No wonder that tabloids automatically assume first-name terms with the rest of us (**DORIS, 90, MUGGED**).

(THEIR) NAMES ARE LINKED Term of innuendo. The male partner may be an ESCORT.

NIGHTMARES Newsmen are uneasy sleepers (and who can blame them?) Their very journey to work probably starts with a "nightmare drive" - all part of the SHOCK/HORROR trade.

NITERIES Where tabloid gossip columnists and *DIARISTS* dance the night away after FREELOADING at EATERIES. And BUMP INTO people.

NO COMMENT Allegedly newsworthy persons pursued by reporters believe that by using this formula they can avoid being (mis)quoted. They are wrong. A quotation can always be manufactured: see *FALSE VERBATIM*.

NOSH From the German word *naschen*, meaning to nibble, which in Yiddish (i.e. modified medieval German) is pronounced with a short "o" sound, "noshen". The Americans turned this into the verb "to nosh", and then the noun "nosh" for food in general. See TUCKING INTO and WASHING DOWN.

NOT OUT Stock description of an old person's age - especially centenarians who CLOCK UP a century (**"Mabel: 100 Not Out"**). If notably fat they do not "weigh 20st" but WEIGH IN AT... like boxers or jockeys. See MATCH OF THE DAY.

NOTE(S) Provide endless fun for non-musicians: low notes, sour notes, flat notes, right notes, wrong notes - though most of all HIGH and sour notes, and, nonsensically, high and low keys. See LEITMOTIF, UPBEAT, DOWNBEAT.

NUDE Newspapers prefer "nude" to "naked", because nakedness can be artistic or innocent but nude is thought to be lewd or rude. See BAREFACED CHEEK, BARING ALL, MODEL.

O

OFF THE RAILS See MAKING TRACKS.

... OF THE YEAR An often meaningless accolade which has superseded the mere "prize". Everybody is somebody's something of the year, but in the media industry the title enables people or papers to call themselves AWARD-WINNING for no special reason: "Read all about it in tomorrow's award-winning *Daily Post!*" See also BEST/WORST DRESSER.

OH BROTHER! Dual-purpose headline- or *STORY*-cliché, for trades unions or (after a TV SOAP) priests or monks.

OLDEN DAYS Facetious *ARCHAISM*.

OLÉ See OO LA LA.

OLYMPIAN Considered interchangeable with olympic. It is not. See also GOLDEN GIRL.

ON A WING AND A PRAYER One of the FLYING HIGH aviation clichés, especially for an allegedly precarious flight - whether in a jumbo or microlight - even a balloon, which has no wings but goes UP, UP AND AWAY! For - the "Sky's the Limit!"

ONCERS See CRISP.

ON/OFF CUE Cliché for snooker and its players. These may also "get a BREAK." See MATCH OF THE DAY and other sporting entries.

ONE-TIME Ambiguous but common way of saying "former", as in "He is Elizabeth Taylor's one-time lover". "Two-time" ("the two-time Oscar winner Meryl Streep") is even less satisfactory.

ONGOING Adverb describing a continuing *STORY* reported in the press and often twinned with SAGA.

ONSLAUGHT *ARCHAISM* used in often wildly inappropriate applications like "Everton survived a relentless reds onslaught..."

ON THE CARDS Presumably from fortune-telling, i.e. something predicted or expected. Hence "A white Christmas is on the cards..." *ad nauseam.*

ON THE CREST OF A WAVE A project ON COURSE for SAILING HIGH - unless SCUPPERED or SUNK: in other words a maritime cliché.

ON THE HOP See HOPPING MAD.

OO LA LA A signal that the *STORY* concerns France or FROGS and their curious habits. HACKS also think that Spaniards go round all day exclaiming "OLÉ" (though the acute accent, as in PATE and EXPOSE, is considered optional). The phoney *le* in front of English words is also now fashionable, e.g. "le Car" for a French motor.

OPENLY Like UNASHAMEDLY, usually twinned with newsworthy grief. Before tears start flowing (ar at any rate are claimed to be flowing) the subject is VISIBLY MOVED. If Our Correspondent had been present at Gethsemane, Peter would - REPORTEDLY - have wept not bitterly (Matthew, 26.75) but "openly".

ORDEAL Any slight discomfort, as in "TOT trapped in 10-minute lift ordeal".

ORGANISER New word for diary.

OUR MAN IN ... Cliché description of an ambassador or other diplomatic representative, from Graham Greene's *Our Man in Havana*, but presumably a Foreign Office term long before that.

OUTLETS Retail shops: "corner" shops run by ordinary people and the "high street" stores of large conglomerates. See also STREET VALUE.

Food outlets shrink

Co-ops, multiples, voluntary | wholesalers and grocers began
chains and other retail organiza- | rationalize their stocks

OVER[1] Journalese for "more than...": "He waited over six years".

OVER[2] The geographical or positional connotations are surely so strong that it sounds foolish and absurd in abstract use: MAN HELD OVER WOMAN, HEAD HELD OVER PUPIL,DOCKERS MARCH OVER IMMIGRANTS, NURSES TO STRIKE OVER CUTS, etc.

OVERALL "Workers demand overall cover..." And a BLANKET BAN?

P

(A) PACK OF LIES Lies, like wolves, huskies and American cigarettes, always come in packs, as surely as race-horses come in STRINGS.

PARAMETER Favoured by journalists, broadcasters, politicians and businessmen, but nothing more than a pretentious way of saying "limits" or "boundaries". For its proper meaning consult a scientific dictionary. See also EQUATION and QUANTUM LEAP.

PENSIONER Media word for *any* old person or OAP, whether in receipt of a pension or not - just as any rich man's daughter is automatically an HEIRESS. To call all elderly people pensioners may stir readers' emotions but could offend an active person of around 65. Conversely, "pensioner, 92" is stating the obvious. At that age he is unlikely to be a boy-scout (though he may be a BOYFRIEND or even a LAD and still looking for BROWNIE POINTS). Pensioners can even be POLITICAL FOOTBALLS: whenever the government announces some new law or measure, however unrelated to the daily life of the elderly, it is immediately condemned by the opposition with the words, "Pensioners will suffer". See GRANNY and UNEMPLOYED.

PETITE When being coy about women, SCRIBES may resort to French, hoping to add a SAUCY *soupcon* of OO LA LA.

PETTICOAT Feminising prefix word indicating an unexpected or inappropriate presence of women: " Petticoat Miners", "Petticoat Soldiers", etc. An *ARCHAISM*: women seldom say "petticoat" but prefer "underskirt".

PHEW WHAT A SCORCHER! Stock headline for a hot summer's day. Also "Sizzler". But see also BRRR!

PHOTO OPPORTUNITY An invention of the Public Relations Industry, whose workers offer these "opportunities" to journalists as if doing them a favour. The purpose is of course to get a product, or the VIP they represent, publicised.

PICKING UP THE BILL Just as prison sentences are always HANDED DOWN, so bills ("tabs") are invariably picked up: "picking up the tab for a hundred grand".

PICTURE CLICHES The press photographer did not invent these well-tried aids to communication - he merely built on painters' time-honoured tricks. Think of the contrivedly-posed 18th-century CONVERSATION PIECES; the cut-off "kit-kats"; the pious symbolism of Murillo's "eyes-turned-to-heaven" pictures; or the stiff postures of 19th-century political worthies: even Leonardo da Vinci's *Last Supper*, for which he evidently insisted that Christ and the Disciples line up on one side only - the far side of the table (whereas people dining with friends would naturally sit opposite each other). I can just hear Leonardo say (only in Italian) "Would you mind all sitting in a line, lads, so I can get you all in the picture?" The modern photographer also makes demands on his subjects:

Jumping for Joy The subject is requested to leap in the air, if possible with his or her legs spread out, while the photographer grovels on the FLOOR to give the impression of a very high jump. Especially suitable for actors, dancers, etc.

The One Leg stuck out in Front Pose This is now such a universal cliché that I do believe people stick out a leg without being asked (and would probably stick out two if they could) because they know they are being photographed for a paper.

The Silly Chorus/Conga Line As above but used when two or more subjects stick their legs out in front, like the chorus of a musical; or form a conga line, when they all stick out one leg each. The more incongruously unsuitable the subjects, i.e. TODDLERS or toothless PENSIONERS, the better pleased the photographer.

The Inappropriate Hat The younger the subject the better and all the more effective if the hat is ill-fitting. Policemen's, soldiers' and firemen's hats, boaters and Fred Astaire toppers are the most common pretend head-wear. Hats are also DOFFED for the camera, perhaps in a big sweep, with some sort of punning cliché about "pudd'n' on the Ritz" never far behind.

Singing in the Rain Photographers always seem to have a large umbrella handy, which the subject (e.g. a cricketer during a rained-off test match) holds over his head while sticking out a hand, palm upwards and eyes cast towards the heavens. This can mean either, "Is it going to rain?" or "Will it stop raining?"

Big Feet Footballers and other athletes are shown reclining with the soles of their feet closest to the camera lens and therefore enormous - a small grinning head in the distance.

Thumbs Up A favourite since it was a gesture of optimism in the face of defeat during World War II, e.g. when returning from Dunkirk. Now it can mean that the subject has won £5 in a competition.

The Vee Sign Also from World War II, popularised by Winston Churchill and, with the first and second fingers of one or both hands, spelt out "V for Victory". In this the hand is held aloft, palm facing forward and kept still. When used in this "still" manner by pickets, protesters, hijackers, "urban guerillas", pseudo-revolutionaries and many kinds of rabble-rousers, it means either "we've won" or "we've lost but are still defiant".

The Demonstrators' Vee Sign Two fingers as above, the palm facing forwards but the arm makes a forward-batting gesture. Seen in mass demonstrations, in football grounds (where it may mean "Send 'im off!"), and by religious (!) fundamentalists, who use it as a gesture threatening the entire free world (and what a far cry from the sign of the cross...).

The Rude Vee Sign Photographers used decently to avert their cameras from this, as it was tantamount to printing a rude word, the intended meaning being "F... You!" or "Go away!", or "I've lost my temper and I hate my fellow-men, especially you"; or, when given by a car user, "I'm a lousy driver". But curiously enough it was also a recognised discussion gesture among medieval philosophers, as may be seen in the painting Christ disputing with the Doctors, by Butinone (National Gallery of Scotland).

The Italian Tenor Gesture The subject's arms are spread wide, palms facing upwards. It can mean, "Look, all *this* (shown in the background) belongs to *me*!", or "Aren't I lucky to be working in such a fine place?" or simply, "Am I not an idiot to let some silly photographer tell me to stick my arms out?" But when a footballer is shown making this gesture to a referee who is holding aloft a red or yellow card, it is a spontaneous gesture of feigned innocence, as if to say, "Look 'ere ref, I never touched 'im, 'is leg wuz already broke!".

The Mermaid A few yards of aluminium foil wrapped round the lower end of a topless or under-dressed young woman is the standard picture cliché for matters maritime and fishy. See also FISHY TAILS.

The Al Fresco Concert However inappropriate the instruments, e.g. a grand piano, photographers request that it be dragged into the open air so that a contrivedly posed photograph can be taken as though in performance. I have seen them in the streets, on a (closed) motorway and even on the beach. Pity the patient artists, desperate for publicity, who agree to do this so that it might bring in a couple of extra customers. *COLONIC IRRITATION* captions about "hitting high notes" or "stringing along" are obligatory.

The Clean Sweep A new man in a new job? Borrow a broom and pose him outside the premises.

The Sideways-on Kiss (single or double):   When congratulations are indicated, the subject is posed with at least one colleague, family member, well-wisher, etc. planting a pouting kiss on his cheek(s). One on each cheek is customary, and if he had a few more cheeks (at any rate visible), they, too, would have people planting kisses on them.

The Swept-off-the-feet Pose This shows a woman celebrating a happy event - engagement, marriage, examination success, etc. - who is lifted up and carried by at least one man.

The Timely Telephone Call Those who receive joyful news seldom do so in the presence of a photographer. No matter - when he does arrive a telephone handset is stuck in the person's hand and an accompanying grin requested, to re-enact the happy event for the picture.

Drinking to Success Has there ever been an announcement of yearly profits figures from, say, Guinness or some other big brewers without a posed picture of a foaming pint held aloft by the chairman, Sir Arthur T. Tootal (who probably normally never touches the stuff)?

Sharing (enjoying) a Joke Caption for any two people talking to each other at a cocktail party or reception. They do not need to look amused.

Squirting Champagne Every celebration seems to have the victor shaking, squirting (and cruelly wasting) most of a bottle of BUBBLY. Bystanders never appear to mind having their clothes ruined. And the most common of all is the -

Stock Photo This is of a well-known subject, e.g. the prime minister or (in the locals) the mayor, shown day after wearisome day at his/her mere mention. The face only is pictured, often heavily cropped, with only eyes, nose and mouth visible (thus giving the impression the subject is peering through a cat-flap). It is done not for representational purposes but "to break up the page" - or else for the benefit of recent arrivals from outer space: everyone else already *knows* what Mrs Thatcher or Councillor Twirp looks like. Also, stories concerning death or disaster are often embellished by an old picture of the subject grinning inanely.

The Smile that Says it All Caption cliché, used even for scowling subjects.

The Grieving Relative No report of a disaster, murder, or other event leading to loss of life is complete without a *FOLLOW-UP* by *DOORSTEPPING* photographers seeking out widows, orphans and other mourning relatives. In the funeral procession or at the graveside these are shown supporting each other or better still, WEEPING OPENLY, their crumpled faces in a dramatic close-up of grief. And when the memorial service (SAD FAREWELL) or anniversary comes round - the *RATPACK* is sure to be there again.

The Studious Look Suitable for head-only shots - the subject cups chin in hand, forefinger vertical on one cheek. Useful for "brainy" children, to hide double chins, etc.

The Dolly Bird Young women, especially aspiring models or beauty queens, are always shown with one leg ludicrously placed in front of the other, the knee of the front leg slightly bent. But they probably do this of their own accord.

PINTA What we put into our CUPPA. From a slogan of the 1950s: "Drinka Pinta Milka Day". Even real newspapers print it, and some less discriminating broadcasters use the word - which sounds especially silly spoken.

PIP/PIPPED The apples/oranges cliché: "British apple growers were pipped at the post yesterday by the French golden delicious..." See also GIVING (SOMEONE) THE PIP.

PIPELINE An imaginary conduit through which wordblind newsmen can pass things solid, liquid and abstract, e.g. "A lifeline plan for three doomed tower blocks in Birkenhead could be in the pipeline." *Liverpool Daily Post.*

PITCHED BATTLE A "pitched" battle is strictly one in which opponents fight from prepared and defined territorial positions: an archaic kind of military operation suggestive of rows of redcoats facing equally carefully placed enemy forces. In the media the word "pitched" is merely a makeweight.

PIZ(Z)AZ(Z) "Zest, vim, vitality, liveliness, flashiness, showiness" says the *OED:* "origin unknown". It gives eight alternative spellings. See also its unlovely cousin RAZ(Z)(A)MATAZ(Z) and *MEDIA UGLIES.*

PLUCK (verb) In normal life fowl are plucked, but in news language this is what helicopters do to people when rescuing them - always "plucked to safety".

PLUMMET See HURTLE and SOAR.

PLUMPING/OPTING "Plump: of a full and rounded form; having the skin well filled or elastically distended; chubby", from the Dutch *plomp*, ungainly, clumsy. "Plumping" in the sense of an emphatic choice, or of "falling for" something, is probably derived from the French *plomb*, a piece of lead - and also gave us PLUMMET (above). Plumping was a favourite election word in the 19th century, and a plumper was a kind of voter.

Girls plump
for new
university

POISED See SET - also the *MediaSpeak* section.

POLITICAL FOOTBALL Media BALLGAME.

POP Only questions of matrimony are popped. The Leader of the Opposition never "pops" a question to the Prime Minister.

POWERFUL BINOCULARS "Police scanned the horizon through powerful binoculars." (Doubtless because of TIGHT security). News binoculars are never plain, just as battles must be PITCHED, banknotes CRISP and political parties not merely split but SPLIT DOWN THE MIDDLE.

PRACTISING Kneejerk prefix for catholics and homosexuals, as members of the more left-wing political parties are always CARD-CARRYING.

PRICE TAG The cost of anything UP FOR GRABS, i.e. for sale. As in "The Renoir is believed to be up for grabs with a price tag of a cool £2m". Price tags are usually SLAPPED ON.

PROBE To investigate, and, as a noun, an investigation. See also LIFT THE LID.

PROBLEMS Usually twinned with "grave" or "mounting" -

MAN FOUND IN MERSEY HAD DRINK PROBLEM	Mounting problems for young couples	Newly-weds, aged 82, have problem

PRONOUNCED The first leg of a pair of inseparable news-twins - the second being "limp". No gait-impaired man appears in the papers who does not "walk with a *pronounced* limp". Sometimes also applied to "stammer" or "squint".

PROTEST (verb) The Americans like to prune from their sentences any words they consider unnecessary (turning "write to me" into "write me", really from the German *schreib' mir*). But in their zeal to save time they cause confusion to the English. To protest something is not the same as to protest *against* something. An accused person in a British court who "protests his innocence" would be thought by an American to be speaking *against* it.

PULL-OUT SUPPLEMENT See FALL OUT.

PUMP (SHOTS/BULLETS) INTO... Emotive and sensationalising term ("The SAS man then pumped six shots into him..."). Shots are *fired*, not pumped - though there exists a pump-action shot-gun, which refers to the way it is loaded, not fired.

PUNCTURED What happens to cyclists' plans when they fail to RIDE HIGH, or FALL FLAT.

PUNDIT See MANDARINS.

PURRFECT! Kneejerk joke for any *STORY* involving - but oh, you've *guessed*! How clever of you.

Q

QUAFFING See FAVOURITE TIPPLE, MINE HOST, SAMPLING THE LOCAL BREW, SIPPING, SLAP UP, WASHING DOWN, etc.

QUANTUM LEAP A *quantum* can be any size, even something very small indeed. Like PARAMETERS it has an exact scientific meaning, devised by scientists for scientists who know what they are talking about. What *SCRIBES* mean by a quantum leap is merely a big advance.

QUIPPED See SMILED.

QUOTH (I/HE/SHE etc.) One of the stilted *ARCHAISMS* with which columnists, *DIARISTS*, etc., HASTEN THITHER to enliven their prose.

R

RAP Short for "reprimand", with the implication "over the knuckles". May be confused by blacks, for whom "rapping" means an expressionles, uninflected way of rhythmic speaking with pretensions to both poetry and song.

MAUDE RAPPED OVER ARTICLES

RATPACK Any group of journalists or posse of press photographers in pursuit of a story. They themselves use the term.

RAUNCHY Women writers' favourite word to indicate a kind of aggressive sexiness, more often in women: outspoken, sandpaper-voiced American comediennes spring to mind.

RAZ(Z)(A)MATAZ(Z) One of the *MEDIA UGLIES* used to describe GLITZY celebration and HYPE, with much KERFUFFLE, PIZZAZZ and TOHUWABOHU, all favoured by *DIARISTS*. "On the razzle" is now as dated as the old "girlie" magazine *Razzle*, which used to delight soldiers, sailors, airmen and schoolboys - though there was never a nipple to be seen.

RECORD BOOKS Imaginary volumes used in many unimaginative ways, e.g. "Hot air balloonist Per Lindstrand soared into the record books as he..."

RED CARD See KICKED INTO TOUCH and WHISTLE-BLOWING.

RED FACES The newsman's idea of embarrassment.

RED LIGHT See GETTING THE GREEN LIGHT.

RED LIGHT DISTRICT Overdramatised description of any area where a prostitute has been seen loitering. See also SMACK CITY.

REDUNDANT Euphemism for "unemployed"; as in "Last year my husband became redundant".

REPORTEDLY A wretchedly clumsy way of saving a couple of words. "The army is reportedly monitoring the ethnic background of recruits" is intended to mean, "The army is *reported to be* monitoring ..." etc. One cannot monitor anything in a reported manner. Similarly there are many things that are *important* or *large* but none that can be described as IMPORTANTLY or "largely". See also HOPEFULLY in *MediaSpeak*.

REVERSAL Not the same as (nor a more elegant way of saying) "reverse". Your dictionary will explain.

RIDING HIGH Cliché for cyclists, more rarely horses, on which one does ride higher. Both may FALL FLAT and cyclists' hopes be PUNCTURED. Rides may also be "bumpy".

RIDING ROUGHSHOD A form of ancient mounted warfare and an *ARCHAISM* even when Charles Kingley wrote "We are an ancient house laid low, with mammon and fashion riding roughshod over our heads" (1843).

RING OF CONFIDENCE Cliché derived from an old advertisement for Bravington's, the jewellers, later also for toothpaste.

ROBIN HOOD Denotes alleged "good" intentions in a miscreant, e.g. "Robin Hood thief".

ROCK (verb) What explosions are always said to do to a place, e.g. "An explosion *rocked* Beirut yesterday as..."

ROCK CORRESPONDENT To paraphrase someone's (whose?) memorable statement, a rock correspondent is someone who can't write, writing for the benefit of those who can't read, about singers or players who can't sing or play. In other words, the paucity of genuine musical talent, compositional and interpretative, in today's pop music, is mirrored by the pretentious, inflated nonsense written about it. But even "real" newspapers feel the need to pander to their immature readers by employing journalists to write critiques of what is musically beneath criticism. Since the pop music scene is demonstrably bound up with narcotics (i.e. crime) the subject could be adequately covered by a paper's sociological and medical correspondents. But then it would lose lucrative advertising from the record industry.

ROLLER A Rolls Royce motorcar. Unless facetiousness is intended the nickname betrays the writer's Mini mentality.

ROMEO Supposedly amorous (or lecherous) male, often one discomfited by rejection of his unwelcome advances, and if these are made at his place of work he is an "Office Romeo". A glance at Shakespeare's *Romeo and Juliet* reveals that Juliet welcomed her Romeo with open arms. Occasionally "Casanova" serves the same purpose, but most tabloid readers are probably unaware that such a person ever existed.

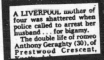

A LIVERPOOL mother of four was shattered when police called to arrest her husband . . . for bigamy. The double life of romeo Anthony Geraghty (30), of Prestwood Crescent,

Unions join drive on office Romeos

ROMPING (verb) In sports reporters' jargon, either a bit of HORSEPLAY or, in football, winning decisively. In horse-racing winners "romp home"..

ROMPS (noun) Usually preceded by SEX(Y): "MP denies Sex Romps with MODEL". Also sometimes "sexy frolics".

ROUGH RIDE Horse- and cycle-riders' discomfiture kneejerk, as in "Rough Ride for Queen's Jockey".

ROWING Media word for "quarrelling" but better in spoken use, when the pronunciation leaves no room for ambiguities - e.g. "The couple rowed all the way across the atlantic..."

RUFFLED See IN A FLAP.

RULED OFFSIDE One of the footballing clichés: "Everton's plans for restricting entrance to card-holders were ruled offside yesterday..." Also KICKED INTO TOUCH,(THE) RED CARD, SENT OFF, CRYING FOUL, etc

RUMPUS Hack word for a row or argument, as in **"UNBURIED DEAD IN CITY MORTUARY RUMPUS "** - *Liverpool Echo*.

RUN As in "running a *STORY* with an *EXCLUSIVE TAG*". To publish something in a paper. See also *FOLLOW UP* and *SPOILER*.

RUS(S)KIES Tabloid word for Russians.

S

SACRED COW COPY *COPY* that is sacrosanct - safe from the attentions, cuts or re-writes of SUBS - and negotiable by only the most famous writers.

SAD FAREWELL Kneejerk for a memorial service: "Stars' Sad Farewell to TV Comic". The accompanying *PICTURE CLICHÉ* may show some of the "stars" ENJOYING A JOKE - though others may be WEEPING OPENLY.

SADLY "Sadly she died before her son became Prime Minister". Was *she* sad when she died, or did the *writer* find it sad that she died when she did? See REPORTEDLY and HOPEFULLY.

SAIL See SUNK.

SAILING HIGH What is said - absurdly - to happen when a maritime project is ON THE CREST OF A WAVE or going FULL STEAM AHEAD - before it is SCUPPERED and SUNK. See also THAT SINKING FEELING.

SAGA Any STORY or DRAMA to which repeated reference is made.

SAMARITAN *Any* helper who gives even the most trivial aid (possibly at the end of a "mercy" DASH) or even merely takes a cup of tea to a neighbour.

SAMPLING THE LOCAL BREW What is done at an HOSTELRY (by courtesy of MINE HOST), etc. Only three from a large stock of facetious *ARCHAISMS* for *HACKS* to choose from when writing about QUAFFING.

SAUCY Now almost exclusively a sexually suggestive word, seldom used by anyone except *SCRIBES*. When ordinary people speak of "sauce" they mean either the substance accompanying food, or impertinence ("He's got a sauce!"). "Saucy" has lost that meaning. See also BUXOM, HANKY PANKY, HORSEPLAY, KISS AND CUDDLE, ROMPS, SHAPELY.

SAYING IT WITH... Probably from an advertising slogan that invited people to "Say it with Flowers". In news jargon it is just a silly cliché.

SCALING News jargon for "climbing". Had a *SCRIBE* written *The Sound of Music* the famous song would have been "Scale every mountain..."
SCENARIO In the language of the theatre, ballet or opera, the outline of the story, action or plot. In news jargon an all-purpose word for any sequence of events.

SCI-FI Abbreviation of "science fiction". See ALIEN.

SCORCHER See PHEW.

SCREAMER Old journalistic word for an exclamation-mark. Editors who care about style have for decades deplored their use, but to no avail. The current tabloid fashion is to use huge single-word headlines followed by an exclamation-mark, e.g. STRANDED! or BLASTED! or OUTRAGE!

SCRIBE Journalists' mock-deprecating self-description.

SCUPPERED See SUNK.

SEEING RED Angry.

SENT OFF "City magistrates yesterday sent off a young Everton supporter who..." See RULED OFFSIDE and other football-based clichés.

SERIOUS See CRITICAL.

SET In the ordinary English spoken by all social or educational groups, events are *expected* or *about to* happen. But for *HACKS*, and only for hacks, forthcoming or predicted events are always "set" to happen. (See also in **MEDIASPEAK**). For "setting" in the typesetting sense see under *COPY*.

SEX AND THE (SINGLE GIRL) Stock cliché varied for different applications. From a book by Helen Gurley Brown.

SEXY A newspaper-selling word, stronger than SAUCY and followed by words like pin-ups, ROMPS, photos, etc.

SHAME Sensationalising hyperbolic headline-word promising salaciousness and scandal, e.g. "Royal Comic in Rent Boy Shame" - a headline which incidentally was also a blatant misrepresentation of the "royal" element. It merely referred to someone who had once appeared at a Royal Command Performance, so the sub-headline "Gay Shock for Queen" was even more misleading.

SHAME ABOUT... Cliché, e.g. "Nice Car, Shame about the Driver".

SHAPELY Of a woman with big breasts, possibly also big hips. The word, like BUXOM, WELL BUILT, and many others listed here, is seldom used except by *HACKS*.

SHELLING OUT What housewives are said to do when paying for eggs; and suffer from SHELL SHOCK when prices rise. No *SCRIBE* can resist an egg "joke" - from "eggs-actly" to "eggs-perts" and "eggs-ercise". Juvenile twaddle like that is actually *taught* in journalists' training-courses!

SHELL SHOCK An illness suffered by World War I HEROES but now debased into a cliché, especially for eggs - see above. And see also FLAK.

SHOCK *HACKS* are not easily shocked, but they think their readers are, so they describe even a faintly surprising event with this word, or "shocker". Nor are they horrified by HORROR.

SHOT DOWN (IN FLAMES) A surely tasteless allusion to wartime aerial combat, like SHELL SHOCK. "A rescue plan for Liverpool Airport was shot down in flames yesterday as..."

SHOT IN THE ARM Clichés come and go, and this form of shooting is, mercifully, going. The expression had its heyday in the 1970s among businessmen as well as journalists, and was meant to indicate a boost of morale or capital. It came from one of the many euphemisms for taking a SNORTER or "snifter" in one gulp, which was called "a shot in the neck". Not to be confused with "shooting (oneself) in the foot".

SHOWING THE RED CARD One of the footballing clichés ripe for being KICKED INTO TOUCH or having the WHISTLE blown on it.

SICKENER Manufactured dramatising noun for something the writer claims to find "sickening", e.g. in football a foul.

(WITH A) SICKENING THUD The traditional way for newsmen to report the arrival of letters, tax demands, etc. which always "landed on my desk/doormat with a sickening thud." Maybe from schoolboy literature, for it has a ring of *Just William* or *Biggles*. CRUNCHES can be sickening, too.

SIEG HEIL The old rabble-rousing Nazi cry is used by tabloids as if it were still a common German exclamation, like the Spanish OLÉ and OO LA LA by the French. It may be printed in various ways: "Seig Hiel" or, in one instance, even "Zieg Hiel" (for the *ie/ei* sequence has a 50/50 chance of correctness in *English* words, let alone foreign ones). See also KRAUT and FROGS.

SIGHED See SMILED.

SIGNALLED A railway cliché. See END OF THE LINE, MAKING TRACKS, JUST THE TICKET, etc.

SILVERWARE Sports-writers' jargon for trophies. See also MATCH OF THE DAY.

SIP One of the QUAFFING group, like TIPPLE and WASHING DOWN.

SIR A teacher. If in some way discomfited or reprimanded he GETS A CANING.

SITUATION A cliché killed by over-use and ridicule! Even a few football commentators have stopped using it. HO HUM. Or should I say "Hallelujah!"?

SIZZLER See PHEW WHAT A SCORCHER.

SKOOL One of several mis-spellings - intentional for once - heralding some facetious *STORY* about education or SIR.

SLAM To condemn, RAP, TONGUE-LASH, or otherwise adversely comment. See also HITTING OUT.

SLAP ON What people are supposed to do when deciding the price of an object, etc. "A PRICE TAG of £3m was slapped on the painting." See *INSTANT VALUATIONS*.

SLAP ON THE WRIST Punishment considered to be inadequate for the offence committed: "FURY at judge's slap on wrist for rapist".

SLAP UP An expensive meal (never, of course, when it appears on an expenses claim, which is always described as "modest"): "Guests were sitting down to a slap up meal as ..."

SLAY One of the most enduring news *ARCHAISMS*. In OLDEN DAYS people used to slay each other - there are some thirty slayings in the texts of Shakespeare and about four hundred in the Bible. "Slay" may just be appropriate in a tight headline, but elsewhere the word sounds stilted and silly. Who would say, "Heard this fantastic joke? It'll slay you."

SLICE OF THE CAKE A share of what is available. Probably from *GRAPHICS* representing proportionate figures or amounts as segments of a circle. So stupefying is the power of clichés that people can in all seriousness compose statements like "This settlement has to come out of the overall cake available within the social GUIDELINES".

SLIDE RULES "Barratts, the ever expanding house builders, will be running a slide rule over the situation..." (*Observer*). If they really used such outdated equipment in this computer age, the contractors would not expand but quickly contract. An *ARCHAISM*, like CARBON COPIES and MILESTONES.

SMACK CITY Overdramatised term for any part of a town where drugs are sold, especially "smack" (heroin): see RED LIGHT AREA. Residents can live for years in such areas without noticing that there is much of a problem:

and often there isn't.

SMELLS/SCENTS These come in various forms, most often in combinations like "The Sweet/Sour Smell of Success": a cliché floggable in many permutations.

SMILED With CHUCKLED, ENTHUSED, GRUFFED, LAUGHED, QUIPPED, SIGHED, time-saving ways of writing a story: "Smiled WELL BUILT mother of six..." indicates the manner in which she said what she is ALLEGED to have said. A SEXY Sunday paper used BITCHED when reporting an allegedly controversial statement by a man they clearly wished to brand as LIMP WRISTED. TRILLED is reserved for utterances by bright and chirpy females. But see also *FALSE VERBATIM* and BLAST.

SMOKES Cigarettes; not, usually, pipes or cigars. For old people "baccy" is thought appropriate, as in "The Chancellor has threatened to STUB OUT the OAPs' baccy concession".

SNEAK PREVIEW See *MediaSpeak* but the same applies in print.

SNORTER A quick short, strong drink, probably taken in one gulp; also "snifter".

SNOW JOKE! One of the oldest in the *HACKS'* armoury, but still (BRRR!) tediously trotted out, winter after winter. See PHEW WHAT A SCORCHER!

SOAP TV "soap opera".

SOAR Birds and gliders soar gracefully through the air, but in the papers rising prices, incomes, the cost of living, etc. "soar" - but may later HURTLE or PLUMMET.

SOCIAL DISEASES In this age of the condom and AIDS, a strangely namby-pamby journalistic euphemism for venereal infections. They are transmitted by sexual, not social encounters. Even by CLOSE FRIENDS.

SOUR NOTES See HIGH NOTES.

SPEAKING OUT Expressing an opinion with force, real or imagined, as in "Maggie Speaks Out". See also SPELLING OUT.

SPED "Speeding" is an everyday word, but the past tense has survived only among poets and hacks: "Ted was injured when he sped over the grass bank into the railings..."

SPELL(ING) OUT Usually warnings - LOUD AND CLEAR.

SPIN See IN A (FLAT) SPIN.

SPINSTER An unmarried single woman and (it is implied) one no longer marriageable. Women are right to object to such pejorative, irrelevant descriptions - a double *ARCHAISM* (from *spinning* - "When Adam delved and Eve span") so why not "single woman"? "bachelor", of a man, implies (just as deplorably) that he is "gay". And see also GRANNY and PENSIONER.

> ## Spinster is committed
>
> SPINSTER Jose Hill, aged 84, who shot BBC commissionaire Kim Sultan, has been committed to hospital for treatment under the Mental Health Act.
> She pleaded guilty at London's

SPLASH(ING OUT) "Mrs Thatcher splashed out on a duckpond yesterday": money spent on maritime or aquatic projects: They may, however, be SCUPPERED, TORPEDOED or SUNK.

SPLIT (RIGHT) DOWN THE MIDDLE Few ordinary splits are admitted in the papers, just as no binoculars are less than POWERFUL, no battles other than PITCHED.

SPLIT INFINITIVES An unnecessarily contentious subject. Although it is not a crime to split, and many do it, the result always sounds awkward and impedes the flow of a sentence, both in spoken and written English, e.g. "He was the first man to ever win an honour for darts"; or "Liverpool hope to at the very least finish in the top three". The *best* writers and speakers, past and present, do *not* split infinitives (although the "rule" is rooted in Latin grammar and may well be described as archaic) and thus set standards of euphony. Perhaps the only "rule" should be one of manners: as no-one ever complains of an *unsplit* infinitive (just as nobody minds *CON*TROVERSY but many do mind "con*tro*versy" - see *MediaSpeak*) it is surely better not to split - if only to avoid offending. Besides, as with other contentious English usages, the resourceful user can always meet the challenge: he simply shows his verbal ingenuity by re-phrasing.

SPOILER One paper's reaction to another's EXCLUSIVE.

SPYING See HASTENING (THITHER) and other *ARCHAISMS*.

SQUAD A team, especially football - one of the pseudo-military words sports journalists use, for mindless FANS like to imagine their sport in terms of violence and war: "Kenny Dalglish's red army continued their relentless march towards the championship when they annihilated the Manchester United squad" etc. Players are "called up", like soldiers, into their team. [Nb Dalglish is right]

SQUEEZE Financial or fiscal hardship or stringency. This kind of squeeze was invented by Sir Eric Geddes, who said on 9 December 1918: "We will get everything out of her that you can get out of a lemon and a bit more... I will squeeze her until you can hear the pips squeak." He was referring to the defeated German nation, not Lady Geddes.

SQUINT See PRONOUNCED.

STABLE A word seldom used except for horses and, as an adjective (especially when coupled with "condition"), for bringing news of a sick person. See also CRITICAL.

Roy Rogers, the singing cowboy star, was taken ill in Hollywood yesterday but is now said to be in a stable condition. His agent

STALKING *ARCHAISM*. Usually only fear "stalks" the streets - perhaps in SMACK CITY.

STAMMER See PRONOUNCED.

STAMP OF APPROVAL Kneejerk for any *STORY* concerning the mail. A favourite *COLONIC IRRITATION* quip for headlines or picture-captions.

STAMP OUT Over-dramatised way of saying "end", or "abolish".

COUNCILLORS
TO STAMP OUT
DOG DIRT

STAND FIRM To act with determination or resolve or, if viewed from an opponent's side, with stubbornness.

STATE GRAB Nationalisation.

STEAMING Mass robbery, e.g. in trains or shops, by rampaging gangs, a crime imported from Caribbean countries. See also MUGGING.

STEAMY Obligatory qualification for "sex sessions", which according to tabloids always take place in a hothouse atmosphere.

STIFF DRINK News twin, like a GOOD CIGAR, a PITCHED BATTLE and POWERFUL BINOCULARS, etc.

STOMACH (verb) One of the food clichés, as in "The government finds the egg revelations hard to stomach..."

STORM A SHOCK/HORROR word of overdramatisation. A mild disagreement in Parliament is always a "Commons Storm". See also FURY.

(A) STORM IS BREWING Usually over something to do with beer, pubs or publicans. See also MILD/BITTER.

STORM OUT Leaving in alleged anger, e.g. a meeting - possibly TIGHT-LIPPED AND ASHEN FACED. Applied even to quiet, slow and dignified departures. See also SMILED.

STORMY WATERS See SUNK.

STORY A news item, whether fact, fiction (or, more likely an unadmitted combination of both). The *OED* defines it, with unintended aptness for this book: " A narrative, true or presumed to be true, relating to important events and celebrated persons..." - adding later "An incident, real or fictitious, related in conversation or in written discourse in order to amuse or interest... an allegation or statement. Colloquially, a euphemism for a lie."

STRAFE See FLAK.

STRATEGIC PLACES In the papers these always have sexual connotations, denoting areas of the body normally kept from public view. In the HACKS' Bible, Genesis III/vii would read: "They sewed fig leaves together and made themselves aprons, strategically placed." In the arms race, strategic weapons are for long-range bombardment, tactical ones short-range. Or, to return to the earlier interpretation, "Come up to my place for coffee" is strategy, but the hand travelling up from a lady's knee is tactics.

STREET VALUE Only illicit drugs have this: no other goods.

STRINGS ATTACHED Journalese for conditions; also a musical cliché - see HIGH NOTES.

STRUCK Like ARRESTED to be used with caution, especially when coupled, as both usually are, with "immediately". "When I met the Prime Minister I was immediately arrested..." makes uneasy reading, even if followed with "by her charm." Similarly avoid "On entering the church the visitor is immediately struck by the mediaeval door..."

STRUCK DOWN Usually by a MYSTERY BUG: taken ill.

STUB OUT The SMOKES and BACCY idiotism, e.g. "Two million Britons are expected to try to stub out the habit after next week's National No-smoking Day."

STUMPED See HIT FOR SIX.

STUNNING Vogue word for beauty or excellence which has joined BRIL-LIANT and FABULOUS. Women's magazines and fashion pages especially are now full of these metaphorical blows to the head.

SUBS In real life stands for submarines or loan but in the press for sub-editors. An imaginary advertisement might call for one able to "work fast and under pressure; who is able to grasp the essentials of material he is called upon to edit; has impeccable grammar, spelling and punctuation; is know-ledgeable in many subjects, has a feeling for foreign languages and an knows the best reference-books". For a sub is often called upon to edit the work of an author writing on his own, narrow, specialist subject but may nevertheless be obliged to cut his *COPY*. If he does this by length rather than by sense he has failed in his job. Some, instead of *correcting* a writer's mistakes, change what was correct in the first place (because they *suspect* a mistake) and turn sense into nonsense. If you put prostate, they make it "prostrate"; you put apposite, they put "opposite". Causal becomes "casual"; censured/"censored"; complement/"compliment"; dandle/"dangle"; discomfit/"discomfort"; Deirdre/"Dierdre"/"Deidre"; empathize/ "emphasize"; foment/"forment/ferment"; genus/genius; grievous/"grievious"; impresario/"impressario"; mischievous/"mischievious"; Ku Klux Klan/ "Klu Klux Klan; mettle/metal (and vice-versa); pedal/peddle (and vice-versa); predilection/"predeliction"; pus/"puss"; racialist/racist; relict/ relic; restaurateur/"restauranteur"; sacrilegious/"sacreligious"; supposititious/suppositious; tamped/tampered; tortuous/"torturous"; Windermere/"Winde-mere"; who/whom (and vice-versa), etc.etc. Writers (other than those able to negotiate *SACRED COW* copy) have no say in the subbing process, get no redress, consultation or correction - but must field FLAK from readers who complain about "their" mistakes. The stock excuse is pressure of time. Subs should also be able to act as *FACT CHECKERS*, telephone contributors to question such minutiae as the correct slant of a foreign accent and verify all dates and numbers. However, there are many shining exceptions to the depressing rule, especially among those carefully chosen for some of the newer or relaunched national papers, although these, too, occasionally suc-cumb to the tired old kneejerks (for it is the subs who compose all those silly headlines). Alas, I have never met a sub who understands that paragraphs are a form of *punctuation* (in ascending order of strength: comma, semi-colon, colon, full-stop, paragraph) . They crudely divide *all* written matter into short, bite-sized chunks, "to break up the page" and "make it easier for the reader". In fact it separates conjunct ideas and makes it harder.

SUNK For any maritime project which after going FULL STEAM AHEAD and having money SPLASHED OUT on it (perhaps while ON THE CREST OF A WAVE or - absurdly - SAILING HIGH) is cancelled or SAILS into TROU-BLED WATERS. Or it may CAPSIZE, be SCUPPERED or TORPEDOED.

SUPER- All-purpose prefix for anything bigger, better, more dangerous, prolific (or more repulsive) than normal, e.g. superdads, supergrasses, super-rats, superbees, etc. Showbiz, which gave us Superman, managed to elevate even Jesus Christ into a superstar.

SUPREMO A Spanish/Latin American ruler or commander; but, since the 1960s, news jargon for any departmental boss. Other fancy phoney foreign titles include MANDARIN, GURU, PUNDIT, etc.

SUSTAIN A formal word now largely confined to news use. Injuries and damage are sustained.

SWEEPING IN How important people arrive: "Television presenter Anne Diamond swept in in a company LIMO" See also WHISKING AWAY.

(THE) SWEET SMELL/TASTE OF (SUCCESS) Cliché relentlessly flogged when sugar, honey or any fragrant substances are in the news. But when sourness is mixed with sweetness a Chinese connection is indicated -

SWEET AND SOUR The WURST hacks have now been dragged, KICK-ING AND SCREAMING, away from the olgd Chinese laundry jokes, but they still try to twist every story into some tasteless "flied lice" type quip. Every robbery or burglary suffered by a Chinese person becomes a TAKEAWAY, see below, and their mixed fortunes are invariably "sweet and sour".

SWINGEING Twinned with "cuts" and "increases" but seldom heard from ordinary people. See the *MAD AXEMEN OF "FLEET STREET"*.

SWOOP What policemen do when making arrests or POUNCE (see DAWN RAID). In the sports pages football managers swoop when "approaching" a player employed by another club.

SYNDROME Properly a medical term, *not* a show-off synonym for a person's state, condition, position, etc. Like CRESCENDO, PARAMETER, QUANTUM LEAP and other professional terms it is best left to the professionals. They do not thank us for devaluing their language.

T

TAB See PICKING UP THE BILL.

TAG Twinned with "price", e.g. "UP FOR GRABS at a price tag of £30m".

TAKEAWAY Theft from a Chinese person. And see CURRYING F(L)AVOUR and SWEET AND SOUR for other race "jokes."

> LIVERPOOL'S Chinatown has become a target for "take-away" thieves who are eating into restaurant profits.

TAKE TO THE CLEANERS Cliché of financial exploitation.

TAKE A SPILL What members of the VROOM VROOM fraternity do when faced with a setback, just as railwaymen go OFF THE RAILS.

TALKING IN TERMS OF ... See IN TERMS OF.

TALKING TURKEY A cliché no hack can resist, however unsuitable the context. Thus when the *Daily Telegraph* (not habitually an offender) printed a picture of the British and Turkish prime ministers in discussion, the *COLONIC IRRITATION* caption began - "Talking Turkey".

TASTE/ TASTING This comes in various forms, from "Ice Cream Firm Tastes Success" (*Daily Telegraph*) to the inevitable "SWEET taste of success" (every tabloid). It can turn into a sour one when appropriate. Media tastings go back to Shelagh Delaney's play, *A Taste of Honey* (1958).

TEETHING TROUBLES Common in infants but commoner still with projects; babies are lucky that *their* teething troubles are not "ironed out".

THAT SINKING FEELING From an old advertising slogan, now a facetious kneejerk cliché for stories about aquatic mishaps.

THE GOOD LIFE Kneejerk (from a TV series) for domestic comfort, self-sufficiency, happiness or prosperity, often absurdly misapplied.

> A GOOD LIFE family of four have been found shot dead in their blazing cottage home.

THE PROVERBIAL... Introduces not a proverb but a cliché. Afterwards it can be apologised for with a deprecatory TO COIN A PHRASE (see *MEDIASPEAK*).

THIGHFUL Obligatory pun for mini-skirted women.

> WIRRAL'S butchers have been put through the municipal mincer by trading standards officers.
> Findings on a minced beef survey have been less than tasty.

(PUT) THROUGH THE MINCER For a discomfited butcher, who may also be GIVEN THE CHOP.

THROWING IN THE TOWEL Boxing metaphor for giving up, though not confined to boxing. See also NOT OUT, CLOCKING UP A CENTURY, etc.

THUD See SICKENING. Also CRUNCH.

TICKET TO RIDE One of the MAKING TRACKS transport clichés.

TIGHT Obligatory prefix for "security". Tight security means police scanning surroundings through POWERFUL binoculars.

TIGHT LIPPED AND ASHEN FACED What newsworthy people (e.g. newly-sacked football managers) are said to be after suffering some kind of REVERSAL or humiliation, and they always STORM OUT. Even if their faces are ruddy with anger (or drink), their lips loose enough to utter a stream of four-letter words and, far from "storming", they are WHISKED AWAY.

TINKLING CASH REGISTERS *ARCHAISM*, as in "The melodious tinkle of cash registers is heard in high street shops..." Cash registers have not tinkled for a long time now. Their sounds vary, but most emit electronic peeps and squeaks, and some actually play tunes that would do credit to the BBC Radiophonic Workshop.

TIP OF THE ICEBERG Cliché unknown before the *Titanic* disaster (1912) which should have been SUNK, SCUPPERED or TORPEDOED long ago. See also BREAKTHROUGH.

TIPPLE See under its unheavenly-twin, FAVOURITE.

TIRED AND EMOTIONAL Lawful euphemism for drunk. Derived from the parliamentary rule that MPs are not allowed to attribute drunkenness to each other. Instead many euphemisms have been devised which make their meaning just as clear. The politician Aneurin Bevan was pissed as a newt but got damages from a journalist by shamelessly perjuring himself.

TITLES The titled have forenames like everyone else but their use is governed by a quaint convention whose observance is not snobbery but conveys information. Thus the wife of Sir John Potter (whether he is a knight or baronet) is Lady Potter, not Lady Shirley Potter. If one needs to use her forename to distinguish her from another Lady Potter it should be given in brackets. If there *is* a real Lady Shirley Potter, perhaps the daughter of the Earl of Wapping (family name Potter), *she* is entitled to her forename without brackets. The same goes for barons, hereditary or life. If you need to mention Lord Oatcake's forename you should refer to him as Lord (John) Oatcake. It is a solecism to call a priest "the Rev(erend) Jones"; as is "the Rev. Mr Jones". Usage demands that "Rev(erend)" is followed by a forename *and* surname, e.g. "The Rev. Arthur Jones" but without "Mr" - although "the Rev. Sir Mark Jones" appears to be acceptable. Another old convention suggests that married women adopt their husband's forename, e.g. Mrs John Smith, not Mrs Joan Smith (and indeed Princess Michael of Kent). This is abhorred by feminists (and does sound as if a woman had changed sex), but some married females who send letters to *The Times* reveal their husband's first name. They sign the letter "Joan Smith" but add ("Mrs John Smith"), to enable the letters editor to follow his paper's old convention of putting at the head, *"From Mrs John Smith"*. Newspapers have recently taken to referring to women by surname only, like males: this is to be preferred to the ugly (sexually-politically-motivated?) "Ms" but looks and sounds unchivalrous. Further titular quirks may be found in *Debrett* and other reference-books. Foreign titles are another MINEFIELD - e.g. when to use Monsieur, Signor, Señor or Herr (von). See also *HERALDIC MOTTOES*, DON, GURU, PUNDIT, etc.

TODDLER TOT bigger than a BABE but smaller than a teenager. All KIDS when ill are BRAVE, and may qualify for the MIRACLE prefix.

TOHU(WA)BOHU Now rarely seen among *MEDIA UGLIES*, this has a respectable biblical ancestry, Hebrew for chaos and desolation. The SCOTS' word for disorder is KERFUFFLE. There is also BROUHAHA, of which HOO-HAA is surely the abbreviation, although the OED has so far not pronounced on this.

TOLL Probably preceded by its twin-word "heavy". Loss of life.

TONGUE LASHING The fiercest possible verbal attack. I can imagine only an ant-eater doing such a thing. See also FURY, HITTING, SLAMMING AND LASHING OUT.

TOP GEAR Kneejerk for motoring success: "Cheshire-based Volvo dealer John Ballwork is POISED to move into top gear following an £8m restructuring of the company..." See FAST LANE.

TORPEDOED See SUNK, TURBULENCE.

TOWERING INFERNO Film-based kneejerk for a BLAZE (INFERNO) in a building taller than two storeys. Even the best papers could not resist it for *COLONIC IRRITATION* under a photograph of a fire in New York.

TRADITIONAL Means old-fashioned, especially in consumer goods and buildings. Also used like "customary", as in "Rubbish is traditionally dumped in black plastic bags..."

TRAGEDY Any unfortunate occurrence reported in the papers. See also FURY and HORROR.

TRAVEL WRITERS FREELOADERS who write about holidays (euphemism: FACILITY TRIPS) provided free-of-charge by travel agents, tour operators and even foreign governments. It is difficult to see how else readers could be informed about holiday and travel, but the phrase "City of Contrasts" (paying lip-service to slums while enthusing about sunshine and scenery) occurs suspiciously often. Yet some papers, like the *Independent*, manage to refuse such inducements. In the smaller tabloids these trips are in the gift of the editor, who distributes them among his staff like favours.

TRAUMA Greek for wound. Freud used it to describe mental anguish, since when everybody has been using it for any mildly unpleasant (or "traumatic") experience.

> The Motherwell episode sticks in my mind the clearest — like an insidious trauma that refuses to die. It all started at Stirling Station where I jumped on a train thinking it

TRILLED See SMILED, SIGHED, QUIPPED, etc.

TRIOS See DUOS. Also *(THE) FAMOUS FIVE*.

TROUBLE AT MILL For any difficulty in Northern England.

TROUBLE BREWING For publicans or brewers: "TV Advert Brews Trouble For Danish Lager". They may feel BITTER about it, but as clichés go this is comparatively MILD. Curiously enough publicans and maltsters are seldom if ever HOPPING MAD, like FROGS - perhaps because hops do not always figure among the chemicals of some drinks sold as beer.

TROUBLED WATERS See SUNK.

TROUBLES Civil unrest, especially in Ireland, where there have been "troubles" since the time of Cromwell.

TRUNK CALL The elephant "joke", whether telephones are apposite or not. Direct dialling has in any case made the term "trunk call" obsolete.

TUCK INTO All journalists, from the lowest tabloid HACK to the most upmarket *DIARIST* and best-connected gossip columnist, insist that people who eat "tuck into" even the finest SLAP UP food or NOSH. They also have us DEMOLISHING, CHOMPING, QUAFFING and "WASHING DOWN a Chateaubriand steak".

TUG OF LOVE CHILD A child (though not necessarily a LOVE CHILD) whose custody is disputed, possibly in a LOVE NEST. (See also *In-Words*).

TURBULENCE What aerial - rarely maritime - projects run into when not FLYING/SAILING (!) HIGH.

U

(THE) UNACCEPTABLE FACE OF... (Also "the two faces of..." and "the ugly face of...") Unthinking clichés, most based on the titles of books or films, though Mr Edward Heath's famous "Unacceptable face of Capitalism" has much to answer for. The *Liverpool Echo* printed a picture captioned "The Ugly Face of Soccer Violence" - showing a hooligans' victim whose face (all but the eyes) was swathed in bandages - and quite invisible.

UNASHAMEDLY See WEEPING.

UNCORKED The UNVEILING of news about vintners, wine merchants and their wares, "The Chancellor has uncorked a new package of tax concessions for common market wines..." When wine is really opened, the bottles are CRACKED.

UNDER WRAPS Something supposedly secret, waiting to be UNVEILED but kept MOTHBALLED. But a SNEAK PREVIEW may be ON THE CARDS.

UNEMPLOYED   With an improving (though still too high) rate of unemployment it is inevitable that more people without work figure in the news than would in times of full employment. Like those in work, the unemployed have accidents, commit suicide, beat (in extreme cases kill) their wives, mistresses and friends, fall from windows, and generally suffer the troubles man is heir to. But their unemployed status is often described in ways that suggest that *it* was the cause of his misfortune. Jobless, OAP and PENSIONER are other loose and emotive descriptions.

UNLEASHED   Spoken and written *ARCHAISM*, as in "the ASSAILANT unleashed four bullets..." Suitable for the DOGS OF WAR - but *bullets*?

UNVEILED *ARCHAISM*. "The local council yesterday unveiled plans for new public toilets in the square". Monuments are formally unveiled, and so was Salome (who incidentally did not give a SNEAK PREVIEW to St John the Baptist) but for more mundane matters "revealed" or "made public" is surely sufficient. See also UNDER WRAPS.

UP (verb) To increase. Sailors used to speak of upping the anchor, sails and there is an annual "upping" of swans. But in the sense of increasing (usually pay) it sounds foolish, and "jacking up" worse, e.g. "jacking up the wages and salaries infrastructure." Trades union leaders keep telling us that unless wages are upped tools will be downed.

UP FOR GRABS For sale, or available: often coupled with a rather low temperature: *this* book is up for grabs at a COOL £7.99. See also PRICE TAG and SLAPPED ON.

UPSTAIRS DOWNSTAIRS Heralds a domestic DRAMA whose SCENARIO concerns a master-servant relationship, possibly with a JEEVES.

UP THE CREEK With or without a paddle: one of the maritime kneejerks, like ALL AT SEA, SCUPPERED, TORPEDOED, SUNK, etc.

UP UNTIL As in "Up until yesterday..." - a *REDUNDANCY* of the "off of" kind. See also *MediaSpeak.*

UP, UP AND AWAY! The ballooning cliché. See also IN A (FLAT) SPIN, ON A WING AND A PRAYER and FLYING HIGH.

V

VIOLATION Like the catch-all ABUSE this USA legal term is entering British English. In America mild misdemeanours like overstaying one's time on a parking-meter or crossing the road where no crossing is marked are "traffic violations". We have enough violence as it is.

VIP Abbreviation of allegedly "Very Important Persons". Airports have VIP lounges, which are often peopled by Very Unimportant Starlets FLYING IN, usually wearing skins of a dead animal and carrying those of several more draped over their arms. After offering a PHOTO OPPORTUNITY they are WHISKED AWAY. Unlike VAT and AKA ("vat" and "acka") the word is still said as an abbreviation ("vee eye pee") not "vipp".

VISIBLY MOVED What people are before WEEPING OPENLY. The invisibly moved are not worth mentioning in the papers.

VOLGA *HACKS'* "joke" way of spelling "vulgar" whenever a Russian context presents itself, e.g. "Volga Joke", etc., *ad nauseam.*

VOW Any decision, however trivial, mundane, unimportant or unsolemn, is by *HACKS* elevated to a solemn vow: "He vowed to consult his solicitor"; or "She vowed to lose another six pounds."

VROOM VROOM The motor-cycling cliché, as in "Vroom Vroom Romance TAKES A SPILL". There is no comparable noise for car-drivers. Do motor-bikes bring out the childish in their devotees?

W

WALKING AWAY Emerging uninjured from an accident. People "walk away" even if they have been cut - unhurt - from the wreckage or run like hell because they stole the vehicle they crashed; just as they "walk free" after a court acquittal, even when WHISKED AWAY in a LIMO.

WALTER MITTY "My client is a rather pathetic Walter Mitty figure". Defence put forward on behalf of an accused person. Mitty was the hero of a story by James Thurber, in the *New Yorker* (1939) later a film with Danny Kaye. The *OED* defines Mitty as "a person who indulges in day-dreams; one who imagines a more adventurous or enjoyable life for himself than he actually leads..." See JEKYLL AND HYDE and ROBIN HOOD.

WANTED MAN Wanted by the police for "interviewing". This would not be remarkable were it not usually "Most Wanted Man" - though the grading stops there. There is no "Second Most Wanted Man", let alone a third or fourth. When a wanted man is arrested he is always said to be BUNDLED AWAY, perhaps in a DAWN RAID.

WASHING DOWN Alcoholics are said to be good at finding ingenious excuses for drinking and hiding their embarrassment behind facetious language. If newsmen drink as much as even the most cursory research in nearby HOSTELRIES suggests this would explain why they always use coy *ARCHAISMS* or ancient euphemisms of conviviality when they write about drinking. They do not drink but QUAFF, IMBIBE or PARTAKE OF. The pub landlord gets the Dickensian description MINE HOST - and they SAMPLE THE LOCAL BREW. Champagne is BUBBLY, perhaps more delicately SIPPED: though even the finest wines can come in LASHINGS.

WATCHDOG BODIES These dogsbodies are non-canine but come with or without teeth. They supposedly guard our interests and may be composed of PUNDITS and WISE MEN - even GURUS.

WED Press *ARCHAISM*, as in "Darling, when I'm a sub-editor will you wed me?" No doubt after a WHIRLWIND COURTSHIP.

WEEPING OPENLY/UNASHAMEDLY A person can be described as weeping in this manner even when turning away from the camera and fully covering his face with a handkerchief. Nevertheless he will be VISIBLY MOVED. Needless to say, press photographers and television cameramen love to get close-ups of such personal occasions. They justify this by explaining that they are "providing a service". To whom? After the Lockerbie air disaster the *Liverpool Daily Post* printed two whole pages of photographs showing grieving relatives. The big-circulation tabloids did worse - but the *Post* had the gall to print them under the headline **A TOWN WHICH WANTS TO BE LEFT TO GRIEVE!** By everyone except the *RAT-PACK* and their several million readers? And such papers write about HEARTLESS THIEVES! See also SAD FAREWELL.

WEIGHING IN Media persons, on radio, television and in print turn to boxing when announcing the weight of a new-born infant. Not "the young prince weighed 8lb" but "...weighed *in at* 8lb." According to other sporting metaphors centenarians are a hundred NOT OUT and have CLOCKED UP a century (such clock-ups are always linked with centuries, from cricket). But when a person is dying he is never described as having "thrown in the towel": far from it - however weak, feeble and probably unconscious, he is said to be FIGHTING FOR HIS LIFE.

WELL BUILT A woman with big breasts: unlike BUXOM, SHAPELY, CURVACEOUS this makes her sound like a car.

WE NAME THE GUILTY MEN! Catchpenny, sales-generating tabloid headline.

WENDING *ARCHAISM* used by *DIARISTS* and gosssip columnists: "Wending my gleeful way across the bridge..." Such writers are untouched by any Plain English campaigns: they hie themselves hither and thither and know not whither or from whence their next idea will issue forth.

WHEELS OF FORTUNE Cliché regularly trotted out when writing about motor-cars, bicycles, or any other form of wheeled transport. Shakespeare has several allusions to the wheel which the mythical figure of Fortune was supposed to have turned, but hers was a lottery-wheel: she did not ride it like a kind of monocycle before its time. See also RIDING HIGH and the nautical kneejerks SUNK, SCUPPERED, TORPEDOED, etc.

WHEN THE ... HAD TO STOP From Robert Browning's *A Toccata of Galuppi's* in which occur the lines: *What of soul was left, I wonder/When the kissing had to stop?* and constantly, tediously and endlessly adapted by the media.

WHIRLWIND COURTSHIP (or ROMANCE) Brief acquaintanceship resulting in marriage.

WHISKED AWAY What is done to people in the public eye who do not wish to speak to the *RATPACK*, or be seen on television; also what happens to people whose *STORY* has been bought by one paper, whose representatives do the whisking, in a motor-car of course, while the rest think of *SPOILERS*. But when someone arrives in a LIMO, he is said to have "swept in". See HUSTLED AWAY.

WHISTLE-BLOWING Public exposure, perhaps by a "mole", of an ALLEGED racket, etc. Also a footballing kneejerk - KICKED INTO TOUCH.

WHOLESALE On a large scale, often followed by words like "slaughter".

WISE MEN GURUS serving on a committee to investigate some matter of moment. Their number is not limited to three.

WORDS-PLITTING Schools used to teach us how words were derived and made, and therefore how we should break them at the end of a line. It was part of elementary English: we not only learnt about syllables but also prefixes, suffixes, stems, etc., with perhaps a little Latin to explain word origins. Today word-splitting is haphazard in newspapers and magazines: the break comes where the line runs out of space, not between syllables. While this is not as bad as misusing or mis-spelling words (as meaning is not generally impaired or confused) non-words and nonce-words result, e.g. "tran-sport", "mans-laughter", "girlf-riend", "screwd-river", "ins-pector", "winds-creen", "bew-itching", "screwd-river", Newham as "Ne-wham" and even "new-spaper". They distract the reader, offend the eye - or can be downright laughable: as when an article about am-putations repeatedly mentioned a "leg-end", and another referred to a rape counsellor as "the-rapist". The *Liverpool Daily Post* makes even the godhead divisible: "Jesus Chr-ist"! It is symptomatic of the creeping unconcern for standards that afflicts many professional word-users, who seem to have lost all pride in their craft. There is no excuse: most print is now produced with the help of computers able instantly to diagnose and correct mis-hyphenated words.

WURST Stock spelling of "worst", suitable for KRAUT "jokes."

WRITS These always FLY, like FUR and FEATHERS.

Y

YA Tabloid spelling of "you", according to context or headline space. ("Who loves ya?"). But the notorious "GOTCHA" headline in the *Sun* had more to do with *YOD-DROPPING*, for which please see *MediaSpeak*.

YEN Cliché for the achievements, cravings or aspirations of Chinese and Japanese persons. *Yen* comes from the Chinese *yüan*, a round thing - so those who use this clapped-out old joke for *both* nationalities are inadvertently correct. Both peoples are immensely industrious and "have a yen" (i.e.

yearning) for money.

YESTERDAY... Almost invariable ingredient of every newspaper *STORY*: "British apple growers were PIPPED at the post yesterday as..." etc. To be able to read yesterday's stories today is better than in OLDEN DAYS, when news took days, weeks or even months to reach the press. But now television-watchers expect instant news, and by the time the papers bring it it is stale. Which is perhaps why journalists feel they must entertain readers with constantly recurring feeble quips, puns and "jokes" as derided here. Or could it be that red noses and clowns' attire disguise a terminal desperation?

Y-FRONTS Almost generic term for men's underpants, but in fact a registered trade-name. In 1988 they celebrated their golden jubilee. See also FORMICA.

Z

ZANY Like EXTRAORDINAIRE and IRREPRESSIBLE, seldom used except by newsmen to describe a kind of amiable exhibitionism, as in "Zany flautist James Galway..."

ZIZZ See *MEDIA UGLIES*.

The End

But now turn the book over and read

MediaSpeak

for more shock-horror revelations.

Correction

Last week, we described the new Convenor of the teacher education sector of the London Students' Organisation, Val Furness, as "a Communist Party candidate." She feels this description is ambiguous and needs to be clarified. She is a member of the Communist Party of Britain (Marxist-Leninist). She is not a member of the Communist Party of England (Marxist-Leninist), or the Communist Party of Great Britain, the Communist League, or the Communist Federation of Britain (Marxist-Leninist). She would like to say that she is not in the Broad Left either.

Due to a misunderstanding over the telephone we stated that the couple would live at the home of the bridegroom's father.

We have been asked to point out that they will in fact live at The Old Manse.

We regret that owing to a typographical error the closing sentence of Sir David Llewellyn's article yesterday appeared as "Blessed are the merciful, for they shall receive money." "Money" should have read "mercy."

The word "unfortunate" in the letter from Lord Wedderburn of Charlton yesterday should have been "fortunate".

Israel weighs the risks: in a Leader on June 17 the reference to "Mr Begin's plan" was a mishearing for Mr Reagan's plan.—Ed, Gdn

Correction

Shaikh Muhammad al-Fassi is not a nephew of King Fahd of Saudi Arabia, as stated on July 14. He is related to the king by the marriage of his sister to Prince Turki.

Mr. Stephen Boulding, whose name was inadvertently misspelt in last week's report of the Young Conservatives' conference at Eastbourne, asks us to state that the phrase he used in his speech in a harmless, mock-serious vein was "Frogs and Italians". Owing to an error in transmission this was reported as "wogs and Italians".

Correction

The caption to an item headed "New bishop enthroned" on September 22 incorrectly stated that the Bishop of London, Dr Graham Leonard, had performed the traditional ceremony of knocking on the main door of St Paul's Cathedral. The ceremony had been deleted from the order of service by the Dean and Chapter, and the main door was opened in advance of the bishop's arrival, as a gesture of welcome.

Correction

The omission of a sentence from Frank Johnson's column on May 12 made it appear incorrectly that the Speaker had declined to take a point of order from Mr Andrew Faulds in the previous day's proceedings in the House of Commons.

A CORRECTION

IN A CAPTION in last night's *Evening Gazette* Miss Dorothy Duffney, conductor of the Cleveland Musical Society, was described as Mrs Vera Beedle. She is, of course, Mrs K. Atkinson, of Hartburn Lane, Stock-

We apologise to Roger Pincham, Chairman of the Liberal Party, for a "not" that was misprinted as a "now" in the seventh paragraph of his letter of April 7. The clause concerned should have read ". . . but (the Falkland Islanders) must not be expected to face the total destruction of their community . . ."

An Advertisement in the Evening Chronicle of 19th September, 1972, carried the sentence "Pot in the Park" — This should have read "Pop in the Park." We apologise to the Ian

Correction
The photograph on April 21 of the Duchess of Gloucester's visit to the Aleck Bourne maternity unit at St Mary's Hospital, Paddington, should have referred to the Elm unit, not the Elm unit.

MR ARTHUR RUBBRA
In Saturday's obituary of Mr Arthur Rubbra he was inadvertently referred to as Sir Arthur Rubbra.

In this column last Friday, ing the BBC's Borgias, that The "I thought the snow just was made to observe, concerning as bad as the critics had said." The misprinting of "snow" for "show" was obviously caused by the adverse weather conditions prevailing

IN yesterday's leader the name of Anthony Burgess should of course have read, Anthony Blunt. We apologise to readers for the error.

On Page 39 of today's Colour Magazine there is a reference to Nigel Burgess and his brother Anthony, "the spy". We should of course have referred to Guy Burgess. We apologise to Anthony Burgess, the distinguished author, for this mistake.

CORRECTION
A caricature of Mr Norman Willis, deputy general secretary of the TUC, was incorrectly described yesterday as being of Mr Alan Sapper.

PS: Instructions for last fortnight's fresh lemon cake read three teaspoons of salt instead of half a teaspoon. Apologies to anyone who found it too salty?

In our recipe for Banana Trifle last week we inadvertently omitted the bananas. We apologise a

IN the Manweb supplement on Tuesday, Cook up a taste of 1883! the ingredient of white fat in the pastry recipe for Perfect Apple Pie should have read 1oz and not 10oz as stated.

Correction
In the penultimate paragraph of the Whitehall brief article yesterday the word "for" was inadvertently omitted from the following sentence: "The safeguard is the media members of the committee, who are very sharp and fight for the press.

I fail to understand the argument that if you want to look at pictures you can only do so if it is free, and if it is not free you shall not go. It is a false analysis and false thesis that the future of the artistic world depends on going into places free. You expect to pay for going to the loos.

Correction

Because of a telephone mishearing the Prime Minister was incorrectly quoted in later editions. of *The Times* yesterday on museum charges. His remark should have read . " You expect to pay for going to the Louvre."

APOLOGY AND CORRECTION

Apologies to the Seventh-Day Adventist Church, Chiswick. In our "church notes" last week we stated that the church had observed a day of prayer and feasting. This should have read "a day of prayer and fasting."

Correction

The caption of a photograph which appeared in *The Times* on May 14 incorrectly identified Mr Teng Hsiao-ping, the Chinese First Deputy Prime Minister. He was standing on the left of the photograph, not in the centre, as stated.

Correction

A tribute to Mr Edward Burney in *The Times* of May 18 referred to his visit to the Ionian islands soon after their annexation by Greece. This reference should have been to the Aegean islands.

In Merrily Harpur's Diary, on November 24, it was wrongly stated that the dog buried at the top of the Duke of York's steps was that of von Ribbentrop. The dog .Giro was owned by Ambassador von Hoesch.

THE TITLE of a lecture given by William Henry Altor. of New York, at the. First Church of Christ Scientist. High Wycombe, was incorrectly. given in last week's *Free Press* as "How to bore and be bored." In fact Mr. Alton spoke on the subject of "How to love and. be loved." The *Free Press* regrets the error which was a misreading of contributed copy.

wife B a r b a r a , at Hoylake, it was stated that Mrs. Hodson had left the marital home to live with a lover. In fact, Mrs. Hodson and her children left to live with her mother.

Our apologies to Dr John F. West, the last sentence of whose letter (July 6) should have read : " I strongly recommend prospective visitors (to the Faroes) to travel by the Smyril from Scrabster, unless they have plenty of time to spare."

CORRECTION

A report yesterday on the Irish church leaders' meeting at Dundalk should have stated that Cardinal Conway's use of the word "horizon" was in a way prophetic. Because of a mishearing in transmission this word appeared as "pathetic."